THE DIALOGUES OF PLATO

Kylix (wine cup), Attic red-figured, early fifth century B.C. Louvre AGR G. 144. © Photo R.M.N. Potter: Hieron. Height 0.12 cm, diameter 0.315 cm. Formerly in Campana Coll. Hoppin, *Handbook of Attic Red-Figured Vases,* no. 23*. Signature painted on handle: HIEPON.

TOP: Dionysus between two ithyphallic satyrs with wine pot and flute, and two maenads with castanets, thyrsus, and cup.

BOTTOM: Satyr with flutes between four maenads, two with thyrsus, one with lyre, one with mixing bowl. The posture of the last is twisted, in a triumph of composition, as though to represent not only motion but the mixing.

Such a cup might have graced Agathon's tables the evening of the banquet. (The medallion is reproduced on page xii.)

THE DIALOGUES OF
PLATO

VOLUME II
THE SYMPOSIUM

TRANSLATED WITH COMMENT BY
R. E. ALLEN

YALE UNIVERSITY PRESS
NEW HAVEN AND LONDON

Designed by Sally Harris and
set in Baskerville types by
Brevis Press, Bethany, Connecticut.

Printed in the United States of America by
Vail-Ballou Press, Binghamton, New York.

Library of Congress Cataloging-in-Publication Data

Plato.
[Symposium. English]
The symposium / translated with analysis by
R. E. Allen.
p.   cm. — (The Dialogues of Plato ; v. 2)
Includes index.
ISBN 0–300–04874–2 (cloth)
0–300–05699–0 (pbk.)

1. Love—Early works to 1800.   2. Socrates.
3. Imaginary conversations—Early works to 1800.
I. Allen, Reginald E., 1931– . II. Title.
III. Series: Plato. Dialogues. English. (New Haven, Conn.) : v. 2.
B358.A44   1984   vol. 2
[B385]
184—dc20   90–26725

10 9 8 7 6 5 4 3

CONTENTS

v

PREFACE

The *Symposium* is the most widely read of Plato's dialogues with the single exception of the *Republic*, and this for good reason. Its literary merit is unsurpassed, and beneath the shining splendor of its surface it is constructed with the precision and something of the intricacy of a Swiss watch. Its philosophical, psychological, and religious force is revolutionary, offering a vision of what it means to live a human life founded on a transcendent principle of Beauty which, itself intelligible, is the source of all intelligibility and the ultimate aim of all loving. The *Nachleben* of the dialogue, as the Germans call it, its afterlife and influence, is very nearly as broad as the breadth of humane letters in the West; in the matter of *Quellenstudien*, it is not a spring, but a mighty river. Aristotle's theory of contemplation in the *Nicomachean Ethics*, as well as his theology in *Metaphysics* XII, where God is the primary object of both intellect and desire, and moves by being loved, is indebted to Diotima. So is Plotinus's account of beauty. Through Plotinus and, in aftertime, Aristotle, the indirect effect of the *Symposium* on medieval philosophy and theology, on Augustine and Bonaventure and Aquinas, was very great. Ficino picked up Pausanias's muddled distinction between sacred and profane love, which the *Symposium* clarifies in the contrast between the speeches of Aristophanes and Alcibiades and the speech of Diotima, and, combining with it much that is borrowed from Plotinus, forged it into a theory of the relation of art and beauty which guided the mind of Michelangelo and helped sustain the Renaissance. In nineteenth-century Germany, Aristophanes and Romanticism triumphed over Diotima's rationalism, and the triumph of the drunken comedian was ratified by Nietzsche in *The Birth of Tragedy*, which presents an incongruous counterpart of the symposium, inverted. After Nietzsche came Freud, to make the divorce between desire and reason final and to proclaim that sacred love is in its inner essence profane, even as Diotima had proclaimed that profane love is in its inner essence sacred.

An account of the afterlife of the *Symposium* might easily grow into a general survey of Western culture—and a very large book. A commentator may properly be excused from such a task. What follows is an introductory account of this singularly powerful dialogue, along with some cursory remarks on its Nachleben, and a translation meant to allow the Greekless reader to follow the thought of the dialogue for himself with some degree of literalness. In making the translation, I have relied on Burnet's text, occasionally departing from it where variance seemed trivial, or where manuscript readings seemed to me to preserve a satisfactory sense without emendation. I have constantly consulted R. G. Bury's edition, which is especially valuable for its insight into structure and its sensitiveness to rhetorical shading, as well as Kenneth Dover's, from whom I have silently adopted many suggested translations of words and phrases. Among translators, I have usefully consulted W. R. M. Lamb in the Loeb Classical Library, Léon Robin in the Budé edition, and the fourth edition of Jowett, revised by D. J. Allan and H. E. Dale; the version by Alexander Nehamas and Paul Woodruff, eagerly anticipated, proved unhelpful.[1] I must also acknowledge with gratitude the criticism and suggestions of students and friends, Dougal Blyth, now lecturer in classics at Auckland, and David Ambuel of Northwestern, as well as the helpful comments of such colleagues as John Anton, Daniel Garrison, David Konstan, Stuart Small, and David White.

A word needs to be said, I suppose, even in so short a preface as this, about Platonic love. The late Renaissance made that love a kind of companionship between persons of opposite sex in which there was no element of sexual desire, and the notion has stuck. But for Plato, or if you will, Diotima, love implies active concern for the virtue and goodness of another soul, founded on the love of Goodness itself; it also implies sexuality, since sexuality finds its purpose in the intercourse of man and woman for the procreation of children and the continuation of the race. Still, there is an important truth encapsulated in the Renaissance mistake. Freud, analyzing the neurotics of Vienna at the end of the Victorian era, concluded that much mental disorder arose from sexual repression. It is

---

1. R. G. Bury, ed., *The Symposium of Plato*, 2d ed., Cambridge, 1932 (hereafter cited as Bury, *Symposium*). Kenneth Dover, ed., *Plato: Symposium*, Cambridge, 1980 (hereafter, Dover, *Symposium*). *Plato: Lysis, Symposium, Gorgias*, trans. W. R. M. Lamb, Boston, 1926. *Platon: Le Banquet*, trans. Léon Robin, Paris, 1929. *Plato: Symposium*, trans. Alexander Nehamas and Paul Woodruff, Indianapolis, 1989. Compare *Plato: The Symposium*, trans. Walter Hamilton, New York, 1951.

not a cause likely to have troubled an Athenian of the fifth century B.C., and the *Symposium* may be read, at one level at least, as an argument that a bit more in the way of sexual repression might prove conducive to mental health. The *Symposium,* indeed, offers an argument for a degree of abstinence verging on asceticism.

A further word, both literary and logical, about Eros as personified and as a relation in the speech of Diotima. It may be said that Plato treats Eros as the domain of a relation, taken distributively. The personification of Eros in the speech of Diotima is not merely a literary device: Eros is the lover qua lover, each lover just insofar as he loves. It will be evident that the lover qua lover cannot be identified with the lover considered apart from that relation. If the soul is immortal, as Socrates argues in the *Phaedo,* then, given Diotima's claim that the lover qua lover lacks immortality and desires to possess it, this must imply that Eros is not Psyche, and it is a root of error to confound them.

The numbers and letters in the margins of the translation represent a conventional way of locating and referring to passages in the dialogue. They derive from the Stephanus edition of 1578, succeeding the Aldine edition of 1513: Henri Estienne edited and printed, in three volumes, a folio edition of numbered pages, with columns divided on the page— whence the letters. The edition is set in type whose design had been commissioned by Francis I, king of France. It is a very beautiful book.

Medallion of kylix reproduced as frontispiece: Satyr seizing a maenad. She holds by the tail a spotted panther who before death was a nursing female: the hunted hunter, dead mother of life, an iconographic representation of the coincidence and clash of opposites characteristic of Dionysiac religion. Elsewhere, the spotted animal becomes a dappled fawn, or a spotted creature ambiguous between a fawn and a panther.

THE SYMPOSIUM

COMMENT

Prologue: Apollodorus to a Companion (172a–174a)

The narrative scheme of the *Symposium* is complex—more complex than that of any other Platonic dialogue except the *Parmenides*. Apollodorus is asked by an unnamed friend to describe a meeting between Socrates, Agathon, Alcibiades, and others at a banquet that took place many years before, where there were speeches about love. Apollodorus himself was not present, but has been told about it by Aristodemus, a follower of Socrates who was there; Apollodorus has also asked Socrates about it, and Socrates verified Aristodemus's report.

A symposium is a "drinking together," a formal banquet. But it is more than that. It is a ritualistic drinking, a private religious ceremony, the Greeks being free of the unlovely assumption that religion to be religion must be no fun at all. Dedications were offered, the company sang a paean, libations were poured to divine patrons, traditionally to Olympian Zeus and the gods, to the heroes, and to Zeus Savior. But other gods might be substituted, and here the appropriate god, at the Lenaea, is Dionysus, whose festival it is (compare 176a). The drinking itself was conceived as a religious act, an acknowledgment both of divinity through wine and of mutual fellowship.[2] A modern dinner party with toasts and speeches is analogous in its sense of occasion, but present-day celebrants would not think of their drinking as involving religious ritual or the invocation of gods; the Greeks did.

The banquet celebrates Agathon's first victory in dramatic competition at the Lenaea in 416 B.C., while still in his twenties (compare 198a). Soc-

2. See E. R. Goodenough, *Jewish Symbols in the Greco-Roman Period*, vol. 6, *Wine*, Princeton, N.J., 1956, pp. 9–10.

3

rates was then in his mid-fifties and Alcibiades about thirty-four, at the height of his brilliant career and influence. It was the year before the Sicilian Expedition of 415 B.C., which Alcibiades instigated; from it, Athens lost a fleet and an army and began her long decline.

The narrative date, as distinct from the dramatic date, is less precise, but determinable. Since Apollodorus checked the accuracy of Aristodemus's account with Socrates, it falls before the death of Socrates in 399 B.C., and indeed before the death of Agathon in about 401 B.C.,[3] but some years after Agathon left Athens (172c), which was after 411 B.C., when he heard Antiphon's defense[4] and was caricatured in Aristophanes' *Thesmophoriazusae*, and probably after 407 B.C., when Agathon went to the court of Archelaus in Macedonia. So the date of Apollodorus's narrative, and Aristodemus's, must be over a decade after the banquet, around 402 B.C. The story is fresh in Apollodorus's memory—he told it to Glaucon only a few days before—and he now agrees to tell it again to an unnamed companion.

Plato's introduction to the *Symposium* emphasizes the importance of the speeches to follow, and specifically the accuracy of Apollodorus's account of the speech of Socrates (199c–212c). Apollodorus is concerned to learn and repeat a conversation that took place when he was merely a boy, and there have been at least two recent reports of the speeches (172b).[5] That he has checked Aristodemus's account with Socrates implies the accuracy of his account so far as the doctrine of Socrates is concerned, though not (178a) of others.

The *Symposium* apart, only in the *Phaedo* and the *Parmenides* is a dialogue narrated by someone other than Socrates, and then for the excellent reason that Socrates is dead. He is not dead in the *Symposium*. But it would have been impossible to put into Socrates' own mouth the scene with Alcibiades at the end, because it is an encomium of Socrates. Plato has at the very beginning of the *Symposium* fashioned the narrative structure of the dialogue around that final scene, which must therefore be important to its interpretation.

---

3. This is implied by the perfect ἐπιδεδήμηκεν in 172c 4.

4. Aristotle, *Eudemian Ethics* III 1232b 8.

5. It is gratuitous to take this reference to a second report as evidence that Plato in the *Symposium* meant to reply to some other story about the banquet circulating at the time he wrote (Bury, *Symposium*, p. xvii); this collapses time frames, confusing the date of Apollodorus's narration, which is before the death of Socrates in 399 B.C., with the date of Plato's composition of the *Symposium*, which is surely after the death of Socrates, and almost as surely after 386 B.C.; it assumes that the banquet was a historical event, for which there is no adequate evidence; and it neglects the dramatic function of the story about Phoenix's version of the conversation, namely, to indicate the interest taken in it and thereby its importance.

That the *Symposium* is narrated by someone other than Socrates does not by itself explain the fact of double narration, Apollodorus telling his companion what Aristodemus told him. This scheme is frequently recalled in the body of the dialogue (for example, at 180c, 223c–d), and if it again emphasizes the importance of the conversation, it serves also as a continuing reminder to the reader of the temporal distance between the conversation and its narration. One effect of that distance is to suggest that the conversation of 416 B.C. is not, as a whole, reported with precise accuracy; this is not left to inference, for Apollodorus directly states (178a; compare 180c) that Aristodemus did not remember all of what was said by every speaker, and that he himself does not remember everything Aristodemus said. So the double narration suggests not only importance but incompleteness. Perhaps this emphasis on remoteness and incompleteness is further meant to suggest, as in the *Parmenides*, that the banquet itself is a fiction, an inference supported by the occurrence of several clear anachronisms (182b, 193a).[6]

But there is something else. The device of double narration throws the figure of Apollodorus into high relief. As readers, we have met him elsewhere. He was present at the trial of Socrates (*Apology* 34b), where he offered to stand surety for him (38b), and the depth of his distress at Socrates' death is observed at *Phaedo* 59a–b. But he is indelibly present after Socrates drinks the cup at the end (117b), when his tears cause the others to break down and Socrates to reprove them. As the *Symposium* (173d) tells, Apollodorus had the reputation of being "soft."

The figure of Apollodorus leads the reader from the *Symposium* to the *Apology* and the *Phaedo*, to the trial of Socrates and his execution, and within the *Symposium* itself to the concluding scene with Alcibiades, which anticipates the trial. The very narrative structure of the *Symposium*, with the choice of Apollodorus as narrator, reminds the reader from the very beginning of this brilliant, vibrant dialogue that in life we are in the midst of death, and that this is not least true of the true lover, the philosopher who loves the good to be his own forever.[7]

This is but one example of what will be shown over and again in what follows: the *Symposium* is a dialogue of powerful symbolic effect. It suggests that the *Symposium* was written after the *Phaedo*.

---

6. Which also strongly suggests that the *Symposium* was composed after 385, as a *terminus a quo*. This conforms to the stylometric evidence, as far as it goes. Aristotle's two references to the *Symposium* (*Politics* 2.1262b.12, *De anima* 2.415a 26) shed no light on the date of composition.

7. See Paul Friedländer, *Plato*, vol. 3, Princeton, 1969, p. 5.

Aristodemus's Prologue (174a–175e)

Aristodemus is short, shoeless, and contemptuous of riches, a modest and unbidden guest, invited by Socrates rather than his host to the banquet he describes. As a follower of Socrates, he stands in ironical contrast to the final speaker whose speech he will report, Alcibiades—also an unbidden guest, but self-invited, and outwardly possessed of all that Aristodemus lacks: good looks and wealth, noble birth and political power. The two men have this in common: each loves Socrates for his wisdom and lacks the wisdom he loves. When morning comes and Socrates leaves, Aristodemus will leave with him. Alcibiades will have gone to sleep.

A word should be said about dining arrangements. The participants do not sit at table but recline on couches, propped on their left elbows, eating and drinking with their right hands from low tables; the couches are broad enough to hold two men lying obliquely, one below the other; presumably the couches are arranged in a semicircle, so that the diners can see each other. The participants deliver their speeches from left to right, beginning with Phaedrus.

Agathon, as host, reclines alone on the last couch, farthest to their right, and would have spoken last but for Socrates' abstracted delay in arriving at the banquet. This not only characterizes Socrates and his bent for contemplation, but puts him beside Agathon and makes him speak last, with the result that he is able to comment not only on the speech of Agathon but by implication on everything that has gone before—a simple example of what is everywhere evident in the *Symposium,* namely, how tightly and intricately the dialogue is constructed as a work of art.

With great economy of means, Plato in this prologue not only draws a remarkable portrait of Socrates—his kindly wit, his courtesy, his abstractedness and habit of contemplation,[8] the affection and respect in which he is held—but also comments on the action to follow. Agathon calls Socrates outrageous, a charge Alcibiades will later repeat (215b; compare 219c) because he supposes Socrates' praise of his wisdom is ironic; he suggests to Socrates that Dionysus, the wine-god, will later judge their wisdom—*in vino veritas.* But the argument itself, the *logos,* not Dionysus, will prove the judge, and it is a sign of this that in the concluding scene, Socrates, still arguing, will drink everybody else under the table, get up and go to the Lyceum and wash, and spend the rest of the day in his accustomed way: Socrates will vanquish the wine-god.

---

8. A habit of which Alcibiades will give a striking example at 220c–d.

Eryximachus Proposes Speeches in Praise of Eros (176a–178a)

Eryximachus suggests that since everyone had too much to drink the day before, the company should drink only as they please instead of having rounds of obligatory toasts, and they should dismiss the flute-girl and entertain themselves with conversation. Phaedrus once remarked to him that no one has ever composed an encomium to Eros; he suggests that they remedy this by giving speeches in honor of the god, proceeding from left to right starting with Phaedrus, as father of the discourse. Socrates approves the suggestion, and the others agree.

The dialogue that follows falls into three main parts. The first (178a–197e) consists in a series of speeches in praise of Eros by Phaedrus, Pausanias, Eryximachus, Aristophanes, and Agathon. Of these, the speeches of Aristophanes and Agathon, with whom Socrates will argue till dawn of the following day (223c), are incomparably the most important. The second part of the dialogue (198a–212c) consists in Socrates' criticism and refutation of Agathon, and his narration of the speech of Diotima, which carries the argument beyond refutation to a vision of Beauty itself as the ultimate object of love. The third part (212c–end) consists in a drunken encomium to Socrates himself by Alcibiades, the beloved transformed into a lover.

Eros meant love in the sense of romantic love, and included sexual passion. But Eros could be used broadly enough in Greek—Diotima will so use it—to include desire in all its forms. It may be contrasted with Philia, love in the sense of affection or friendship or liking.[9]

The project Eryximachus proposes is to "adorn" Eros, to give speeches in praise of him.[10] Eros might well have been thought to stand in some need of adornment. Sophocles in one of the great choruses of the *Antigone* (781–800) addresses "Love unconquered in battle," who sleeps on the maiden's cheek and roams in savage places, whom neither men nor immortals can flee, who introduces madness and forcibly turns the minds of just men to injustice and their own disgrace. Euripides in the *Hippolytus* (525–564) tells how Eros bewitches the heart of those he would destroy;

9. At *Laws* 8.837a, *eros* is distinguished from *philia* by its overgreat or inordinate (σφοδρόν) intensity.

10. Cf. Aristotle, *Rhetoric* I 1367b 27ff. Aristotle especially emphasizes the ethical implications of praise: "To praise a man is in one respect akin to urging a course of action. The suggestions which would be made in the latter case become encomiums when differently expressed. . . . Consequently, whenever you want to praise anyone, think what you would urge people to do; and when you want to urge the doing of anything, think what you would praise a man for having done" (*Rhetoric* I 1367b 36–1368a 8, trans. W. Rhys Roberts).

he is author of ruin, tyrannical in violence, with destruction in his breath. Plato in the *Republic* (III 403a) knows of a right Eros, "by nature a temperate and cultivated love of good order and beauty," but Eros is also the master passion of the tyrant, the sting of *pothos,* unsatisfied longing, allied to drunkenness and a source of madness (IX 572e, 573a–b, d; compare 586c). So it is that the *Phaedo* (81a) can refer to "fierce loves," and the *Laws* (VI 783a) to "lust most keen," and the *Phaedrus* (266a) to a love of ill omen. In the speeches that follow, Eros will indeed be adorned magnificently; but it is well for the reader to remember that there is a dark side to Eros, associated with madness and wrongdoing and destruction. In Alexandrian times, Eros became a winged child with a bow, companion of Aphrodite, mischievously smiting lovers with his arrows—the Cupid of Saint Valentine's Day. In origin he was more powerful and more terrible.

Given this nature, it was no accident that Phaedrus failed to find encomia of Eros. The speeches that follow offer praise of Eros and ignore his dark side; it is therefore mistaken to suppose that they represent ordinary Athenian opinions about Eros. They are exercises in rhetoric, and they show the influence of sophistical culture on upper-class Athenians, who could afford the fees of the sophists; they are, as Phaedrus implies, in the nature of sophistical displays, *epideixeis.*

The *Symposium* is a great work of argument, but there is also a mythopoeic element in it: argument is carried forward and completed by metaphor and symbol, rhetoric and myth. The dialogue is both a masterwork of philosophy and a masterpiece of literature, and each because it is the other; for in it Plato chooses to imply some part of his philosophical meaning by artistic means.

If Eros is the subject matter of the *Symposium,* rhetoric is one of its major themes, and Plato's choice of characters, and the speeches they make, indicates that the dialogue is aptly connected with the *Protagoras.* Léon Robin, indeed, suggested that the *Symposium* is a companion piece of the *Phaedo,*[11] a claim eloquently supported by F. M. Cornford:

> The *Symposium* is held to be near in date to the *Phaedo,* in which the deliverance of Socrates by a self-chosen death from the Athenian prison becomes the symbol of the deliverance of man's soul from the prison-house of the body by its own passion for wisdom. Whichever of the two dialogues was finished first—and I suspect it was the *Phaedo*—Plato felt the need to hang beside the picture it gave of Socrates another picture as different as possible.

11. *Platon: Le Banquet,* trans. Léon Robin, Paris, 1929, pp. vii–viii.

Every genuine drama has a physical atmosphere. The storm is as necessary to *King Lear* as the stillness after the storm is to *The Tempest*. The atmosphere of the *Phaedo* is the twilight that precedes the night: 'the sun is still upon the mountains; he has not yet gone down.' It ends at sunset, with Socrates' mythical discourse about an Earthly Paradise for purified souls. The atmosphere of the *Symposium* is steeped in the brilliant light of Agathon's banquet, celebrating the victory of his play in the theatre. . . . And the *Symposium* ends at day-break, with Socrates arguing with the two drowsy poets till they fall asleep and he goes off to take a bath and to argue all the rest of the day at the Lyceum.

The *Phaedo* had brought out the ascetic strain in Socrates, the man of thought to whom the body with its senses and appetites is at best a nuisance. There was that strain in him. The Cynics were destined to fasten upon it and follow the track that leads from the denial of the flesh to a point where the sage will be found taking refuge in a dog-kennel—the tub of Diogenes the dog—and advertising his sin-gular virtue by outraging not only the graces but the decencies of life. Plato's word for such men is *amousos*, uncultivated, ungracious, un-musical. Socrates was not such, but rather the chief and indispensable guest at the elegant young poet's table. If he was a man of super-human self-restraint, that was not because there was nothing in his nature to restrain. He could drink more wine than anyone else, but no one had ever seen him drunk. He had not, as some later critics said, ignored or 'abolished' the passionate side of human nature; he had done something else with it. The man of thought was also the man of passion, constantly calling himself a 'lover', not in the vulgar sense—the speech of Alcibiades was to make that perfectly clear—but still a lover. The *Symposium* is to explain the significance of Eros to the lover of wisdom.[12]

This is finely said, and its estimate of Socrates is important, but it con-nects the *Symposium* and the *Phaedo* through their differences. The *Sym-posium* is linked to the *Phaedo* through the figure of Apollodorus,[13] and through its implied asceticism, but its main philosophical filiation is with the *Republic*: the account of Beauty itself at 210a–212a anticipates the ac-count of the Good in *Republic* VI (506b–509b). It is also important to ob-serve that the *Symposium* is directly connected with the *Protagoras* through its cast of characters. With the single exception of Aristophanes, all of its

12. *The Unwritten Philosophy*, Cambridge, 1950, pp. 68–69. Greek transliterated.
13. See above, comment on 172a–174a.

speakers figure there, and this could scarcely be so had Plato not meant
to recall that dialogue to the minds of his readers.

When Socrates and Hippocrates go to the house of Callias to visit Protagoras, they find Eryximachus and Phaedrus listening to Hippias of Elis
lecture on nature and astronomy; Pausanias and Agathon are seated with
Prodicus of Ceos (*Protagoras* 315c–e). Alcibiades is present too, arriving
after Socrates (316a). Prodicus of Ceos was a sophist best known, to Plato's
readers at least, for his genius in distinguishing the meanings of words
and determining the correctness of names;[14] his influence is evident in the
speeches of Pausanias and Agathon, whose style, however, is also much
influenced by Gorgias. Hippias was a polymath who put himself forward
at Olympia as willing to answer any question and was never stumped;[15]
he taught young people calculation and astronomy and geometry and music, the "arts" (*Protagoras* 318e), and his influence is present in the wideranging natural history of Eros offered in the speech of Eryximachus. Of
the five initial speakers in the *Symposium*, four—Phaedrus, Pausanias,
Eryximachus, Agathon—exhibit in marked degree the tropes of sophistical rhetoric. The single exception is Aristophanes, who was not present
in the *Protagoras*. Socrates in the *Protagoras* (347c–348a) also exactly anticipates the rules laid down by Eryximachus in the *Symposium* in respect
to drinking parties, flute-girls, and speeches.

The dramatic date of the *Protagoras* is nearly twenty years earlier than
that of the *Symposium*, approximately 435 B.C.; this inference is based on
the youth of Alcibiades, who was just then getting his beard (*Protagoras*
309a–b). The relationship between Socrates and Alcibiades is an important thematic link between the two dialogues: the *Protagoras* opens with
Socrates being quizzed by an unnamed companion about his pursuit of
Alcibiades; the nature and consequences of that pursuit are explained by
Alcibiades himself in the *Symposium*.

There is a further connection between the two dialogues. The central
issue of the *Protagoras* is the worth of sophistic education, culture, *paideia*,
and this as represented, not by the likes of Euthydemus and Dionysodorus, but by men of stature such as Hippias and Prodicus and the great
Protagoras himself. Hippocrates comes to Socrates before first light, in
great excitement: Protagoras has come to town, and Hippocrates wants
to study with him for the sake of *paideia*. Socrates warns him of danger.
Knowledge is the food of the soul,

---

14. *Protagoras* 337a, 340a, 341a, 358a, d; cf. *Charmides* 163d, *Laches* 197d, *Euthydemus*
277e, *Meno* 75e.
    15. *Hippias Minor* 363eff.; cf. *Protagoras* 315c.

and we must take care, dear friend, lest the sophist in praising what he sells deceive us, as grocers and hucksters do with food for the body. Though they don't at all know which among their wares benefits or harms the body, they praise everything they sell; and those who buy of them don't know either, unless they happen to be physicians or trainers. It's the same with these people who tour our cities peddling knowledge to whomever desires it; they too praise everything they sell, but it may be, dear friend, that some of them are ignorant whether the things they sell are good or bad for the soul. So too for those who buy from them, unless they happen on the other hand to be physicians of soul. So if you know what is good and what is bad, you can buy your knowledge safely from Protagoras or anyone else; but if you don't, look to it, dear friend, lest you risk and hazard things of greatest value. For the risk is immensely greater when you purchase knowledge than when you purchase food. You can buy food and drink from a huckster and carry it away in another container, and before you take it into your body by eating or drinking, you can set it aside in your house and summon an expert to consult about what should be eaten and drunk, and what should not, and how much, and when; so there's no great risk in the purchase. But knowledge cannot be carried away in another container. Having paid the price, you must necessarily take what is learned into your very soul, and depart either benefited or harmed.[16]

Protagoras will claim to teach virtue, the excellence of a man and a citizen; the remainder of the *Protagoras* shows—literally exhibits—that this particular huckster of learning does not know whether what he sells is good or bad. The speakers of the *Symposium* have paid their fees and carried home the learning of the sophists in their souls. The dialogue not only provides specimens of rhetoric, but exhibits the effects of rhetorical *paideia,* culminating in the speech of Alcibiades at the end.

The speeches that follow have a ring structure, a structure peculiarly suited to combining varied and diverse themes and holding them together in the mind of the reader: it is a structure Plato repeatedly uses, with astonishing success, in the *Republic.* Phaedrus makes Eros a god, and the eldest; Pausanias makes him two gods; Eryximachus makes him two natural forces; Aristophanes makes him a single natural force in men; Agathon, returning to Phaedrus, makes him a single god, but the youngest. This structure is so effective that, though the individual speeches, with

16. *Protagoras* 313c–314b.

the exception of Aristophanes', have severe logical and stylistic weaknesses, the overall effect is one of great brilliance, and the reader is left with a sense of intellectual satisfaction. The whole is golden, despite the dross of its parts: it is pure alchemy of style.

The Speech of Phaedrus (178a–180b)

In the traditional manner of encomia, Phaedrus begins by describing Eros's excellence of birth: Eros is a god and, along with Earth, eldest of all gods except Chaos; this is attested by ancient tradition. Eros is also of great benefit to mankind, for a man in love wants to appear καλός, beautiful (or noble), to his beloved, and is ashamed to seem ugly (here cowardly). Eros then causes the ἐραστής, the lover, to feel shame and ambition, thereby gaining ability to do great and noble deeds in public and private, and becoming inspired with courage even to the sacrifice of his own life for his beloved, the ἐρώμενος or παιδικά.[17] An army of such men would be invincible.[18] Not only men but also women are willing to die for their beloved, as Alcestis for Admetus and Achilles for Patroclus. But Orpheus, a musician, was too soft to die for Eurydice: because he journeyed to the underworld alive, he was sent back by the gods empty-handed. The gods themselves honor those who die for love.

In the *Phaedrus*, Phaedrus will read to Socrates a discourse on Eros he has taken from Lysias (*Phaedrus* 230e–234c; compare 262d–264d), arguing that sexual favors should be granted, not to lovers, but to those who are not in love. Love is only another name for intemperate sexual desire; it is a sickness (231d), and Lysias argues on prudential grounds that sexual intercourse without love is much to be preferred. Impoverished in content, void even of the generosity of passion, the speech of Lysias is tedious and repetitive in style, and also ill organized—Socrates will later compare it to the epitaph of Midas the Phrygian, the lines of which may be taken in any order (263c–d). It is a poor specimen of rhetoric, whose only virtues are brevity and clarity (234e). Yet Phaedrus, the encomiast of Eros in the *Symposium*, recites it with manifest approval.

The portrait of Phaedrus in the *Phaedrus* is of a piece with his speech in the *Symposium*, admirably analyzed by R. G. Bury:

Phaedrus's speech, though not without merit in point of simplicity of

---

17. τὰ παιδικά literally means "things having to do with children," especially boys, but often refers to the beloved, and is used broadly enough in Plato (cf. *Republic* VI 485b 8) to mean any object of love.
18. Compare *Republic* V 471c–d.

style and arrangement, is poor in substance. The moral standpoint is in no respect raised above the level of the average citizen; the speaker pays little regard to consistency, and the method of argument, with its want of logical coherence, savours much of the sophists. As examples of this self-contradiction we may point to the statement that Achilles, as younger than Patroclus, must be beloved not lover, whereas Alcestis, though younger than Admetus, is treated as the lover not the loved; we may point also to the other inconsequence, that the self-sacrifice of Achilles, the beloved, is cited in support of the contention that only those who are lovers are capable of such self-sacrifice. The arbitrary handling of the Orpheus myth is another striking illustration of the sophistic manner.[19]

Phaedrus in the *Protagoras* (315c), it will be recalled, was portrayed as a pupil of the sophist Hippias.

Phaedrus's attitude toward Orpheus is dismissive, mere upper-class prejudice against musicians. But Orpheus, more than a man, was a hero, and the source of a religious movement in Greece whose exact nature remains unclear. He is already described as famous by Ibycus in the sixth century, and again by Pindar, and Herodotus refers to τὰ ὀρφικά, Orphic rituals or writings. It is certain that Orphism, or at least some versions of it, required rites of initiation and a way of life which required abstention from the eating of flesh (*Laws* VI 782c). Plato in the *Republic* (II 364e) refers to the "babble of books" attributed to Orpheus and Museaus,[20] "children of the Moon and the Muses," by wandering pardoners and oracle-mongers who claimed that their ritual purifications could relieve the consequences of wrongdoing. In book X (620a) the soul of Orpheus chooses to return as a swan. Plato, in his own way, was as dismissive as Phaedrus—but for a different reason.[21] It is to be observed, however, that Socrates looked forward to meeting Orpheus and Musaeus in the afterlife (*Apology* 41a); one must distinguish between Orpheus and Orphics.

It is worth remarking on the connection between Eros and beauty in Phaedrus's speech. Love induces one to live καλῶς, beautifully, which

19. *Symposium*, p. xxv. Greek terms translated.

20. The contents of these books are unclear. There is a wealth of Hellenistic testimony to Orphic doctrines, including Orphic cosmogonies, and lively controversy about whether those doctrines date to classical times.

21. Viewed from this perspective, E. R. Dodds's claim that Orphism involved a "Puritan psychology" (*The Greeks and the Irrational*, Berkeley, Calif., 1951, p. 149) implies a highly unusual sense of "Puritan" (cf. *Republic* II 363c, 364b, *Phaedrus* 244d–e, 265b). In general, the notion that Orphism was a reformation movement, meant to purify the excesses of primitive Dionysiac religion, is doubtful; to judge from the *Republic* and the *Symposium*, the news had not reached Athens.

here primarily means bravely and nobly. A lover wants to appear καλός to his beloved, and is loath to do anything αἰσχρός, shameful or ugly or cowardly. The power of love goes beyond this life to the next, as the examples of Alcestis and Achilles show, and Phaedrus implies that it is the lover, not the beloved, who is καλός: "For lover is more divine than beloved: the god is in him and he is inspired" (180b). The use of καλός to describe the lover rather than the beloved is also evidenced by vase paintings that label ithyphallic satyrs καλός. This cannot be merely linguistic, for the use Phaedrus rejects is embedded in his language.

The Speech of Pausanias (180c–185c)

Pausanias of Cerameis speaks next. Though doubtless a historical person, we know him only through the *Symposium* and the *Protagoras,* where he is associated with the sophist Prodicus and found in bed with a boy; he is also mentioned in passing in Xenophon's *Symposium.*[22]

Phaedrus claimed that Eros is eldest and most honored of the gods, a source of virtue and happiness to mankind. Pausanias, in the manner of Prodicus, distinguishes. There are two Erotes, for Eros is the partner of Aphrodite, goddess of sex, and there are two Aphrodites, one Heavenly, the other Vulgar or Popular.

Pausanias is in fact attempting to divide the substance of a goddess who is one: Aphrodite Ouranios is also Aphrodite Pandemos:

> It is reasonable to take her as an adaptation of one of the great goddesses of the type of Ishtar, who were worshipped throughout a great part of Asia. Wherever she came from, she was certainly worshipped practically in every place where Greek was spoken. Generally she was the goddess of love, beauty and marriage, but also, in Sparta especially, a war-goddess, a conception of her which seems originally to have come from Cypress itself (warlike goddesses are not uncommon in Asiatic cult), by way of the ancient worship of her just off the Lako-

22. VIII 32–33, Socrates speaking, trans. O. J. Todd: "Yet Pausanias, the lover of the poet Agathon, has said in his defence of those who wallow in lasciviousness that the most valiant army would be one recruited of lovers and their favorites! For these, he said, would in his opinion be most likely to be prevented by shame from deserting one another,—a strange assertion, indeed, that persons acquiring a habitual indifference to censure and to abandoned conduct toward one another will be most likely to be deterred by shame from any infamous act." Xenophon has conflated the speeches of Pausanias and Phaedrus in Plato's *Symposium;* his account is not independent of Plato's. But see further W. K. C. Guthrie, *History of Greek Philosophy,* Cambridge, 1969, vol. 3, pp. 340–344, vol. 4, p. 365n3; and A. E. Taylor, *Plato,* New York, 1934, p. 209.

nian coast, at Cytheria (hence her very common title, Kythereia). This is no doubt the real reason why she is so commonly united with Ares, who is her cult-partner here and there, and in mythology her lover and sometimes the father of Eros. . . . To the same desire we may attribute her mythical position as mother of Eros. This was a respectably old god, worshipped at Thespiai in Boiotia, and at Parion in Mysaia. Despite the constant association of 'Venus and Cupid' in literature, Eros has nothing whatever to do with her in anything but late cult, and little in any literature before the Alexandrian period; although in Hesiod he attends Aphrodite, he is not her son, but an ancient cosmogonical power, which indeed he continued to be in theological and philosophic speculation. In the places where his worship is of importance, he is quite markedly the deity of the loveliness of young men and boys, to which, as is well known, the Greeks were exceedingly susceptible. In Alexandrian times, however, the idea of romantic love (not mere desire) between the sexes took possession of literature, which is why most of the famous love-stories date from this time. Eros therefore became more and more important, at the same time losing his dignity; for whereas he was previously shown for the most part as a handsome young athlete—his famous bow dates only from the fourth century B.C.—he is now generally shown as a pretty child, a little winged archer, capricious and mischievous, delighting in working magic (by shooting an invisible arrow at them) on gods and men alike. In literature, therefore, he appears for the most part late and in a subordinate part, as part of the divine machinery for making someone fall in love with someone else.[23]

Pausanias means to correct Phaedrus, who claimed that Eros is καλός. No action is beautiful or ugly in and of itself, but beautiful if done beautifully, ugly if done shamefully; Eros is beautiful or ugly according to the kind of love it is. Vulgar Eros is directed toward women and young boys, and to the body rather than the soul, and it is as inconstant as its objects. Heavenly Eros is associated with Heavenly Aphrodite, who is motherless, and directed solely toward the masculine, a principle superior in strength and intelligence to the feminine. That is, it is directed not toward young boys but toward adolescents, youths whose intelligence is beginning to sprout with their beards. Vulgar Eros has brought pederasty into disrepute and should be forbidden by law, like adultery.

The νόμος—custom or law—concerning pederasty is in most places

---

23. H. J. Rose, *A Handbook of Greek Mythology*, New York, 1959, pp. 122–123.

simple. Some Greek cities allow it, others forbid it, especially those in Ionia under barbarian rule. In Athens, the law or custom is more complicated and difficult to understand: people generally approve of the lover's suit, no matter how extreme his importunity, and law permits this to be done without reproach, its license even extending to the breaking of oaths and promises, since a sexual vow is not binding as an oath. On the other hand, parents in Athens prevent their sons from talking with lovers, and boys are criticized by their contemporaries and their elders for allowing themselves to be seduced. So in Athens, pederasty seems to be regarded both as beautiful and as shameful. But no act is simply beautiful or shameful in itself, but beautiful if done beautifully, shameful if done shamefully— Pausanias is a master of the ringing tautology. It is shameful to gratify an unworthy lover, who is inconstant because he loves the bloom of the body, which fades; but the worthy lover loves the soul and its virtue, the attributes that constitute the excellence of a man and a citizen, and this love is permanent and not inconstant.

And so, Pausanias avers, Athenian law provides a test for distinguishing worthy lovers from those who ought to be shunned: it is the test of time, which shows whether lover and beloved are moved by love of virtue and education, παιδεία. If Eros is good and founded on virtue, it justifies any action including deception, since it is good to gratify a lover for the sake of virtue. So Heavenly Eros is of the highest value both to private citizens and the city, for it compels both lover and beloved to be concerned for their own virtue.

"Aphrodite," in ordinary Greek usage, meant sex, and the verb ἀφ-ροδισιάζω, used in the active of the man and in the passive of the woman, meant to have sexual intercourse. One may distinguish Eros from Aphrodite as one may distinguish love from sex, as something more than sex and perhaps other than sex; so there is merit in Pausanias's distinction. Unfortunately, in his zeal for pederasty, he muddles the distinction between sex and love by offering two Aphrodites and two Erotes: Vulgar Eros and Vulgar Aphrodite aim at women and boys for purposes of sexual intercourse; Heavenly Eros and Heavenly Aphrodite aim only at older boys for purposes of virtue and education—and sexual intercourse, "gratification."

Something is lost in all this. Vulgar Aphrodite, "who in her birth partakes of both male and female," is treated as Venus Meretrix; but she is also of course Venus Genetrix, by whom, as Diotima will suggest in the speech of Socrates, men are able to achieve a kind of vicarious immortality through their offspring. Heavenly Aphrodite, a goddess, but one who yet "partakes not of the female but only of the male," is inherently sterile.

Pausanias's speech is a rhetorical defense of pederasty on the ground that it is noble and good to gratify lovers for the sake of virtue.[24] That is, it is good for adolescent boys, emotionally and intellectually immature, their character unformed, inexperienced in judgment of men and the world, to submit to anal copulation,[25] and play the woman's role,[26] for the sake of masculine self-improvement. And it is appropriate for a man to indulge in every extremity of slavish and groveling behavior, to forswear his own oaths, to practice deceit and seduction, in order to induce a boy so to submit—as long as the man is virtuous.

The frankness with which Pausanias commends pederasty may seem surprising to a modern reader, though perhaps less so than formerly; the love that dared not speak its name tends nowadays to shout it from the rooftops, and hold parades. It will be observed that Pausanias is not praising homosexuality, nor even pederasty broadly defined, but a specific variant of it: the love of pubescent boys just getting their beards. The attachment is essentially romantic and idealized; it is explicitly contrasted with outrage, wantonness, or lust, and it is intended to be permanent. Pausanias himself appears to have been the ἐραστής, the lover, of Agathon as ἐρώμενος, the beloved, and their relationship has continued into adulthood (177d, 193b–c). The ἐραστής was often not an older man but a young man in his first maturity, not separated by many years from the boy he loved.[27]

Plato condemns homosexual intercourse both in the *Republic* (III 403a–c; compare Aristotle *Politics* II 1262a.32–37, *Nicomachean Ethics* VII 1148b.27–30) and in the *Laws*. At *Laws* VIII 838e (compare 841d, 836c–e, I 636c) homosexual intercourse is condemned because of its sterility, and because the practice of it can render men unfit for marriage, and because it is contrary to nature and a shameless indulgence. Plato accurately portrays, in the *Symposium*, common fifth-century Athenian senti-

24. See, by contrast, *Euthydemus* 282a–b.

25. K. J. Dover has suggested, on the basis of vase paintings, that homosexual copulation in Athens was solely intercrural (*Greek Homosexuality*, London, 1978, p. 103). But as he himself acknowledges (p. 99), the literary sources in comedy and Hellenistic poetry assume anal copulation, and Gregory Vlastos for this reason suggests that prevailing artistic conventions screened out the depiction of what was in fact the usual mode of gratification. "Socratic Irony," *Classical Quarterly* 37 (1987), p. 96.

26. Cf. *Laws* VIII 836e.

27. For example, Hippothales' love of Lysis (*Lysis* 204b–d); though in the *Charmides* (155d), Socrates professes himself excited by a glimpse inside Charmides' cloak, and this, though ironic (see below, 216d–e, 222b), must gain its irony by congruence with customary gallantry. The irony in this dialogue persists: at the end, Charmides and Critias, later to be numbered among the Thirty Tyrants, are described as plotting together against Socrates— as in aftertime they did, undertaking to send him to his death (*Apology* 32c–e). Charmides, when young, was καλός in body; he proved not to be καλός in soul.

ment in the matter of homosexuality; but that sentiment was not his own, any more than it was Socrates', as may be inferred from Alcibiades' failure to seduce him. In the *Symposium*, Diotima will treat the intercourse of man and woman as a divine thing, an immortal element in the mortal living creature (206c); men fertile in body turn to women and are lovers in that way, aiming at immortality and remembrance and happiness through the begetting of children (208e). Diotima will also recognize a different kind of pederasty, which is not sexual but aimed solely at education (209b–c); it is a stage in the ascent to Beauty itself (211b).

To understand pederasty in Athens, it is perhaps helpful to understand something of the status of women.[28] Pederasty of the sort Pausanias describes was primarily an upper-class phenomenon, and it was encouraged by the position of upper-class women, who were in purdah, segregated from men since childhood. Athens was a great port city and faced toward Asia; oriental influence may have counted for much in its treatment of women, which, if we may rely on the example of Homer's Penelope, was not historically Greek.[29] An Athenian aristocrat found in marriage a wife who would be mistress of his house and mother of his children, but not an intellectual and moral companion, and marriage was not a matter of love or romance but of dynastic continuity based on family alliances. It is an indication of the status of women that, among the citizen class, seduction was a more serious crime than rape;[30] it was plainly not the woman's interest in personal safety nor the integrity of her body that was protected by this rule, but the proprietary interest of her husband or guardian, his interest in stability of possession, legitimacy of offspring, and quiet enjoyment of title.

So love and marriage had very little to do with each other, though no

28. Helpful, but not dispositive; it may put the cart before the horse. So far from the position of Athenian women explaining Athenian homosexuality, it may be that Athenian homosexuality goes some way toward explaining the position of Athenian women. Pausanias's contempt for women and heterosexual intercourse suggests an attitude toward the female principle that is consistent with, if it does not imply, the subjugation of women, and may be connected with the worship of Dionysus.

29. Neither was homosexuality, of which there is no trace in Homer. Between the eighth century and the fifth century something happened—something perhaps associated with the Thracian Dionysus.

30. A. R. W. Harrison, *The Law of Athens: Family and Property*, Oxford, 1968, p. 34; cf. p. 38, summarizing criminal offenses allied to adultery, such as procuring and prostitution: "Two features of these rules concerned with sexual behavior especially strike us. First, the woman and her chastity are hardly protected in their own right, but only because she is the humble but necessary vehicle for carrying on the οἶκος. Second, sexual acts of males outside matrimony are only punished if committed with free-born Athenians; it was not the acts themselves, but the involvement of two citizens in them which made them sufficiently abhorrent to entail legal punishment."

doubt, as happens in other cultures where marriages are arranged, love often followed. A figure like Aspasia, the mistress of Pericles, to whose intellectual brilliance Plato pays ironical tribute in the *Menexenus,* is significant: she is a *hetaira,* a companion, a courtesan—not a common prostitute, but also not a wife—and she is foreign-born. Indeed, the presence of a woman at a symposium such as Agathon's was prima facie evidence in a court of law that she was not a citizen. Women were readily available, of course—there were the flute-girls, for example. But they were slaves or foreigners, or children rescued from exposure for purposes of prostitution, and seldom objects of an idealizing love.

Upper-class Athenian men turned for romance not to women, who were either unavailable or ineligible, but to boys of their own class. These relationships were perhaps not primarily sexual—romantic love in general is not primarily sexual—but doubtless they were often so.

Bury remarks:

> The speech of Pausanias is a composition of considerable ability. Although, like Phaedrus, he starts by grounding his conception of the dual Eros on mythological tradition, yet when this conception is once stated the distinction is maintained and its consequences followed out with no little power of exposition. The manner in which the laws regarding pederasty in the various states are distinguished, and in special the treatment of the complex Athenian νόμος, display the cleverness of a first-rate pleader. The general impression, in fact, given us by the speech is that it forms an exceedingly smart piece of special pleading in favor of the proposition that it is good to gratify lovers. The nakedness of this proposition is cloaked by the device of distinguishing between a noble and a base Eros, and by the addition of the saving clause 'for the sake of virtue'. . . .
>
> Pausanias is a lawyer-like person in his style of argumentation; and, appropriately enough, much of his speech is concerned with νόμοι. The term is noteworthy, since it inevitably suggests that antithesis νόμος)(φύσις which was so widely debated among the sophists and thinkers of the close of the fifth century. Is the moral standard fixed by nature (φύσει) or merely by convention (νόμῳ)? . . . Pausanias poses as a conventionalist, and a relativist, and a champion of law as against nature . . . ; and this is of itself sufficient to show that, in Plato's eyes, he is a specimen of the results of sophistic teaching. . . . In literary style the speech of Pausanias displays, in a much higher degree than that of Phaedrus, the tricks and ornaments proper to the sophistical schools of rhetoric.[31]

31. *Symposium,* p. xxvi–xxvii.

If Pausanias's distinction between two Aphrodites and two Erotes is muddled, it was also in aftertime fertile; it suggests that love may be more than physical, and that, insofar as it is directed toward education and virtue, it may become a means to attaining a spiritual end. Ficino in the Renaissance used it to point the contrast between sacred and profane love, a contrast which the *Symposium* anticipates in the differing accounts of love offered in the speech of Diotima and the speech of Aristophanes.

It will be observed that Pausanias thinks that the lover who loves beautifully is beautiful, καλός. In this use of the word he agrees with Phaedrus.

First Interlude: Aristophanes and His Hiccups (185c–e)

Apollodorus now humorously comments on the sophistical isology of Pausanias's speech, his "speaking in equal measures," with repetitive rhythms, neatly balanced antitheses, and frequent use of assonance, including rhyme and alliteration. This ties the speech of Pausanias to the speech of Agathon: the rhetoric of both is in the manner of the sophist Gorgias (compare 198c).

The story of Aristophanes' hiccups, the most famous hiccups in literature, performs a variety of dramatic functions at once. It provides comic relief; it calls attention to the drinking habits of Aristophanes and the medical lore of Eryximachus; it emphasizes the importance of the speech of Aristophanes by mentioning it and deferring it, thereby increasing expectancy and dramatic tension. At a subliminal level, it reminds us once again of the brooding presence that haunts the *Symposium*, the presence of Dionysus, the wine-god, whom Agathon has prayed in aid as a judge.

Dionysus

The banquet takes place at night, and all through the night. It is lit by lamps, burning wicks in pools of olive oil, for there were then no candles. Unlike daylight, this light comes from many different directions at once, from many lamps, for it is a large room in a great house to hold so many couches, and on this winter night of the Lenaea the lamps provide not only light but heat. The light is not intense. It is a golden light, softening outlines, warming, flattering, making luminous the faces of the speakers. They may recall, as they look at one another and listen, that gold is the color of divinity.

The modern reader of the *Symposium* senses the light without seeing it, and senses in it, half in shadow, the movement of numinous forms. They are the forms of gods he barely comprehends—Eros, of course, and Aphrodite, Uranus and Cronus and Zeus, Apollo and the fated musician-hero Orpheus. And everywhere in the shadows, the flickering, haunted figure of Dionysus, whose festival it is. In the corners of so large a room, perhaps, there is darkness—or only so much light as to make darkness visible. Dionysus was of fiery origin.

In the *Cratylus* (406b), Socrates makes the name Dionysus mean Wine-Giver and connects him with Aphrodite, born of the foam. He was in origin a god of fertility, and chief of his symbols, other than wine, was the phallus, ritually symbolized as the thyrsus, or wand. His rites were celebrated at three main Athenian festivals, the Lenaea in winter and the Anthesteria[32] in spring, festivals of great antiquity whose origins lie shrouded in the archaic age, and the Greater Dionysia, a civic festival that perhaps dates from the mid-sixth century, as distinct from the more ancient country dionysia held locally around Attica. The Greater Dionysia, if it was celebrated with a bout of public drunkenness of which Plato heartily disapproved (*Laws* I 637a–b), was also celebrated by drama, and from it came not only the comedies of Aristophanes, always in Dionysus's company (*Symposium* 177e), but the tragedies of Aeschylus, Sophocles, and Euripides. The Lenaea was an occasion for drama too, usually comedy, though Agathon has just won the competition there with a tragedy. Athens no doubt was the city of Athena, but in the fifth century B.C. Dionysus was one of its primary gods. One might read long and hard in Plato before discovering this to be true; yet it is important to the *Symposium* and, indeed, to Plato's criticism of the positive morality of his time.

A κῶμος is a revel, and a comedy a revel-song; the revel often ends in a γάμος, a union of the sexes, and throughout the classical period the chorus and actors in comedy wear artificial phalli and sing phallic songs. Tragedy is a goat-song, and distinctly less jolly; the goat-song may originally have been sung over a goat as sacrificial victim, torn alive and eaten raw as a representative of Dionysus himself. Tragedy sends suffering and

---

32. The Anthesteria was a festival of flowers, at which the jars of new wine were opened; but it also was a time of exorcising the ghosts of the dead, very like Halloween. This may explain the connection between Dionysus and Hades in Heraclitus, Fr. 93: "If it were not to Dionysus that they made procession and sang hymns to the pudenda, they would be doing most shameful things; Hades and Dionysus, for whom they rave and celebrate the rites of the winepress, are the same." Aristotle preserves record of a rite of great antiquity still practiced in his own day: The King Archon, the chief religious magistrate of Athens, had a building called the Bucoleum, or Bull Stall, near the Prytaneum, where his wife, in an annual ceremony at the Anthesteria, married and had sexual intercourse (σύμμιξις) with Dionysus (*Athenaion Politeia* 3.5). No details of the ceremony are recorde 1, and it is treated as a sacred mystery, but if we keep to the name of the building, it suggests ritual intercourse with a bull, the characteristic bestial form of Dionysus. See, however, H. W. Parke, *Festivals of the Athenians*, Ithaca, N.Y., 1977, p. 112.

violent death to a hero or heroine in a manner worthy of lamentation, and it assumes a characteristic psychology of ὕβρις, arrogant refusal to keep within the metes and bounds of one's own place in the scheme of things, coupled with νέμεσις, or allotted destruction. Modern drama is meant for entertainment. Attic drama, in origin at least, served a religious purpose: to obtain for the community the divine blessings of fertility and, connected by way of crop failure, release from sin. Back of it all, perhaps, is not only the goat but the scape-goat.

Dionysus in Athens at the dramatic date of the *Symposium* in 416 might have been regarded as a genial god, as wine is genial. The Athenian in the *Laws*, written at the end of Plato's long life, enacts that Dionysus may be invited by men over forty years of age; he is partner of revels, cheering the heart against old age, and his gift is not to be censured. But in 406 B.C., approximately the date of Aristodemus's narration of the *Symposium*, Euripides' *Bacchae* was posthumously produced in Athens, and the first readers of the *Symposium* may have remembered that Dionysus was also something other than a wine-god, and more terrible.

The *Bacchae* is the story of how the worship of Dionysus came to Greece from Lydia and Phrygia. It is a disturbing play, especially in its representation of the god, who is portrayed as powerful, effeminate, pitilessly cruel, licentious, and, specifically in respect to Pentheus and Agave, who oppose him, moved by motives of humiliation and revenge. The play, in part at least, answers to known ritual: womens' societies at Delphi engaged in mountain dancing, ὀρειβασία, in historic times and were joined by delegates from Athens. These *orgia*, which were certainly acts of devotion and may or may not have involved orgies, took place in midwinter, in alternate years,[33] at Delphi, by night. Carrying the thyrsus, a long rod tipped with a clump of ivy, with wreaths of ivy on their heads and clad in fawnskins, some of them handling snakes, some of them giving nurse at the breast to small animals they would later tear to pieces, the women danced to the very summit of Parnassus, over eight thousand feet high. They danced as possessed, to the music of shrill flutes and timbrels, tossing their heads back and exposing their throats, psychologically in a state in which the boundaries of normal self-awareness and self-control were lost, their human personality replaced by another which they took to be that of the god himself. Religious dancing, in the case of these bacchae, produced an ecstatic state in which the worshipper experienced communion or even identity with Dionysus. This state was induced by a cul-

33. Celebration in alternate years strongly suggests that the god of ecstasy and the wine-god are not the same, but in origin different gods given the same name; for the wine-god is a god of the returning seasons, a year-god.

minating ceremony, the tearing apart alive and eating raw, σπαραγμός and ὠμοφαγία, of a sacrificial victim, often a bull or goat in addition to fawns and small animals and helpless nurslings. In Euripides' *Bacchae*, the victim is Pentheus, prince of Thebes; the σπαραγμός ends with Agave, his own mother, carrying Pentheus's head on a thyrsus, mistaking it for that of a young lion and exulting in her ability as a huntress. It is, as L. A. Post remarked, a song of triumph for her own ruin.

Such a state of possession clearly implies extreme pathology, a brief reactive psychosis involving emotional turmoil, delusions, and hallucinations. In short, these women were temporarily mad. One may well think of Lucretius on the sacrifice of Iphegenia: "tantum religio potuit suadere malorum."

We are left with the question of what the *Bacchae* meant to Euripides, and to his audience. E. R. Dodds remarks that "as the 'moral' of the *Hippolytus* is that sex is a thing about which you cannot afford to make mistakes, so the 'moral' of the *Bacchae* is that we ignore at our peril the demand of the human spirit for Dionysiac experience. For those who do not close their minds against it such experience can be a deep source of spiritual power and εὐδαιμονία. But those who repress the demand in themselves or refuse its satisfaction in others transform it by their act into a power of disintegration and destruction, a blind natural force that sweeps away the innocent with the guilty."[34] If this trivializes the *Hippolytus*, its account of the *Bacchae*, and of εὐδαιμονία, is decidedly unclear: what does εὐδαιμονία consist in? "To resist Dionysus is to repress the elemental in one's own nature; the punishment is the sudden collapse of the inward dykes when the elemental breaks through perforce and civilization vanishes";[35] but in the same paragraph Dodds suggests that the ritual "may have developed out of spontaneous attacks of mass hysteria." Dodds is able to describe the state of Euripides' mind when he wrote the *Bacchae*: "It is as if the renewed contact with nature in the wild country of Macedonia, and his re-imagining there of the old miracle story, had released some spring in the aged poet's mind, re-establishing a contact with hidden sources of power which he had lost in the self-conscious, over-intellectualized environment of late-fifth-century Athens, and enabling him to find an outlet for feelings which for years had been pressing on his consciousness without attaining to complete expression."[36] So εὐδαιμονία and spiritual power, it seems, are to be identified with the "elemental" in one's nature as expressed in psychosis—Freud's "primary process."

34. *Euripides: Bacchae*, 2d ed., Oxford, 1960, p. xlv.
35. Ibid., xvi.
36. Ibid., xlvii.

We know nothing of Euripides' consciousness apart from the proper interpretation of his plays; but the Athens Euripides left for Macedon in 408 B.C. had been hammered by almost twenty-five years of war, and war, to recall Thucydides, is a harsh task-master, which tends to reduce men's character to their conditions. So far from being overintellectualized, Athens had become increasingly benighted, as superstition, magical practices, and private orgiastic rites increased.[37] If the *Bacchae* is directed to Athens, it is better understood not as an acceptance of Dionysiac licentiousness and unreason, but as a rejection of it.[38] The play contains perhaps the greatest recognition scene in all literature, as Cadmus, Agave's father, brings her to consciousness of what it is she holds in her hand. The power of the scene is intensified by the fact that it implies a double recognition, for the audience is brought to recognition too. Up to this point the religion of Dionysus has been made to seem attractive and joyful, as dancing is joyful, as wit is attractive. Now, pity for Agave combines with revulsion at the cruelty of the god who has possessed her.[39] Is it too Socratic to suppose that Euripides held a mirror up to his audience and brought them to examination of their own lives?

Interpreting the thought of a poet is speculation, as Socrates in the *Protagoras* (347c–348a) points out, and one must beware, in discussing Greek religion as in discussing our own, of the fallacy of accident. A visitor from Mars, observing the handling of rattlesnakes in the name of Christ in Harlan County, Kentucky, would be mistaken in using that ceremony as evidence for the ritual observance of Christian churches generally; bumper stickers reading "God said it, I believe it, and that settles it" do not show currently and universally accepted canons of biblical criticism and exegesis. The rites at Delphi no doubt represented an aberration from the even tenor of Greek religious ways, and it is difficult at this distance to know how they influenced the minds of the *Symposium*'s first readers; still, it is very likely that Dionysus, accompanied by maenads and silens, decorated the red-figured cups from which the guests at the banquet drank. It may be said of Dionysiac religion generally that it involved extreme emotional ambivalence. Dodds says of rites of the sort of σπαρ-αγμός that they are "at once holy and horrible, fulfillment and unclean-

---

37. See ibid., xxiii. Plato, who punishes sparingly, would in the *Laws* (X 910b–c) punish anyone practicing private orgiastic rites.

38. See E. R. Goodenough, *Jewish Symbols in the Greco-Roman Period*, vol. 6, *Wine*, Princeton, N.J., 1956, pp. 17–18: "The play is a denunciation of popular Dionysiac rites on the ground that they are a travesty of the true nature of the god . . . a protest against those in Athens who would observe the rites in the crude form in which Pentheus accurately describes them." For a review of other interpretations of the play, see Dodds, *Bacchae*, xxxvii–xlii.

39. See L. A. Post, *From Homer to Menander*, Berkeley, Calif., 1951, pp. 150–151.

ness, a sacrament and a pollution—the same violent conflict of emotional attitudes that turns all through the *Bacchae* and lies at the root of all religion of the Dionysiac type."[40] Goodenough remarks:

> No Hellenic god is more controverted than Dionysus, and none more diversely represented. He was a deity of undetermined origin who apparently came into Hellas after many of the other gods were thoroughly settled, or had been assimilated from pre-Grecian peoples. The evidence for him on vases is very large; yet no two people who have examined the evidence have come through with the same impressions. . . . It seems obvious that in early times Dionysus was a god of crude realism, who embodied the contradictions of nature and of man's soul. The contradictions expressed themselves in a series of complete paradoxes: he was the hunted hunter; one who brought life mixed with death, light that darkens, nursing care which tears and devours the nursling, and, himself mad, he maddened his followers with the true madness which finds its highest intelligibility in raving. The god presented himself in just as bewildering a confusion of symbols, of whose every detail historians have found strikingly different interpretations. Dionysus came, without dispute, to be a general god of fertility, with special interest in the vine, . . . the god who rose from the dead in the spring. The original Dionysus who came down from Thrace to Athens was not the same at all but only a god of ecstasy. The Greek vases most vividly agree with comedy in emphasising sexuality in the Dionysiac symbolism.[41]

That Dionysus was both the hunter and the hunted, a unity of opposites, is suggested by his iconography on the pottery: his creatures are the panther and the fawn, both distinctively spotted, and sometimes almost indistinguishable in form. It may be that the unity of opposites included not only hunter and hunted but male and female, that Athenian homosexuality was connected with Dionysiac religion of the ecstatic type described in the *Bacchae*, which had little enough to do with fertility, the image of creation. Dionysus is represented as effeminate or androgynous by Euripides and others, and the alternation of domination and submission, attraction and repugnance, beauty and foulness, is characteristic of the extreme emotional ambivalence found in religion of the Dionysiac type.[42] Pausanias's contempt for women and his pederasty recall the fate

40. *Bacchae*, xvii.
41. *Jewish Symbols*, pp. 13–16.
42. See Walter Burkert, *Structure and History in Greek Mythology and Ritual*, Berkeley, Calif., 1979, pp. 29–120.

of Agave, and the fact that Pentheus is not a man but a boy with beard
just sprouted. But in an area so socially and psychologically complex as
this, it is perhaps better to think in terms not of linear causation or func-
tional relationships, but of constellations or significant conjunctions of elements. Dodds remarks that "the ὠμοφαγία and the bestial incarnations
reveal Dionysus as something more significant and much more dangerous
than a wine god. He is the principle of animal life, ταῦρος and ταυρό-
φάγος, the hunted and the hunter—the unrestrained potency which man
envies in beasts and seeks to assimilate. His cult was originally an attempt
on the part of human beings to achieve communion with this potency.
The psychological effect was to liberate the instinctive life of man from
the bondage imposed on it by reason and social custom: the worshipper
became conscious of a strange new vitality, which he attributed to the god's
presence within him."[43]

The doctrine of Eros in the *Symposium,* so far from accepting emotional
ambivalence of the Dionysiac type as an essential characteristic of the human soul, replaces it with a steadfast and coherent pursuit of goodness
and beauty that culminates in the contemplation of Beauty itself. Rationality is not psychological bondage imposed on instinctive life. It is the
psychological liberation of instinctive life, as leading to its completion and
fulfillment. Human emotions and desires require peculiarly human expression, and envy of brute beasts, from Plato's point of view, implies
deep-seated sickness of soul.

The Speech of Eryximachus (185e–188e)

Eryximachus, son of Acumenus, is a doctor like his father, and he and
Phaedrus are close friends (176d–e, 177a–d). His profession of medicine
shapes not only his speech but his conduct, and his favorite virtue is temperance. He offers advice on drunkenness (176d) and then on hiccups
(185d–e) and champions moderation in drinking (176b, 214b); when Alcibiades and his revelers enter and the party gets rowdy, he and Phaedrus
leave.[44] He serves as an unelected master of ceremonies at the beginning
(176b–177e) and frequently behaves as if he were in charge of the party
(189a–c, 193d–194a; compare 214a–e). It is he who has suggested the
theme of the banquet, the encomium on Eros.

43. Dodds, *Bacchae,* xlvii.
44. The year after, in 415 B.C., both Eryximachus and Phaedrus were accused of being
involved in the mutilation of the herms, along with Alcibiades (Andocides I 15, 35). Plato's
portrait suggests that he thought the charge unfounded.

Given the Socratic Proportion that health is to the body as virtue is to the soul, Eryximachus as a physician is thematically juxtaposed with Socrates.[45]

Eryximachus follows Pausanias in assuming that Eros has a double nature—there are good and bad Erotes—but he thinks Pausanias did not carry the distinction far enough. Pausanias thought that the double Eros is an impulse in souls toward beautiful persons, whereas in fact it is toward many other things and in other things—in the bodies of all animals, all plants, everything that is. Eryximachus extends Eros to the whole of nature, as a cosmic principle which is the basis of arts as diverse as medicine, gymnastics, agriculture, music, astronomy, and the art of the seer.[46] Medicine is defined as knowledge of the desires—τὰ ἐρωτικά, the things of love—of the body relative to emptying and filling (186c). This process involves making opposites friendly to each other, so that they love and are in attunement with each other. That is, the desires are Erotes, but also by implication have an Eros toward each other, associated with friendship and harmony. The aim of medicine is to introduce harmony between Erotes.[47]

As Pausanias had supposed that a person is καλός in having sexual relations with good people and ugly in gratifying libertines, so the physician is καλός in gratifying the healthy desires in the body, the good Eros, but

45. Gildersleeve claimed that Eryximachus is a pedant and a system-monger "who was only on sufferance in that brilliant company and whom Plato holds up to ridicule as incorporating the worst foibles of the professor of the healing art" (*American Journal of Philology* 30 [1909], p. 109); this in reply to Sir William Osler's claim that "nowhere in literature do we have such a charming picture illustrating the position of the cultivated physician in society as that given in Plato's dialogue of Eryximachus" (*Counsels and Ideals*, New York, 1905, p. 24). It has since been fashionable to see Eryximachus as a caricature, a figure of fun, and to discount his importance. This is unsupported by the text, and obscures his thematic role in the dramatic structure of the *Symposium*. See further Ludwig Edelstein, "The Role of Eryximachus in Plato's *Symposium*," *Ancient Medicine* (ed. Temkin and Temkin), Baltimore, 1967, pp. 153–171. Cf. *Phaedrus* 268a–b.

46. In treating Eros as a cosmic principle, Eryximachus was anticipated by Phaedrus, who quoted Hesiod and Parmenides (178b). In assuming two Erotes as cosmic principles, he perhaps also draws on Empedocles' cosmic principles of Love and Strife. Aristotle provides an instructive comment: see *Metaphysics* I 984b 23–985a 6.

47. Dover remarks (*Symposium*, p. 105): "Eryximachus, who feels that the study of medicine qualifies him to go beyond what Pausanias has said, runs together (1) the contrast between good desires or tendencies and bad desires or tendencies, and (2) the contrast between good consequences of reconciling opposites and the bad consequences of failure to reconcile them. In (1) he stretches the denotation of the word 'eros' wide enough to diminish its utility very greatly, and in (2) he stretches it even further by treating an adjustment between two extremes as creating an eros of the extremes for each other." But (1) scarcely diminishes the utility of the word; it anticipates the breadth of Diotima's use, while (2) anticipates her connection of desire with friendship, φιλία. See David Konstan and Elisabeth Young-Bruehl, "Eryximachus' Speech in the *Symposium*," *Apeiron* 1982, pp. 40–46.

not those unhealthy desires that constitute the bad Eros. Love has passed
from the gratification of desire to the principle of all desire and gratification. In so doing it has become normative, as indeed Pausanias had already suggested, in that it implies a distinction between desires and what
desires ought to be satisfied.

Eryximachus extends this account to gymnastic and agriculture. Again,
music is knowledge of desires concerning attunement and rhythm, and
the musician must introduce concord among opposites and gratify the
good Eros of the audience; astronomy is knowledge of desires concerning
motions of stars and seasons of years, their mixture and attunement; ἡ
μαντική, the art of the seer, involves avoiding the impiety that arises if
one does not gratify the orderly and good Eros, and also introduces
friendship between gods and men.

Eryximachus's speech serves an important dramatic function. By extending Eros beyond sexual desire, it anticipates Diotima's treatment of
Eros as desire in all its forms, one of whose works is friendship. By making
Eros a cosmic principle evinced in medicine, a principle found not only
in opposed desires of the body but in their attunement, it anticipates the
main theme of the speech of Aristophanes: that human love is a healing
power, that Eros is the good physician (189d, 193d).

Eryximachus and Greek Medicine

The medical theory Eryximachus expounds is broadly Hippocratean,
though not traceable in detail to any known work; its prose style, and its
impulse toward generalization, perhaps show the influence of the sophist
Hippias.[48]

Hippocrates was not a culture hero but a living, breathing man: Plato
in the *Protagoras* (311b) mentions "Hippocrates of Cos, one of the Ascle-
piads" as a teacher to whom a student might go to learn the art of medicine. In the *Phaedrus* (270c–e), Socrates offers an account of scientific
method that recalls Eryximachus in its concern for the nature of the
Whole, cites Hippocrates in support of the claim that one cannot understand the body unless one follows this method of procedure, and suggests
that medical inquiry is an example of true argument and the method of
collection and division characteristic of Plato's own dialectic. Six centuries
later, Galen would say, "Hippocrates is the first known to us of all those

48. The brief Hippocratic treatise *The Art* has been (conjecturally) ascribed to Hippias;
Eryximachus, who is present with Hippias in the *Protagoras*, here uses the exact phrase
(186b).

who have been both physicians and philosophers, because he was also first to recognize what Nature effects."[49]

The Hippocratic corpus as it has come down to us, however, is certainly not the work of one man or even a committee, but of a tradition extending over hundreds of years, and, in its theoretical aspects, often at variance with itself. The tradition is united in its naturalism, its relentless exclusion of divine intervention as the explanation of disease, including mental disease. The author of *The Sacred Disease*—not only epilepsy, but also perhaps other mental disease including bacchic or corybantic possession—strikes the tone of the whole: "I am about to discuss the disease called 'sacred.' It is not, in my opinion, any more divine or more sacred than other diseases, but has a natural cause, and its supposed divine origin is due to men's inexperience, and to their wonder at its peculiar character."[50] Eryximachus as a doctor, asked at a drinking party to praise Eros as a god, immediately reduces it to a natural power.

Plato attributes to Hippocrates a philosophical concern that is frequently, though by no means universally, exhibited in the Hippocratic corpus. Certainly it is exhibited by Eryximachus, whose claim that ἁρμονία, attunement, is the aim of medicine and the essence of health is strikingly evident in *Regimen I*, where health is analyzed in terms of music and, more specifically, attainment of ratios among the elements of the body of the octave, the fourth, and the fifth, the perfect consonances of Greek music; failure to achieve attunement causes disease. *Regimen I*, again, holds that the elements of the body are composed of fire and water, and these, though opposite, are also treated as complementary: the power of fire is to cause motion, the power of water to nourish, so that fire and water are different in power but work together in their use. Eryximachus's criticism of Heraclitus's doctrine of the warfare of opposites fits with this; the emphasis in *Regimen I* on fire and water is perhaps akin to what Eryximachus has in mind in suggesting that the aim of medicine is to make inimical elements—opposites such as cold and hot, bitter and sweet, dry and wet— friendly by bringing them into attunement. The introduction of these opposites, again, perhaps anticipates the doctrine of opposite humors, phlegm, blood, yellow bile, and black bile, associated with the hot, the cold, the wet, and the dry, whose proportional mixture or blending produced health, and disproportion disease and pain.[51] If these are philo-

49. *On the Natural Faculties* I xiii (translation after Brock).
50. *The Sacred Disease* I 1ff., trans. W. H. S. Jones. The discussion of Greek medicine in what follows owes much to Jones's magisterial edition of Hippocrates in the Loeb Classical Library.
51. Cf. *Timaeus* 81a–86a, with F. M. Cornford's commentary, in *Plato's Cosmology*, London, 1937, pp. 332–343. Hippocrates, *On the Nature of Man*, chap. iv.

sophical conjectures, they are also primitive scientific theories, meant to
explain the factual foundation on which Greek medicine was based, derived from accumulated experience and accurate observation, preserved
in clinical histories and accompanied by clear classification of diseases: in
this connection, observe Eryximachus's emphasis on diagnosis.

Did Eryximachus have an art? He did indeed. In surgery, the Greeks
were in many respects ahead of average medical competence in America
at the middle of the last century, specifically in their emphasis on clean-
liness—of hands, of instruments, of dressings and bandages, of the operating room. They were skilled in the treatment and bandaging of
dislocations and fractures, including depression fractures of the skull;
they could trepan the skull to relieve pressure on the brain; they had excellent knowledge of the treatment and dressing of wounds, and understood the uses of cautery. On the medical side, there was fair knowledge
of the pharmacopia, an astonishing emphasis on the preparation and use
of various kinds of barley water, concern to see that the patient was rested
and kept calm, and a considerable emphasis on diet. Treatment was con-
servative, with trust in the natural recuperative powers of the body—the
vis medicatrix naturae. The Greek doctors were also much concerned with
preventive medicine, and specifically with diet and exercise. They classi-
fied diseases by symptoms rather than causes; they appear not to have
known smallpox, measles, diphtheria, scarlet fever, bubonic plague, or
syphilis; they did know pneumonia, consumption, malaria in manifold
forms, and the common cold. They also knew that medicine was a noble
calling, and their ethical responsibility to their patients, repeatedly insisted upon in the Hippocratic corpus, was of a high order: respect for
their art made them intolerant of apes and clowns, and treatment was
distinguished by humanity to the patient and the curiosity to inquire.
Eryximachus is proud of his art, and with reason. Plato treats the physician's art as analogous to that of the statesman, as body is analogous to
soul.

Second Interlude: Aristophanes Recovered from
His Hiccups (189a–c)

Eryximachus now threatens with humorous self-importance to censure
Aristophanes, and Aristophanes, the comic poet who ridiculed Socrates
on the stage, expresses fear that he will himself become an object of ridicule.

The Speech of Aristophanes (189c–193e)

Aristophanes revises the naturalism of Eryximachus by treating Eros, not as a dual cosmic force at work in the world-process at large which also represents its friendship or attunement, but as a single healing force within human beings. The comic poet offers a story dealing with "human nature and its condition" (189d).

Human beings were once spherical, with two sets of arms and legs, one head with two faces and four ears, and two sets of genitals, male, or female, or both, so that they were any of three kinds: male-male, male-female, female-female.[52] These beings were very strong and, in their strength and pride, challenged the gods. So Zeus, in order to keep them alive but weaken them, had them cut in two by Apollo and their faces turned toward the cut, so that they might become more orderly by contemplating the fact of their own division.

The two halves of each whole were filled with longing ($\pi\acute{o}\theta o\varsigma$) for each other, and when they found one another they embraced and were unwilling to do anything apart; so they died from hunger and inability to act. The race would have perished, had Zeus not taken pity and turned their genitals to the front; they had before got children in the earth as the locusts do, but now in each other, male begetting in female. So this is the origin of Eros: he is inborn in us and unites our ancient nature, making one from two and healing us (191d). Each of us is only the token of a human being, sliced like a flatfish, and ever seeking his matching token ($\sigma\acute{u}\mu\beta o\lambda o\nu$), whether that token is male or female.

When a half meets its other half, they are stunned by friendship and kinship and Eros, and they delight in being with each other. The reason for this is not desire for sexual intercourse (192c); on the contrary, the soul of each wishes for something it cannot put into words. Lovers desire to live a common life and die a common death, to become one in a complete and lasting union. The reason is that this was our ancient nature, and we were once wholes. So Eros is a name for the desire and pursuit of wholeness ($\tau o\tilde{u}$ $\acute{o}\lambda o\nu$, 193a). It both arises from and strives to cure the diremption of human nature.

Both Jung and Freud supposed that the speech of Aristophanes rep-

---

52. This conception is essentially original, without antecedent in Greek mythology, though Empedocles (Diels-Kranz, *Fragmente der Vorsokratiker* B 57–61) assumed that the conflict of Love and Strife had in the course of the ages thrown up various monstrous forms. Aristophanes is a comic poet with a salacious wit, and his image is perhaps drawn not from literary antecedents but from sexual intercourse, and more specifically, to judge from the frequency with which it is depicted in vase painting, coupling *in piedi*.

resented Plato's own view of love, and that it supported their own speculation that love is inherently androgynous or bisexual, that is, that all
men and women have in them an impulse toward both homosexual and
heterosexual relations.[53] As an interpretation of the *Symposium,* this is mistaken. Aristophanes no more expresses Plato's theory of love than Callicles in the *Gorgias* expresses Plato's theory of justice; Aristophanes is a
character in a dialogue, and not the leading character. Jung and Freud
also misinterpret Aristophanes, whose story implies that individual human beings are not inherently bisexual, but inherently either homosexual
or heterosexual; it is the primitive whole, not its halves, which is capable,
on occasion, of being androgynous (189d–e, 191d–192b). Aristophanes,
after all, wrote the *Lysistrata,* and only heterosexual love accords with the
purpose of Zeus, who turned the genitals to the front for the purpose of
reproduction (191c); homosexual intercourse is at one point dismissed as
a means of relieving tension and getting back to work (191c; compare
193e), and Eros in the speech of Aristophanes is not conceived to be primarily directed toward sexual relations at all (192c–d).

In the *Phaedrus* (264c–d), Socrates criticizes the speech of Lysias on
grounds of inconsequence: a discourse should be like a living thing, with
body, head, and foot, the members organized in fitting relation to each
other and to the whole, whereas Lysias's speech can be read in any order,
like the epitaph of Midas the Phrygian. So much might indeed be said,
very nearly, of the speeches of Phaedrus, Pausanias, Eryximachus, and
Agathon. Aristophanes' speech is, on the contrary, well organized and
develops directly to the conclusion at 193b–d. R. G. Bury remarks:

> In point of style and diction the speech of Aristophanes stands out
> as an admirable piece of simple Attic prose, free at once from the
> awkwardness and monotony which render the speeches of Phaedrus
> and Eryximachus tedious and from the over-elaboration and artifi-
> cial ornamentation which mar the discourses of Pausanias and Aga-
> thon. In spite of occasional poetic colouring—as, e.g., in the finely-
> painted scene between Hephaestus and the lovers (192c ff.)—the
> speech as a whole remains on the level of pure, easy-flowing rhythm-
> ical prose, in which lucidity is combined with variety and vivacity of
> expression.[54]

---

53. C. G. Jung, *Psychology and Religion,* New Haven, 1938, p. 68, following Freud, *Three
Essays on the Theory of Sexuality* (1905), Standard Edition, p. 136; cf. *Beyond the Pleasure Principle* (1920), Standard Edition, pp. 57–58; *Outline of Psychoanalysis,* New York, 1949, p. 6n1.
54. *Symposium,* p. xxxiv.

Aristophanes, "whose whole occupation concerns Dionysius and Aphrodite" (177e), has given a brilliant analysis of romantic love, offering an aetiological myth that explains Eros by a quasihistorical account of the division of human nature. Each of us is the product of our ancestors' bisection: just as they were primitively combined with one and only one other person to constitute a whole of which each was half, so we are halves longing to meet one and only one person who is our other half, so that in our union we may become whole.

This implies the uniqueness of the beloved: if Eros is desire for wholeness, there is one and only one other half that will satisfy that desire. Uniqueness and desire for wholeness explain the fact that lovers long to be with each other for life, unwilling to be separated even for a little while, and yet have no words to express what they wish to get from each other by being together. The desire for wholeness is directly connected with intrinsic delight in the presence of the beloved.

The uniqueness of the beloved and intrinsic delight in the presence of the beloved imply that Eros involves much more than sexual intercourse. The beloved is unique, but the sexual organs of lovers are not unique; men and women are in this respect fungible—by night all cats are gray. Again, delight in the beloved implies a desire for permanent association with the beloved, whereas desire for sexual intercourse ceases when appetite is satisfied. Eros is not the same as Aphrodite. Still, intrinsic delight in the beloved seeks sexual expression and issues in sexual passion, an appetite that grows by what it feeds on.

It will be observed that Aristophanes does not claim of Eros that it inherently idealizes the beloved; the beloved is not a god and not divine, any more than the lover is. Nor is there any suggestion that romantic love is a projective veil concealing the real nature of the beloved while revealing the archaic transferences of the lover. Lover and beloved are halves of the same whole, and it is the desire for wholeness that defines the nature of Eros. Love is the good physician, healing the incompleteness of our human nature, curing its diremption.

This view of love is not without dignity, and it is founded on facts of human experience, as Diotima will herself attest (211d–e); if that experience is not so common as advertising copywriters have made it seem, it is also not bounded by given cultures or given constellations of ideas.[55]

55. C. S. Lewis in *The Allegory of Love* (Oxford, 1936, pp. 3–4, 11) argued that romantic love begins with the troubadours and Provençal love poetry, the tradition of courtly love, and that it represents a real, and rare, change in erotic sentiment. Its distinguishing marks are *Frauendienst* and the idealization of adultery, and the transformation of love and the beloved into objects of religious awe and worship. In respect to the last point, at least, Lewis

Aristophanes touches in his speech a primitive and cross-cultural reality. Jacob and Rachel in *Genesis*, Nala and Damayanti in the *Mahabharata*, Orpheus and Eurydice, Pyramis and Thisbe, Romeo and Juliet, are literary representations, from diverse sources, of real emotions.

Zeus divided the united wholes to weaken them, and turned their faces toward their division to remind them of their need for right conduct toward the god. Aristophanes' story is the story of a Fall: we need healing precisely because, when whole, we were impious and not well ordered. Here too there is perhaps an appeal to experience. Lovers, in their concern for one another, are little concerned for anyone else. There is something in love's wholeness which is arrogant (see 190d)—prepared, if need be, to storm heaven.

And not only arrogant, but forever frustrated. For if the aim of love is wholeness and abiding unity, it is an aim that cannot be achieved. I may desire to breathe with your breath, live with your life, die in your death: I cannot do it. Despite the impulse toward union and merger, toward being welded together, becoming one from two, lovers are inherently and essentially separate. And it is the body, by means of which they express their union and their love, which is a cause of their separation.

Aristophanes here touches the very nerve of romantic love. Romantic love makes union with one unique individual the primary value in life: the aim is a wholeness or completion obtainable in no other way, a wholeness that is the very purpose or meaning not only of loving but of living. Yet romantic love is mediated by the body, which is a cause of separation rather than union; so there is a desire fundamental to our nature which cannot in principle be satisfied. Since fulfillment of that fundamental desire is what makes life worth living, and that fundamental desire cannot be fulfilled, life is not worth living: we are creatures of a longing that cannot be satisfied, and romantic love therefore turns back upon itself and is implicated with death.

---

later corrected himself: "Years ago when I wrote about medieval love-poetry and described its strange, half make-believe, 'religion of love,' I was blind enough to treat this as an almost purely literary phenomenon. I know better now. Eros by his nature invites it. Of all loves he is, at his height, most god-like; therefore most prone to demand our worship. Of himself he always tends to turn 'being in love' into a sort of religion" (*The Four Loves*, p. 154). On courtly love in its relation to the myth of Tristan and Isolde, one may consult Denis de Rougemont, *Love in the Western World* (first published in French under the title *L'Amour et l'Occident*), New York, 1956; and M. C. D'Arcy, *The Mind and Heart of Love*, 2d ed., London, 1954. One may also, of course, consult Wagner's *Tristan und Isolde*, with special attention to the Liebestod. The Tristan myth is represented in English literature by Thomas Malory, "The Book of Sir Tristram de Lyones" (ed. Vinaver, *Malory: Works*, Oxford, 1971), which puts the original story told in twelfth-century French romances into the framework of the Arthurian cycle.

Aristophanes offers a myth that begins in extravagant comedy and ends in a vision of the human condition which is, if not inherently tragic, then at least life-denying; in the depths of his speech we may perhaps see both Epicurus and the Stoics—or the Buddha. For it is but a short step to suppose that if the most fundamental desire of our nature cannot be satisfied, if union with the beloved is the very purpose and meaning of our lives, and if that union cannot, and cannot in principle, be attained, desire itself is suffering, and the rational aim of life is not to satisfy desire but to be rid of it, to achieve *ataraxia*, *apatheia*, *undisturbedness*, *lack* of feeling. If romantic love is implicated with death, it is also implicated with despair. The romantic, prepared in the exuberance of his love to storm heaven, ends in a vision of life in which joy has been replaced by an everlasting alpha privative.[56]

But there is another side. Diotima will show that romantic love implies immortal longings, and Aristophanes' claim that lovers wish something besides sexual intercourse, a permanent union that they cannot describe but only hint at obscurely, is perhaps proleptic to Diotima's account of Eros as implicitly love of Beauty itself. If this is true, then the most fundamental desire of our nature is not for another human being, but implicitly for knowledge or contemplation of what always is and never changes. This suggests the doctrine that learning is recollection, a doctrine which in the *Meno, Phaedo,* and *Phaedrus* is taken to imply the immortality of the knowing soul. The *Symposium* does not state the doctrine that learning is recollection, but its argument will prove unintelligible without it: Aristophanes—and Dionysus with him—is a philosopher who has forgotten his aim.

The speech of Aristophanes is by far the best expressed and most powerful in this first part of the *Symposium,* and Plato meant for its force to be felt; the discourse of Agathon that follows, with its incantatory repetition of honorific attributes of Eros, is puerile by comparison. The love that Aristophanes describes will be exemplified by Alcibiades' frustrated love for Socrates, so that, structurally, Aristophanes' speech works at a very deep level of the *Symposium.* Socrates and Diotima will explicitly reject its account of Eros (205e), while acknowledging the emotions on which it rests (211d–e). Aristophanes' account rests on a kind of experience that

---

56. Aristophanes triumphed over Diotima in early German romanticism, and without comedy. Goethe, in *The Sorrows of Young Werther* (1774), portrayed suicide as an appropriate response to frustrated love, with enough conviction to prompt suicides all over Europe, and in *Faust* Goethe made knowledge not the salvation of the soul, but the price of its damnation. The triumph of Aristophanes, drunken comedian and professional servant of Dionysus, was ratified by Nietzsche in *The Birth of Tragedy.*

some people sometimes have, as perhaps Aristophanes would have urged in reply (see 212c). But Diotima treats the analysis of Eros as a matter, not of feeling and emotion, but of desire, and if Eros is so construed, Aristophanes has failed to understand its object.

The thematic importance of the speech of Aristophanes has been obscured by the role Aristophanes' *Clouds* played at Socrates' trial. In the *Apology* (19b–c; compare 18b–d), Socrates ranks Aristophanes as chief among the Old Accusers:

> Very well, what do those who slander me say? It is necessary to read, as it were, their sworn indictment: "Socrates is guilty of needless curiosity and meddling interference, inquiring into things beneath Earth and in the Sky, making the weaker argument stronger, and teaching others to do the same." The charge is something like that. Indeed, you have seen it for yourselves in a comedy by Aristophanes—a certain Socrates being carried around on the stage, talking about walking on air and babbling a great deal of other nonsense, of which I understand neither much nor little.

So the *Clouds* contributed to the prejudice against Socrates which helped cause his death.[57] That we are meant to remember the *Clouds* in the *Symposium* is shown by the fact that Alcibiades alludes to it (221b; *Clouds* 362). Yet Socrates and Aristophanes are on good terms in the *Symposium*, though they disagree about Eros (205e, 212c); they are together at the party, and along with Agathon they are still arguing at dawn (223c–d). Plato draws Aristophanes in bold strokes, but his portrait is neither distorted nor hostile: Aristophanes is made to give a magnificent speech.

The *Clouds* was first produced at the Great Dionysia in 423 B.C., when Socrates was forty-five years old. It took third and last prize in the competition, behind other comedies that have now been lost. The reasons for this ranking we do not know; it was said to be Aristophanes' favorite play. Second prize went to the *Connus* of Ameipsias, which also put Socrates on the stage and lampooned him for his toughness, his poverty, and his lack of shoes.[58] Socrates in the year 423 B.C., a year after the retreat from Delium (see 211a), was in the news.

Aristophanes published the *Clouds* afterwards, probably before the dramatic date of the *Symposium* in 416, in a revised version which was not produced; this is the version that has come down to us. The leading fea-

---

57. See also *Birds* 1282*ff.*, 1554*ff.*, *Frogs* 1491*ff.*
58. Cf. Diogenes Laertius II 28. Perhaps the same Connus who taught Socrates music: *Euthydemus* 272c, 295d; cf. *Menexenus* 235e.

tures of its portrait of Socrates are delineated in the *Apology*: Socrates inquiring into things in the heavens and beneath the earth, which suggested atheism, in his very own φϱοντιστήϱιον, his little thinking-shop, teaching students for pay to make the Unjust Argument triumph over the Just Argument. Aristophanes in no way distinguished Socrates from the sophists, and his Socrates is representative of a type: the *Clouds* is essentially a cartoon. In this Aristophanes confirmed the prejudices of his audience, identifying what his audience failed to distinguish, and for this he might after all be forgiven; a comic poet is a dramatist, and a dramatist, according to the *Gorgias,* is a rhetorician who aims to say what will give pleasure to his hearers without regard to whether it is true or false. Dramatic poetry is a kind of demagoguery, a species of base rhetoric, flattery.[59] The dramatist has the knack of saying what people want to hear. This is a reason to suppose that in the year 423 B.C. the Athenians wanted to hear that Socrates was a sophist. Resemblances are slippery things: Plato in the *Sophist* (231a) will suggest that Socrates resembled the sophists as the dog resembles the wolf, the fiercest of animals and the most tame. Condemn Aristophanes for his lampoon of Socrates? One might as well condemn Athens, the object of Socrates' mission.

Third Interlude: Socrates and Agathon (193e–194e)

Having concluded his speech, Aristophanes now turns to Eryximachus and reminds him that Agathon and Socrates have not yet spoken. Socrates makes light of his ability to speak, and undertakes to engage Agathon in argument. Phaedrus intervenes and tells Agathon to proceed with his praise of Eros.

Socrates' modesty about his own ability to speak compared to Agathon's recalls 175d–e, and Agathon's suggestion that on this point Dionysus will judge between them. The interlude is introduced by Aristophanes, "whose whole business concerns Dionysus and Aphrodite" (177e), and he speaks to Eryximachus, the physician who knows the effects of wine on the body, recommends moderation, and dismisses flute-girls in favor of conversation.[60]

59. *Gorgias* 502c.

60. The thematic tension in the *Symposium* between Dionysus and the λόγος is perhaps the foundation of the distinction between Dionysian and Apollonian, blind and savage energy and measured and harmonious restraint, which Nietzsche offered in *The Birth of Tragedy.* Socrates, whom Nietzsche connects with Euripides and regards as an embodiment of the *Logos,* is there treated as himself a daimon almost on a level with Apollo and Dionysus, who are gods; he is a destructive critic who forces the Apollonian apart from the Dionysian and

The Speech of Agathon (194e–197e)

Agathon, the tragic poet, remarkable for his personal beauty and the beloved of Pausanias (193b), undertakes first to praise the character of Eros, and second, to praise his gifts to men.

Eros is the happiest and most beautiful of the gods, and the youngest, not the oldest, as Phaedrus had claimed; this prepares the way for the leading feature of Agathon's speech, his identification of Eros and its object, the beautiful.[61] Eros hates old age and will not draw near it. He is soft, delicate and supple. He is also good: for he is just, as having no part of violence or injustice; temperate, as master of pleasure in that no other pleasure is stronger than love; courageous, as possessing even Ares, the god of war and the most courageous of gods; and wise, since he is a poet, and his wisdom creates all living things and all the practical arts. Agathon, it will be observed, has ascribed to Eros the so-called cardinal virtues of justice, temperance, courage, and wisdom.

After Eros's character, Agathon recites his gifts to men. He produces peace and kinship, gentleness and goodwill, generosity and graciousness, desire for beauty and concern for good order. His praise should be sung by everyone—and certainly Agathon's own hymn to Eros is incantatory.

The speech of Agathon that follows is very much in the style of Gorgias: it is marked by isology or "speaking in equal units," short parallel clauses, assonance, and rhyme. Denniston remarks:

> But, while the importance of Gorgias has often been exaggerated, it cannot be doubted that he and Thrasymachus, and perhaps other sophists in a less degree, did exercise considerable influence on Greek prose. In the case of Gorgias the influence was, I believe, wholly bad. What he did was, in fact, to take certain qualities inherent in Greek expression, balance and antithesis, and exaggerate them to the point

wrecks Greek tragedy: "In so far as the struggle was directed against the Dionysian element in the older tragedy, we may recognize in Socrates the opponent of Dionysus. He is the new Orpheus who rose against Dionysus, and although he is destined to be torn to pieces by the Maenads of the Athenian court, he still put to flight the powerful god himself " (sec. 12, trans. Walter Kaufmann). This is a penetrating estimate of the thematic tension of the *Symposium*, from which much of its imagery is drawn, and its estimate of Socrates' attitude toward tragedy is accurate; it is also perhaps worth observing that Euripides is the only poet besides Homer whom Socrates in the *Symposium* quotes, and that Apollo is represented by Aristophanes himself as a figure of punishment, carrying out the judgments of Zeus. According to Kaufmann, the young Nietzsche for years carried a copy of the *Symposium* in his pocket; it was his favorite book. But of course, he turned its meaning upside down and perverted it.

61. See also *Phaedrus* 237c, 262d–263e.

of absurdity. To his doctrinaire mind, balance meant mathematical equality. And this was more readily obtained, and more blatantly obvious to the ear, if the clauses were short. Hence his writing is throughout chopped up into the smallest possible units. Further, symmetrical antithesis naturally carries with it assonance at the end of clauses. . . . Gorgias, the ancient authorities tell us, was the first writer of Greek prose to exploit consciously the use of rhyming clauses. Whereas in earlier prose rhymes naturally arose out of symmetrical structure, in Gorgias and Isocrates, and other writers under Gorgionic influence, they are deliberately sought out. . . . Further, with a view to obtaining both rhyme and symmetry, clauses are padded with superfluous synonyms. . . . To the use of short, symmetrical rhyming clauses, we must add the use of similarly derived words in close juxtaposition. . . . Such are the simple ingredients of the manner of Gorgias. Starting with the initial advantage of having nothing in particular to say, he was able to concentrate all his energies upon saying it. And, to an author so fortunately placed, technique offers no especial difficulty.[62]

These features also mark the speech of Agathon. The translation undertakes not to represent but to suggest them.

Agathon begins somewhat frigidly, the conscientious student of Gorgias, but warms to his task in the end. Those who doubt that prose can sing without saying anything may be invited to read the peroration of Agathon's speech in Greek. Bury remarks:

In his speech Agathon claims that he will improve on the method of his predecessors. In his attention to method he is probably taking a leaf out of the book of Gorgias, his rhetorical master and model. Besides the initial distinction between the nature and effects of Eros, another mark of formal method is his practise of recapitulation: at the close of each section he summarises the results. In his portrait of the nature of Eros—his youth, beauty, suppleness of form and delicacy of complexion—Agathon does little more than formulate the conventional traits of the god as depicted in poetry and art. His attempts to deduce these attributes are mere pieces of sophistical word-play.[63]

And yet, the speech of Agathon anticipates in important respects the speech of Socrates and Diotima that is to follow. Agathon distinguishes

62. J. D. Denniston, *Greek Prose Style*, Oxford, 1952, pp. 10–12.
63. *Symposium*, p. xxxv.

between what Eros is and what he causes; Diotima will distinguish Eros from his works. Agathon makes Eros beautiful and a lover of beauty; Diotima will deny that he is beautiful on the ground that he is a lover of beauty. Agathon makes Eros happy; Diotima will make Eros the wish for happiness. Agathon makes Eros a cause of friendship and peace; Diotima will make Eros desire for knowledge of Beauty itself, and thus implicated with the common good. Agathon makes Eros delicate, since his home is in the souls of men; Diotima will exalt beauty of soul above beauty of body. Agathon makes Eros supple in form; Diotima will define Eros in terms of its object. Agathon ascribes to Eros the cardinal virtues of justice, temperance, courage, and wisdom; Diotima will make Eros a philosopher, a lover of wisdom. Agathon makes Eros a poet and creator, responsible for the generation of animals and a teacher of the arts; Diotima will make Eros according to the body responsible for generation, and according to the soul responsible for poetry, law giving, and education.

But in place of Agathon's singing heap of flattering adjectives, meant to adorn the god and please the audience without regard for truth, Diotima will offer, in dithyrambs, the ascent of the lover to Beauty itself. Both speeches are rhetorical. But Agathon's rhetoric deals with appearance, as Socrates' examination of it will show, and Diotima's with reality. The two speeches exhibit the contrast between sophistic *paideia* and philosophy. Diotima's speech, though it contains elements of parody, is in the nature of a protreptic.

Aristotle in the *Poetics*[64] makes clear that Agathon was one of the leading playwrights of his time, so skilled at representation that Aristotle compares him to Homer, and an innovator in that he invented his own plots and did not rely on the traditional stories on which tragedies were based, which are "only known to a few, though a delight to all."

Fourth Interlude: Two Kinds of Encomium (198a–199c)

Socrates now remarks that his fears have been realized: Agathon has spoken so well that he himself is at a loss, turned to stone by the Gorgon of Agathon's version of Gorgias. He was mistaken about offering an encomium of Eros: he thought the point of an encomium of Eros was to tell the truth, whereas it seems it is rather to make Eros appear as beautiful and good as possible, whether what is said is true or not. Socrates will not offer that kind of encomium because he cannot; but he will tell the truth

64. 1451b20*ff.*, 1454b 14, 1456a 18*ff.*

about Eros in his own way if the company wishes. Phaedrus and the others urge him to speak.

Socrates distinguishes two kinds of encomium, one concerned to praise without regard for truth or falsity, the other concerned for truth but picking out its best features. This recalls the distinction in the *Gorgias* between two kinds of rhetoric: the one a species of flattery, concerned with pleasure to the hearers and indifferent to truth or the good of the soul; the other philosophical rhetoric, concerned with truth and the good of the soul and indifferent to pleasure. The rhetoric Gorgias practices is not based on knowledge or truth; it is a knack, not an art, of persuasion, allowing the orator to appear to the ignorant to know more than those who have knowledge (*Gorgias* 459c). Socrates here says almost the same thing of Agathon, Gorgias's follower. Agathon's speech, and by implication the others, is a specimen of flattery, aiming at pleasure but indifferent to truth. Socrates will not offer flattery; he will aim to tell the truth about Eros, while yet, as is proper to an encomium, picking out what is best. If Eros has also a dark side, Socrates will not directly speak of it here.

So the first act of the *Symposium* ends. It has been a feast of rhetoric: five speeches, all pleasing, about Love. Phaedrus led off and treated Love as an ancient god; he in this way introduced a theme that Pausanias developed, Prodicus-like, by dividing Love's divinity. Eryximachus followed, and treated Love as a divided cosmic power. Then Aristophanes, who treated Love as a healing force whose dwelling place is in the souls of men. At the end, in a ring structure, Agathon returns to Phaedrus and treats Eros as a god, but a youthful god. Of these speakers, Aristophanes is a comic poet, and Agathon a tragedian; the *Gorgias* (502a–e; compare *Symposium* 223d) treats tragedy, and by implication comedy, as rhetoric and akin to demagoguery: it aims at pleasing the audience without regard to truth or the good of the soul. As the *Symposium* makes clear, both comedy and tragedy are the special province of Dionysus.

Socrates in his own account of Eros will take something from each of these five speeches, and reject much. It is of the nature of rhetoric, conceived as a species of flattery, that it should consist not in utter falsehood but in half-truth.

The Speech of Socrates (199c–212c): The Elenchus of Agathon (199c–201c)

Socrates approves of Agathon's procedure in discussing the nature of Eros first, and what he causes, his works, afterward. The speech of Diotima will conform to this plan. She will discuss the nature of Eros first, and arrive at a definition: Eros is desire to possess the good forever (206a). Diotima will then turn to discuss his works (206b), which issue in creation in respect to body and soul.

Socrates' approval of Agathon's distinction suggests, if it does not imply, that questions about the nature of Eros, of what sort he is, are prior to questions about his works, what he does: we need to know who, or what, Eros is (201d). This conforms to Socrates' procedure in other dialogues. In the *Meno* (71b; compare 87b, 100b), for example, one must understand what virtue is (τί ἐστι) before one can determine what things are true of it (ὁποῖόν γέ τι), for example, whether it is taught; in the same way here, we must understand what love is (ὁποῖός τις) before we can understand his works (τὰ ἔργα αὐτοῦ).[65] Unlike virtue in the *Meno*, Eros is not a Form or Idea, but if Socrates is right, it must ultimately be defined in terms of an Idea, the Idea of Beauty. There is the further point that since the nature of anything, what it is, is universal, a request for definition cannot be met by mentioning an example of the thing to be defined.

Socrates begins by asking whether Eros is such as to be *of* something or *of* nothing. The sense of the question, in Greek as in English, is not transparently clear, and Socrates immediately undertakes to make it more precise. One cannot say that Eros is *of* a mother or father, for that would be absurd (199d). It is absurd in at least three different senses, all of which are neatly excluded: the genitive here expresses neither the love felt *by* a mother or father, nor the love felt *for* a mother or father; Eros, after all, may mean any sort of love, but especially sexual, not parental or filial love. Nor is this genitive a special case of the genitive of origin. In Greek, to be *of* someone may mean, idiomatically, to be a child of someone;[66] Socrates is not asking for the parentage of Eros, which would be a way of identifying who he is characteristic of an encomium.

It is possible to be more precise. Socrates is not asking about any given father, but about father by itself (199d.4), and so similarly about brother, that which it is by itself (199e.2). That is, he is asking of father qua father, brother qua brother, whether they are *of* something or *of* nothing: asking, not about any given father or brother or sister, but about all fathers just insofar as they are fathers. He will similarly inquire of Eros qua Eros.

The *of* is a genitive of relation: father is father *of* something, namely, a

---

65. The *Meno* contrasts the questions τί ἐστι and ὁποῖόν τι, while in the *Symposium*, ὁποῖός τις is equivalent to τίς ἐστιν, and contrasted with τά ἔργα αὐτοῦ. Plato is characteristically disdainful of technical terminology, but the difference in gender also corresponds to the underlying personification of Eros.

66. As at 204b.6 and 7.

son or daughter. In the same way, brother is brother *of* something, a brother or sister. So too Eros is *of* something, not *of* nothing. That is, Eros, like father, is a relational term. Eros is also desire for what is loved (200a). So Eros is desire *for* what it is *of.* The genitive is adnominal or definitory, specifying the kind of love or desire involved, but it is also objective. Eros is love of some object; to specify that object is to define the kind of Eros it is.

Phaedrus had represented the lover as beautiful, καλός, and there are vase paintings that apply the term to satyrs. But the Greek imagination characteristically represented love as the object of love, desire as the desirable. Eros was pictured as a beautiful youth, Aphrodite a supremely lovely woman. Agathon in his speech praised Love as good and beautiful and divine. It is precisely this conception of Eros that Socrates means to correct. He will not imitate Agathon's encomium because, as he emphatically says, one should always tell the truth about the thing praised (198d, 199a–b). He then proceeds to refute Agathon's claim.

His ἔλεγχος, or refutation, rests on the fact that Eros is relational, that love is always love *of* something, desire desire *for* something. Eros belongs to that class of terms that have their meaning "toward" (πρός τι) something else. If so, then Eros lacks what it loves and desires to possess it: "Everyone who desires something desires what has not yet been obtained and is not present; his love and desire are set on things he lacks, things he does not possess" (200e). Desire arises only in privation or lack,[67] a point brought out by a pretty piece of analysis: no one can desire what he already has, since he necessarily has it whether he desires it or not; insofar as the object is possessed, desire for it ceases. Eros as Eros cannot exist as satisfied, for when it is satisfied it ceases to exist. When it is, its object is not; when its object is, it is not. In this respect, love is like death.

Socrates further assumes that Eros is always love of the beautiful, or the good—the two terms are here used interchangeably (201c; compare 204d–205a). As a dialectical matter, he is entitled to this assumption: Agathon had said that "the world is fashioned by the gods through love of beautiful things; for there is no love of the ugly." It follows that, since Eros is love of what it lacks, it cannot be beautiful or good, and, since the gods possess both attributes, it cannot be divine. Like St. George on the inn sign, Eros is always on horseback but never rides on. Agathon is refuted.

Socrates had requested permission to ask Agathon a few small questions in order to elicit agreements on which his own account might proceed (199b). Socratic dialectic proceeds not by asserting what is true, but by

67. Cf. *Lysis* 221d, *Philebus* 35a.

assuming things which the respondent agrees that he knows (*Meno* 75d), and ἔλεγχος, refutation, is an important part of dialectic, in the nature of a reductio ad absurdum: consistency is the first and primary test of truth. Socrates has relieved Agathon of the false conceit of knowledge, and given him a motive to inquire into what he once thought he knew and now knows he did not know (203e–204a); this has also provided Socrates with premises by which the inquiry can go forward.

Agathon had earlier suggested that he and Socrates would argue their rival claims to wisdom later, using Dionysus as judge (175e). In this brief ἔλεγχος, Agathon has begun to learn to judge for himself.

Since Eros is love of what it lacks, it cannot be beautiful or good, and since the gods possess both attributes, it cannot be divine. It is not, however, bad or ugly or mortal, but "intermediate" between those attributes (202a–e).

The logic of the argument seems obscured by the personification of Eros. Love is a relation. As such, it lacks nothing, and desires nothing. It implies, however, privation or lack in the lover.[68] Socrates has distinguished love from its object; but love must also be distinguished from the lover, and when this is done, the argument to show that Eros is neither good nor beautiful nor divine is inconclusive. The lover, who lacks and is by so much imperfect, cannot be divine; it does not follow that love itself is not divine or good, or for that matter, evil and bad.[69] In the *Phaedrus*, when Socrates comes to describe the upward passage of Eros to the Place beyond the Heaven, he describes it as "a god, or something divine" (242e) because it seeks the divine; but later, when he criticizes the Eros described in his first speech, a love that seeks unworthy objects and leads to evil rather than good, he calls it "sinister" or "left-handed," σκαιόν τινα ἔρωτα (266a), a love of ill omen.

But Socrates and Diotima do not in fact speak of love as a relation considered apart from its terms, nor of the lover considered apart from that relation, but of the lover as lover. It is the lover just insofar as he loves who lacks what he loves and desires to possess it. Diotima will personify Eros, and that personification is not merely a literary device, lending to airy nothing a local habitation and a name, but has a logical point: Eros is the lover qua lover, each lover insofar as he loves (199d–e, 200d–e, 204d). It

68. See further "The Elenchus of Agathon: *Symposium* 199c–201c," *The Monist* 1966, pp. 460–463.

69. Agathon, if he is mistaken in describing Eros as beautiful, is surely not making a linguistic mistake: not only the object of desire but the person desiring could be characterized as καλός, as Phaedrus and Pausanias make clear. Indeed, desire itself, and specifically erotic desire, could be so characterized. Cf. E. R. Goodenough, *Jewish Symbols in the Greco-Roman Period*, vol. 6, *Wine*, Princeton, N.J., 1956, pp. 31–32.

will be evident that the lover qua lover cannot be identified with the lover considered apart from that relation. It helps to introduce some elementary distinctions: between a relation and its terms, between the domain of a relation and its converse domain or range. If we then bear in mind C. S. Peirce's further distinction between *logica docens* and *logica utens*,[70] we may say, for nutshell effect, that Socrates and Diotima treat Eros as the domain of a relation, taken distributively.[71]

If, then, Eros is the domain of a relation, what of its range? We are told that loving is for what is not at hand and not present and what the lover has not got, for things of which there is, as it where, an absence of presence (199e). Furthermore, Eros has as its object, not the things themselves, but the possession of those things, so that it is always involved not in the present but in the future. Socrates assumes, as Diotima will assume after him (200a–e), that to love is to desire, and to desire is to wish (199d). But a desire, or a wish, must be defined in terms of its objects, that is, in terms of the various kinds of thing of which it is a desire.[72] Thirst, for example, is simply desire to drink, and distinct from hunger, desire for food; a particular kind of thirst is desire for a particular kind of drink. By Socrates' account, one should be even more precise: thirst is not only for drink, but for possession of what is drinkable. The object of desire is an ideal object, a future state of affairs.[73]

Eros is of the beautiful. Socrates is entitled to assume this dialectically, because Agathon did (197b), but he plainly supposes it true, and Diotima too will assume it; they both suppose it to mean that Eros is desire for possession of the beautiful, or a wish for it (200b–d), and they also suppose that a desire or wish for the beautiful is a desire or wish for the good. Beauty is the sensuous aspect of goodness, what is good to look at or good to hear, and, by an easy extension, goodness in thought or discourse.

70. Or, as Locke remarked, "But God has not been so sparing to men to make them barely two-legged creatures, and left it to Aristotle to make them rational. God has been more bountiful to mankind than so. He has given them a mind that can reason, without being instructed in methods of syllogizing. The understanding is not taught to reason by these rules: it has a native faculty to perceive the coherence or incoherence of its ideas, and can range them right, without any such perplexing repetitions." *Locke's Human Understanding*, ed. Pringle-Pattison, Oxford, 1924, p. 347.
71. This is in general characteristic of Plato's treatment of relations or relatives, and the source of Aristotle's treatment of relation as a category inhering in primary substance. See Bertrand Russell, *The Philosophy of Leibniz*, 2d ed., London, 1937, pp. 13, 206.
72. Cf. *Republic* IV 439b, 438c–d.
73. On the point that desire always looks to the future, one may compare the distinction taken in the *Philebus* between true and false pleasures: pleasure is always directed at something, like opinion, and therefore is true or false in the sense that expectation may be real or illusory.

The Speech of Diotima (201d–212a)

Socrates now offers as his speech the conversation he once had with Diotima, a Mantinean wise-woman, on love. That Diotima is a fiction, meant to be understood as such, is indicated by the claim (201d) that she enabled the Athenians to delay the onset of the Great Plague for ten years, and by the fact that the analysis of Eros she offers is characteristically Socratic. Her introduction allows Socrates to offer a speech on Eros while preserving his mask of ironic ignorance; it explains his insistence that the only thing he knows about is τὰ ἐρωτικά, the things of love; it emphasizes the importance of his account by suggesting that Eros is the subject of a mystery cult of which Diotima is a wise priestess;[74] it represents what Cornford called "a masterstroke of delicate courtesy,"[75] by which Socrates corrects and yet refrains from criticizing Agathon, his young host, by relating the lesson he himself once learned from the prophetess.

A further reason for introducing Diotima arises from the narrative scheme of the dialogue: it would have been inappropriate for Socrates to offer an encomium on Eros which, when Alcibiades praises him, will turn out to fit Socrates himself.[76]

The discourse of Diotima is rhetorical. But the elevated diction of the speech is required by the occasion and does not detract from its philosophical seriousness, which must be judged by its content.[77] One may com-

74. Cf. *Meno* 81a 10.
75. F. M. Cornford, *The Unwritten Philosophy*, Cambridge, 1950, p. 71.
76. Dover remarks: "There may be other reasons why Plato makes a woman his 'spokesperson' in this work. It tends to allay our suspicion that cunning self-interest might be the mainspring of arguments for what is essentially a male homosexual foundation for philosophical activity" (*Symposium*, p. 137). In this way the speech of Diotima in the *Symposium* is made out to be a masked doublet of the speech of Lysias in the *Phaedrus*; dramatic and structural considerations are ignored, and serious and important philosophical analysis is trivialized. Diotima's own view, which Socrates accepts for the excellent reason that it is his own, is certainly heterosexual and fundamentally ascetic; sexual intercourse is by nature directed to the procreation of children. Plato (see pp. 17–18 above) condemned homosexuality, not only on ascetic grounds, but as contrary to nature. No doubt Socrates sometimes speaks as an admirer of the beauty of boys, for example in the *Charmides* (155c), and in this he adopted the conventions of his culture; but the real meaning of it is explained in the speech of Alcibiades: it is irony (216d–e, 219c–d). As to a male homosexual foundation for philosophical activity, the *Republic* recognizes the intellectual talents of women as equal to those of men and therefore makes women eligible for higher education as guardians; there is a tradition that Plato's own school, the Academy, had not only men but women members (Diogenes Laertius III 46, IV 2). Diotima's presence in the *Symposium* is fully explicable without Dover's conjecture, and inexplicable with it.
77. The rhetorical tone of the speech, and the difficulty, in some places, of reconciling it with doctrines found in other dialogues of the middle period, have led some scholars to claim that the speech represents, not serious philosophical doctrine, but a literary jeu d'esprit. Wilamowitz said, in effect: "The answers of Socrates show that Plato definitely does not

pare the speech of Socrates in the *Apology*, or the speech of the Laws of Athens in the *Crito*. As the *Apology* and *Crito* show, and the *Gorgias* and *Phaedrus* explicitly state, rhetoric and philosophy are not enemies, if rhetoric is directed at truth and the goodness of soul of the hearers rather than flattery and pleasure indifferent to truth. Rhetoric, after all, is power of persuasion, and persuasion can be guided and controlled by rational insight. The speech of Diotima, like the speech of the Laws of Athens in the *Crito*,[78] is an example of implicit dialectic, "dialectic not in dialogue,"[79] in which the form of question and answer is used sparingly, but the argument is developed in a dialectical way. The speech begins with an *elenchus* whereby Socrates, like Agathon before him, is relieved of the false conceit of knowledge; it proceeds to a definition drawn from agreements made in the elenchus; that definition is only partial, and various emendations grow from this original starting point, using Socrates' own admissions, until the nature of Eros is more adequately displayed along with his works.

This dialectical development exhibits three stages. In the first, Diotima undertakes to define Eros, reaching the conclusion that Eros is of the good being one's own forever. In the second, she turns to the works of Eros: Eros aims at immortality, of the body through nutrition and reproduction, of the soul through fame, to be obtained through poetry, law giving, and education; because the immortality achieved is vicarious, it is not real immortality at all, and Eros is in this respect frustrated and vain. The third stage is the Greater Mysteries of Eros, in which the lover ascends as by a ladder from bodily beauty, through spiritual and intellectual beauties, to the contemplation of Beauty itself, and there, if anywhere, becomes immortal.

Eros as Intermediate (201d–202d)

Diotima's argument begins by recalling what was established in the elenchus of Agathon: that Eros has an object, that is, that it is *of* something,

---

want the speech of Diotima to be taken as an expression of his own intellectual conviction. The prophetess no more speaks to the point than the doctor and the poet have done. Demonstrative speeches may contain much that is fine and beautiful, but do not lead us to the truth, which is found only through serious Dialectic. If we wish to understand the philosophy of Plato, we must remember that his poetry must be treated as poetry" (paraphrased by J. Stenzel in *Plato's Method of Dialectic* [trans. D. J. Allan], Oxford, 1940, p. 5). But this misunderstands Plato's use of philosophical rhetoric, as Stenzel saw.

78. See R. E. Allen, *Socrates and Legal Obligation*, Minneapolis, Minn., 1980, pp. 82–83.

79. See P. Frutiger, *Mythes de Platon*, Paris, 1930, pp. 24–26. Frutiger (pp. 113*ff.*) counts the story of Poros and Penia as the only myth in Diotima's discourse, and Aristophanes' story as the only other myth in the *Symposium*.

which it lacks and desires to possess. All gods are happy and beautiful, and those who are happy possess beautiful and good things; Eros does not possess beautiful and good things, because it is desire for them; therefore, Eros is not a god and, by implication, Eros is not happy. Eros is not, however, bad or ugly or mortal; rather, the lover qua lover, the lover just insofar as he loves, is "intermediate" (μεταξύ) between these attributes. Eros will turn out to be the wish for happiness.

Diotima's account seems inconsistent with the *Phaedrus,* where love is sometimes good and sometimes bad. But Diotima implies that, contrary to its usual associations in Greek, Eros is not simply sexual desire but desire in all its forms, and this is later made explicit (205a–d). It follows from this and from its relational character that Eros is to be defined in terms of its objects, that is, in terms of the various kinds of beautiful things it seeks. This analysis is developed in the *Republic* (IV 438aff.), where it is argued that desire, as a relative, is also correlative, and, in F. M. Cornford's brilliant paraphrase, "where there are two correlatives, the one is qualified if, and only if, the other is so." Thus, "each desire just in itself, is simply for its own natural object. Where the object is of such and such a kind, the desire will be correspondingly qualified" (439b). Eros as a correlative takes the value of its objects: desire for a good thing is a good desire, bad if the contrary is true. But if desire is considered in abstraction from any particular kind of object, it is indeed "intermediate," neither good nor bad, beautiful nor ugly, divine or mortal. The *Symposium* and *Phaedrus* are not inconsistent on this point.

Eros as Daimon (202d–203a)

As intermediate, Eros is also a δαίμων, a word for which there is no adequate translation in English—certainly not "demon," whose sense derives, not from etymology, but from the Christian rejection of polytheism. Socrates in the *Apology* (27b–e) treats δαίμονες as "either gods or children of gods." Diotima treats them as intermediate between gods and men, immortals and mortals. The word is here translated "divinity."[80] Diotima's treatment of Eros as a divinity is a consequence of her personification of him.

The intermediate mediates. Its function is to bring together, to bind into a unity, the divine and human realms. In the *Phaedrus* (244aff.), Eros is said to be a kind of divine madness that lends wings to the soul of the

80. For a discussion of Plato's "demonology," with comparison of passages, see Léon Robin, *La Théorie platonicienne de l'amour,* Paris, 1908, pp. 129ff.

lover enfrenzied by beauty: "The natural power of a wing is to lead what is heavy upward, carrying it aloft to where the race of gods dwell; preeminently among things of the body, it in some way has intercourse with the divine. But the divine is beautiful, wise, good, and all such as that" (246d). Eros as a divinity is intermediate in that it exists by reason of need—the wing is "among things of the body"—but for the sake of Beauty. In this, Eros is like right opinion, which is intermediate between knowledge and ignorance (202a), and this is why Eros will prove to be a philosopher, a lover of wisdom (203e–204a).

Plato uses the term *intermediate* in at least two distinguishable senses. Sometimes intermediates are described as having a share of opposite qualities;[81] if Eros were intermediate in this sense, it would be both good and bad, beautiful and ugly, mortal and immortal. In another sense, intermediates instead of possessing both opposites possess neither. In the *Gorgias* (467e*ff*.; compare *Lysis* 216d*ff*.), for example, intermediates are actions and physical objects that take their value, not from their own nature, but from their purpose or use; they are neither good nor bad in themselves. The intermediate character of Eros is of this kind. In itself, it is neither good nor bad; it takes its value from its objects. Thirst, for example, the desire to drink, is neither good nor bad in itself; its value is determined by the effect of its gratification in particular circumstances.

The Myth of Poros and Penia (203a–e)

Eros is the child of Penia, Want, and Poros, Resourcefulness. Diotima's myth describes the parents of Eros, a regular feature of encomia, and gives embodiment to the abstract features ascribed to him, in particular his need, his aim to possess, and his love of wisdom.

Insofar as he is privative, Eros is the child of Penia; but he is the son

---

81. See *Euthydemus* 306a, *Phaedo* 102b*ff*., *Republic* V 477a*ff*., VII 523b–524d. If intermediates are things that may have opposite qualities, it is unhelpful to explicate intermediates in terms of the Square of Opposition and the distinction between contraries and contradictories; the Square, after all, has to do with statement relations, not the things statements are about. If Eros is not beautiful, it does not follow, according to Diotima's account, that Eros is ugly; so beauty and ugliness are not contradictories, since if both cannot be true, it does not follow that one must be true (201e–202a). Are beauty and ugliness then contraries, in that both cannot be true but neither may be true? But contrariety does not obtain if the same things may be both beautiful and ugly. Perhaps then intermediates are subcontraries, in that both may be true. But subcontrariety does not obtain if the same thing may be neither beautiful nor ugly, that is, if it is not the case that at least one is true. Again, where subcontrariety obtains, I propositions are convertible, but O propositions distribute their predicates and are not convertible. This shows that it is a root of confusion to identify opposites with predicates; opposites are not true or false of some subject.

of Poros as well, and represents the human capacity for aspiration. As the comparison of his intermediate character with right opinion foreshadowed (202a), Eros is also a philosopher, a lover of wisdom; so he is a hunter, a metaphor traditionally associated with Eros, and one which Plato elsewhere uses to describe the activity of the philosopher—and the sophist.

Because Eros is the child of both Poros and Penia, Robin held that the nature of love is essentially "a synthesis."[82] Eros exists in privation, but desire is not blind, dumb emptiness: to desire is to desire something of a certain kind, so that desire implies awareness of the kind of thing that will satisfy it. Desire, that is, implies cognition, and cognition of what is universal or common to many things.[83] Again, it is not without significance that Eros was conceived on the day of Aphrodite's birth. It is the revelation of beauty to the bodily senses, the *Phaedrus* claims, which first awakens longing for true being. Eros has its being in a synthesis of need and cognition; perhaps, then, there is a sense after all in which Eros is intermediate as being both good and bad, beautiful and ugly, mortal and immortal.

Plotinus and Ficino

The personification of Eros as child of Poros and Penia is a fiction, its logical force requiring us to consider Eros as the lover qua lover, the lover just insofar as he loves. But there is an ancient tradition of interpretation, descended from Plotinus, which takes it as something more. Plotinus maintained that Eros is a substance (οὐσία), sprung from another substance but nevertheless a being in its own right, and the cause of the affection of love in the human soul ("On Love," *Ennead* III 5.3–4). Plotinus interpreted the myth of Poros and Penia as an allegory meant to represent metaphysical connections:

> But myths, if they are really going to be myths, must separate in time the things of which they tell, and set apart from each other many realities which are together, but distinct in rank or powers, at points where rational discussions, also, make generations of things ungenerated, and themselves, too, separate things which are together; the

82. Robin, *Théorie platonicienne*, pp. 121ff.

83. It may be observed that this is not the least important of the differences between Plato and Freud. Freud treats the instincts or drives on the analogy of steam in a boiler, blind pressures for which an object is afterward supplied by the ego, the managerial or directive element in the personality, which through secondary process has a grasp of reality; satisfaction of desire is relaxation of pressure or (to use a different mechanical metaphor) reduction of tension.

myths, when they have taught us as well as they can, allow the man who has understood them to put together again that which they have separated. Here is the putting together [of the myth of Eros]: Soul, which is with Intellect and has come into existence from Intellect, and then again been filled with rational principles and, itself beautiful, adorned with beauties and filled with plenitude, so that there are in it many glories and images of beautiful things, is as a whole Aphrodite, and the rational principles in it are all plenitude and Plenty, as the nectar there flows from regions above; and the glories in it, since they are set in life, are called the "garden of Zeus," and it is said that Plenty "sleeps" there, "weighed down" by the principles with which he was filled. And since life has appeared, and is always there, in the world of realities, the gods are said to "feast" since they are in a state of blessedness appropriate to the word. And so this being, Love, has from everlasting come into existence from the soul's aspiration towards the higher and the good, and he was there always, as long as Soul, too, existed. And he is a mixed thing, having a part of need, in that he wishes to be filled, but not without a share of plenitude, in that he seeks what is wanting to that he already has; for certainly that which is altogether without a share in the good would not ever seek the good. So he is said to be born of Plenty and Poverty, in that the lack and the aspiration and the memory of the rational principles coming together in the soul, produced the activity directed towards the good, and this is Love. But his mother is Poverty, because aspiration belongs to that which is in need. And Poverty is matter, because matter, too, is in every way in need, and because of the indefiniteness of the desire for the good—for there is no shape or rational forming principle (*logos*) in that which desires it—makes the aspiring thing more like matter in so far as it aspires. But the good, in relation to that which aspires to it, is form only, remaining in itself; and that which aspires to receive it prepares its receptive capacity as matter for the form which is to come upon it. So Love is a material kind of being, and he is a spirit (*daimon*) produced from soul in so far as soul falls short of the good but aspires to it.[84]

---

84. *Ennead* III 5.24–57, trans. A. H. Armstrong. Contrast Dante, *Vita nuova* 25: "You may be surprised that I speak of love as if it were a thing that could exist by itself; and not only as if it were an intelligent substance, but even as if it were a corporeal substance. Now this, according to the truth, is false. For love has not, like a substance, an existence of its own, but is only an accident occurring in a substance" (cited and translated by C. S. Lewis, *The Allegory of Love*, Oxford, 1936, p. 47). Dante treats as accident what Plotinus had substantialized.

Here, along with the great hymn to Intelligible Beauty of *Ennead* V 8, is the core of the Neoplatonic interpretation of Plato's doctrine of Eros. At the height of the Italian Renaissance it was revived by Ficino in his *Commentary on Plato's Symposium on Love*, the *De amore*, written in 1469 for the Medici, some years after Cosimo de' Medici had founded in Florence the Platonic Academy of which Ficino was a member, trained in the new Greek learning. The *De amore* became, at least in respect to its substantialization of Love, a persistent force in scholarly literature on the *Symposium* down to the present century.

Ficino in the *De amore* held that natural beauty implies participation in and imitation of a divine Archetype or Idea, and that art can attain to a more accurate representation of the divine essence than can ordinary physical objects, which are clogged with matter. Art, whose aim is beauty, is an expression of love, and a primary way of apprehending supersensible reality; the artist has an intellectual task comparable to that of the philosopher. It is also a religious task, for Ficino thought that natural beauty, since it derives from an imitation of an Idea in the mind of God, is a reflection of the face of the Father. To see the fruit of this theory, one may consider the *Pietà* of Michelangelo in St. Peter's Basilica in Rome, where a grieving mother holding her adult son dead in her arms is represented in the serene and virginal freshness of her youth, the very ideal of woman's beauty; Michelangelo had not only read the *De amore*, but carried a copy of it with him. Ficino's theory of art is often described as Platonic, but Ficino's Plato is thoroughly soaked in Plotinus. Plato thought that art is three times removed from reality, the imitation of an imitation; it was Plotinus who supposed that art, because it is a product of reason, can produce a representation of reality superior to nature.

The *De amore* is not, in the modern sense, a commentary on the *Symposium*; Ficino feigns a dinner party in which the guests give speeches that comment on passages in the *Symposium*, but the speeches are occasions for invention, and only a few passages are selected. The speech of Pausanias figures prominently, but in the sixth of the seven speeches, the speech of Diotima is discussed, and the chief topic is the myth of Poros and Penia. Ficino's treatment assumes an *amor descendens* as well as an *amor ascendens*, in evident reliance on the distinction taken between heavenly and vulgar Eros in the speech of Pausanias. Sears Jayne summarizes:

> The main argument of the *De amore* as a treatise on love may be paraphrased as follows: the cosmos consists of a hierarchy of being extending from God (unity) to the physical world (multiplicity). In this hierarchy every level evolves from the level above it in a descending

emanation from God and desires to rise to the level above it in an ascending return to God. This desire to return to one's source is called love, and the quality in the source which attracts this desire is called beauty. The human soul, as a part of the hierarchy of being, is involved in this same process of descent from God and return to God; in human beings the desire to procreate inferior beings is called earthly love, and the desire to rise to higher levels of being is called heavenly love.[85]

In all of this Ficino follows Plotinus, who sharply distinguished love of beauty from desire for generation[86]—as Diotima does not. The speech of Pausanias was afterwards taken to anticipate this distinction, and the contrast between sacred and profane love. Kenneth Clark remarks:

> Plato, in his *Symposium,* makes one of the guests assert that there are two Aphrodites, whom he calls celestial and vulgar, or, to give them their later titles, *Venus Coelestis* and *Venus Naturalis*; and because it symbolized a deep-seated human feeling, this passing allusion was never forgotten. It became an axiom of medieval and Renaissance philosophy. It is the justification for the female nude. Since the earliest times the obsessive, unreasonable nature of physical desire has sought relief in images, and to give these images a form by which Venus may cease to be vulgar and become celestial has been one of the recurring themes of European art.[87]

Eros as Philosopher (203e–204c)

The intermediate nature of Eros is shown by the fact that Eros stands midway between wisdom and ignorance. No one who is wise desires to be wise, for he is so already. Nor do the ignorant desire wisdom; ignorance is satisfied with itself, since one does not desire what he does not suppose he lacks. Those who love wisdom are intermediate between knowledge and ignorance, and Eros is of this nature.

For convenience in analysis, the translation has divided a sentence that is continuous in the Greek.

The description of Eros as philosopher precisely fits the portrait of Socrates in the *Apology,* and his claim that the worst ignorance is to think

85. *Marsilio Ficino: Commentary on Plato's Symposium on Love,* 2d ed., Dallas, 1985, p. 7.
86. See *Ennead* III 5.1, and Armstrong's note, Plotinus, vol. 3 (Loeb Classical Library), London, 1980, p. 170.
87. *The Nude,* Princeton, N.J., 1956, p. 71.

yourself wise when you are not. In the *Lysis* (218a–b), those who love wisdom are ignorant, but know that they do not know. If someone values something, he does so by reason of something (δία τι) and for the sake of something (ἕνεκα του), as one values a doctor by reason of disease, and for the sake of health (218d–e); disease is bad, but health is good. Put otherwise, the *Lysis* distinguishes *causa quod* and *causa ut*. So similarly here, Eros is a philosopher by reason of ignorance, *causa quod*, and for the sake of wisdom, which is most beautiful and good, *causa ut*. In the *Lysis*, this pattern of reasoning leads to the claim that there exists something for the sake of which all other things are loved, itself not loved for the sake of something else, an ultimate *causa ut* (219b–220b). In the *Symposium* (210a–212a), it will lead to the Ladder of Love and the ascent to Beauty itself, by which all other beautiful things are beautiful.

Eros, the desire which has for its object the beautiful, is connected in the *Symposium*, as it is in the *Phaedrus* (249bff.) with philosophy, the love of wisdom and knowledge. The claim is proleptic: it will be explained by the further claim that Eros implies a wish for happiness, with which wisdom is implicated.

Eros as Wish for Happiness (204c–205a)

Diotima next maintains that the object of Eros is happiness, and that happiness consists in possession of good things.

The lover loves beautiful things. The reason becomes clear if *good* is substituted for *beautiful*: the lover loves good things to possess them for himself, and this because he wishes to be happy; for happiness consists in the possession of good things. So if one asks why the lover loves beautiful things, the answer is that he wishes to be happy, and this answer is final, in that one cannot ask for what purpose (ἵνα τι) someone wishes to be happy and expect a further answer.

The substitution of *good* for *beautiful* at 204d–e was anticipated at 201c: if Eros lacks beautiful things, and good things are beautiful, then Eros lacks good things. Since possession of beautiful things implies possession of good things (204e), and since lack of beautiful things implies lack of good things (201c), good things and beautiful things are equivalent: anything that is good is beautiful, and anything beautiful, good.

That all men wish for happiness is a fundamental assumption of Socratic, as well as Platonic and Aristotelian, moral psychology. The English word *happiness* suggests a feeling-state that differs from pleasure only in being more serene and prolonged, but its etymological connection with *hap, happen,* and *hapless* preserves the memory of an earlier force. Like the word εὐδαιμονία, and in analogy to health, *happiness* also has an objective sense: well-being, the state of affairs in which things are well with a man, however he feels. In the *Republic* (X 620e), the Fates send with each soul a δαίμων to attend it through life and fulfill for it the destiny it has chosen, and its destiny is itself described as its δαίμων.[88] The state of *eudaimonia* is the state of having a good *daimon*—"good hap," though there is an irreducible connotation of fortune or luck in the English word that is not present in the Greek. Happiness conceived as well-being implies concern for wisdom: Eros is a philosopher.

Diotima treats happiness, which consists in possession of good things, as the ultimate object of Eros. Socrates offers a similar account in the *Meno* (77b–78b). Meno had suggested that men desire evil, some through ignorance, believing it good, and some recognizing it for what it is and desiring it anyway. He readily agreed that the former really desire the good, though their desire is misdirected through ignorance; he was then led to agree that no one can willingly or wittingly desire what is bad, for what is evil is harmful, and to be harmed is to be made unhappy, and no one wishes that. It has been claimed that this argument is fallacious, in that it confuses harm to another with harm to oneself. In fact, the argument is enthymematic, assuming premises made explicit in the *Crito* and the *Republic*: to harm another is to act unjustly, and to act unjustly is to harm oneself, that is to say, one's own soul. Thus, though one may desire to harm another through ignorance, one cannot voluntarily harm another, or wish it. This inference is plainly connected with the Socratic paradox that no one willingly or wittingly does evil, that wrongdoing is involuntary. The good is "what every soul pursues and for the sake of which it acts in everything, divining that it is something, but perplexed and unable to grasp adequately what it is or to form any stable belief about it, as about other things, and for that reason missing whatever value those other things may have."[89]

All men wish for possession of the good and for happiness. But this raises the issue of mistake: what appears good sometimes isn't—there may be poison in the cup. The objects of desire, when possessed, have effects upon the possessor, and it is possible to desire things that are injurious. Apparent good and real good may coincide, and in the virtuous life usu-

---

88. *Republic* X 617dff., cf. *Phaedo* 107d–108c, where the δαίμων functions as an intermediate, conducting the soul to the other world when it finishes its life on earth. Heraclitus said that, for a man, character is fate—δαίμων (Diels-Kranz, *Fragmente der Vorsokratiker* B 119).

89. *Republic* VI 505d; cf. *Gorgias* 499e, 467aff., 505cff.

ally do, but they may also differ. So if men do what seems good to them, they sometimes are mistaken about where their own good lies. Eros, the lover insofar as he loves, has as its object the beautiful, and yet, as the *Phaedrus* claims (266a), may love bad things.[90]

The distinction between the apparent good and the real good is connected with a perspectival shift. It makes sense to say, "It seems good to you, or to him, but it isn't"; it does not make sense to say, "It seems good to me, but it isn't." This shift in perspective, due to difference in the persons of the corresponding verbs, explains a difference in use of nouns for loving, desiring, and wishing: we may say either that (first person) desire and wish are always for what is good, or that (second and third person) desire and wish are sometimes for what is good and sometimes for what is bad.[91] Happiness, which consists in the possession of good things, is the common term through which first person and third person unite, in that from both perspectives it is the ultimate object of love, and one cannot be mistaken in one's belief that it is good.

Plato is entitled to choose between these uses, and does so. In general, he treats the object of desire, ἐπιθυμία, a denominative noun that suggests setting one's heart on something, as the apparent good; on occasion—one must look to context—he treats the object of wish, βούλησις, a denominative noun that suggests intention, counsel, advice, as the real good. Since men do what seems good to them, they do what they desire. But since they are sometimes mistaken about where their own good lies, they sometimes do not do what they wish. Thus Socrates argues in the *Gorgias*[92] that though the tyrant does what seems best to him, he does not do what he wishes, and is therefore least of all men free. Socrates uses a similar argument in the *Meno* (77b–78b) to establish that all men wish for (βούλεσθαι) the good, that no man willingly or wittingly wishes evil.[93] The nature of Βούλησις is explained in a single sentence in the *Gorgias* (467d; compare *Laches* 185d): "If a man does something for a purpose, he does not wish the thing he does, but that for the sake of which he does it." Βούλησις is the rational wish of the self for what is truly as distinct from

90. One may compare *Nicomachean Ethics* III 1113a 15–24.

91. Perspectival shift is marked in another way in Greek idiom: ὡς with the circumstantial participle expresses the belief of the subject of the main verb of the sentence (or some other person prominently mentioned) without implying that it is also the belief of the speaker of the sentence (e.g., *Republic* I 329a.7); οἷον (or ἅτε) with the circumstantial participle asserts on the authority of the speaker (e.g., *Charmides* 153a.2). See H. W. Smyth, *Greek Grammar*, 2d ed., Cambridge, 1959, pp. 2085, 2086.

92. 467a*ff*., cf. *Charmides* 167e, *Republic* IX 577c*ff*.

93. This use of βούλεσθαι is found at *Euthydemus* 278e, where all men wish to do/fare well, and at *Republic* IX 577c*ff*.

apparently good; that is, as Diotima has now made clear, it is wish for happiness, which consists in possession of good things.[94]

If Jones believes the world is flat, that it is not flat does not imply that Jones does not believe it. If Jones desires something because he thinks it is good, that it is not good does not imply that Jones does not desire it. But happiness is a common term: from first-person perspective, desire for the apparent good is desire for the good, and implies wish for happiness and possession of good things. If Eros is desire, and one can desire bad things in the mistaken belief that they are good, one can love bad things in fact though not in intention. If Eros is also wish for happiness, then wish for happiness—and wish to contemplate Beauty itself, in which, according to Diotima, happiness consists—is implicit in every desire.[95] So if Eros and desire are one, the love of Beauty is implicit in the desire for a glass of water.

On the other hand, in third-person perspective, one may distinguish rational wish from desire. If Eros is wish for happiness, and if happiness consists in possession of what is really good, then, if the proximate object of desire is not in fact good, one may desire it, but one cannot not rationally wish it; it will follow that one therefore does not love it. Love is not a feeling or emotion, or a state of mind that may be introspectively apprehended without considering the value of its object. If one is mistaken in believing that what one loves is good, one is also mistaken in believing

94. Cf. *Definitions* 413c: βούλησις is "intention with right reason; well-reasoned intention; desire with reason according to nature." At *Symposium* 200a–e, "to wish" (βούλεσθαι) is not distinct from "to desire" (ἐπιθυμεῖν), and this is perhaps also true in the *Meno* (77b–78b; cf. *Lysis* 207d–e). So there was considerable overlap of meaning in ordinary use, and Dover on *Symposium* 200b.4 suggests they are synonymous, "though the former cannot have a substantive as object." This last, if true (Liddell and Scott, *A Greek-English Lexicon*, 9th ed. [Oxford, 1968], s.v. βούλομαι I.2), proves that they are not synonymous, and their distinction is clearly implied at *Gorgias* 467d and *Symposium* 205a. Desire is neutral with respect to the real as distinct from the apparent worth of its objects, and implies no distinction between what seems good and what is good. That distinction is less linguistic than conceptual—or ontological. Happiness is that for the sake of which other things are desired, an ultimate end.

95. Compare Aristotle, *Nicomachean Ethics* III 1113a 15–30 (trans. W. D. Ross): "That wish is for the end has already been stated (1111b.26); some think it is for the good, others for the apparent good. Now those who say that the good is the object of wish must admit in consequence that that which the man who does not choose aright wishes for is not an object of wish (for if it is to be so, it must also be good; but it was, if it so happened, bad); while those who say the apparent good is the object of wish must admit that there is no natural object of wish, but only what seems good to each man. Now different things appear good to different people, and, if it so happens, even contrary things. If these consequences are unpleasing, are we to say that absolutely and in truth the good is the object of wish, but for each person the apparent good; that that which in truth is an object of wish is an object of wish to the good man, while any chance thing may be so to the bad man . . . ; since the good man judges each class of things rightly, and in each the truth appears to him?"

that one loves it. Love must then imply a kind of infallibility in respect to judgments of worth or value of a sort given to the wise man; if one loves *x*, one is not mistaken in one's judgment that *x* is good. And if such judgments require knowledge of the essential nature of beauty and goodness, Eros requires apprehension of Beauty itself. So if Eros and rational wish are one, the love of Beauty is implicit in the wish for a glass of water.

In her conclusion that Eros is wish for happiness, then, Diotima anticipates the Greater Mysteries of Eros that are to follow, and does so whether or not we identify desire and rational wish.

False Consciousness: Plato and Freud

The object of desire, insofar as it is desired, is apprehended as beautiful or good, $\varkappa\alpha\lambda\acute{o}\varsigma$. So in one sense, analytic but not trivial, to be an object of desire is to be good. Since this sense of good has no contrary—no object is bad for lack of being desired—this is a derivative sense of goodness.

What is apprehended as good may also be described as indifferent or as evil. Consider a desire to drink cold water on a warm day after heavy exercise. No doubt the object of desire, just insofar as it is so, is good. But there are inconsistent desires: in such a case, the desire for water is incompatible with the desire, or wish, not to become ill. Getting the water is an apparent good but an actual evil. This inconsistency is at the root of rational choice, which implies ordering or ranking the objects of desire. Choice is specifically rational in that possession of an object of desire has effects on the possessor, and the estimate of those effects issues in judgments that are either true or false. The apparent good consists in objects of desire described as good because they are desired; the real good consists in objects that are truly described as good by reason of the fact that they coincide with what we wish, that is, what is to our benefit.

Given the dolorous fact that the first thing people want is often the last thing they need, and that human beings constantly mistake apparent good for real good, their state may be described as one of ignorance. But it is not simple ignorance, the bare not knowing of something. It is, on the contrary, a kind of not knowing of something one knows, a kind of false consciousness. People, after all, have an awareness not only of what they desire but of what they wish. If they did not, Socratic dialectic would have no purchase on them, neither point nor direction; it makes no sense to question a man in matters of which he is wholly ignorant. Consistency is a necessary condition not only of truth but of psychological integration, and Socratic dialectic, directed ultimately toward self-knowledge, is directed proximately toward exposing inconsistencies of belief. False consciousness at a logical level implies contradiction among beliefs; at a psychological level it implies conflict and inner turmoil, the turbulence within a man who desires what he doesn't wish and wishes what he doesn't desire. This is a sufficient condition for anxiety, a symptom of psychopathology which Plato in the *Republic* identified with defect of virtue.

One may compare the Socratic concept of ignorance with Freud's concept of a dynamic unconscious, mental contents actively excluded from consciousness by a barrier of repression. Here once again there is not simply ignorance or lack of awareness, but a kind of not knowing of something one knows.[96] The stated aim of psychoanalysis, to make the unconscious conscious—where id was, there let ego be—bears some analogy to the Socratic claim of the primacy of self-knowledge. But there are vast differences. The unconscious in Freud has a historical origin: the contents behind the repression barrier derive from the vagaries of psychosexual development in childhood, and where Socrates would have us understand our purposes, Freud would have us understand our past. Again, Freud supposed that mental life, conscious or unconscious, is conditioned by a principle of psychic determinism which implies that nothing, down to the least detail of the least dream, the most minor slip of the tongue or mislaying of an object, is accidental; every psychic event and all behavior have an efficient cause, and this was a crucial basis for Freud's claim that psy-

---

96. Belief that there are unconscious mental states is so general that it is possible to forget there are logical objections to it. It was maintained, before Freud, by Wundt, Hartmann, and Helmholz, and it led William James to maintain that the assumption of unconscious mental states "is the sovereign means for believing what one likes in psychology, and of turning what might become a science into a tumbling-ground for whimsies." James went on to suggest that arguments to show that unconscious mental states exist involve a variety of fallacies, including failure to distinguish between having an idea at the moment of its presence and subsequently knowing all sorts of things about it—the distinction between knowledge by acquaintance and knowledge by description, the basis for his rejection of the incorrigibility of sense perception, as well as memory. James would specifically have dismissed the notion of a dynamic unconscious, on the ground that it involves knowing and not knowing the same mental fact at the same time: "There is only one 'phase' in which an idea can be, and that is a fully conscious condition. If it is not in that condition, then it is not at all. Something else is, in its place. The something else may be a merely physical brain-process, or it may be another conscious idea. Either of these things may perform much the same *function* as the first idea, refer to the same object, and roughly stand in the same relations to the upshot of our thought. But that is no reason why we should throw away the logical principle of identity in psychology, and say that, however it may fare in the outer world, the mind at any rate is a place in which a thing can be all kinds of other things without ceasing to be itself as well." James admitted the distinction between actual and potential knowledge, but cashed out the notion of potential knowledge in terms of (learned) modifications of the brain; his analysis is inconsistent with dynamic repression (*The Principles of Psychology,* Boston, 1890, pp. 163–175). It may be observed that James was familiar with the phenomena of hypnotism, multiple personality, and hysteria, phenomena which prompted Freud and others to assume the existence of unconscious mental states, and for which James provided other explanations.

choanalysis is an empirical science.[97] But false consciousness for Diotima has a purposive origin; it derives from a failure of aim, and from such a perspective many things are accidental, as being inexplicable in terms of purpose, while explanation can be scientific only if science allows explanation in terms of purpose as irreducible in human affairs. Freud's assumption of psychic determinism is then not science but a lively source of superstition very like astrology, and his analysis of "the Unconscious" mainly an artifact of his determinism.

Diotima's Definition of Eros (205a–206a)

By defining Eros as love of the beautiful and the good, Diotima had implied that, contrary to its usual associations in Greek, Eros is not simply sexual, but desire in all its forms; she now makes this explicit. Although we say that all men love good things always, since they all love happiness, we also say that some love and some do not; the reason is that one specific kind of love, sexual passion, has been given the name of the whole. Eros

97. Whether psychoanalysis can be called a science is a matter of considerable dispute. The issue turns on empirical confirmation, testability. Freud thought that unconscious repression caused mental disease, that this could be confirmed by clinical observation—case studies—and he eschewed experiment. Karl R. Popper objects that the theory is only too well confirmed, in that its explanatory power is so great that no conceivable human behavior could contradict or refute it. What is irrefutable is also untestable, and Popper therefore compares psychoanalysis to astrology; it is a pseudo-science (*Conjectures and Refutations: The Growth of Scientific Knowledge*, New York, 1965, pp. 37–39). Adolph Grünbaum objects that *if* the theory of unconscious repression as a cause of mental illness admits of empirical confirmation, that confirmation cannot be obtained from clinical observation, which is ineradicably contaminated by interpretations offered the patient on the basis of the theory; on this Popper and Grünbaum agree. Grünbaum, however, supposes that the theory might be given enough empirical content to be testable extraclinically, by experiment or epidemiological studies, though those studies and experiments have yet to be performed; he holds, that is, that the theory is not irrefutable but rather extremely improbable, as lacking empirical evidence to support it (*The Foundations of Psychoanalysis*, Berkeley, Calif., 1984, passim). This is not a game in the academy: ideas have consequences. Either view, if true, inevitably raises questions about the clinical effectiveness of psychoanalysis and psychoanalytically based psychotherapy, and may even suggest that to hold them out as forms of medical treatment, in the present state of knowledge, raises issues of tort liability for negligent misrepresentation, to which insurers are perhaps a party. It is unlikely that courts will be moved by the claim that those who reject the theory do so because their repressions are still unanalyzed and need treatment—a manifest begging of the question. It is relevant to inquire whether psychoanalysis does not contain or imply an ethical theory, an attribute not usually thought characteristic of empirical science; see the discussion of this by Donald C. Abel (*Freud on Instinct and Morality*, New York, 1989), who argues that Freud, at least in his early and middle periods, offers a moral theory that consists in hedonism and psychological egoism. For a more favorable view, see Gerasimos Santas, *Plato and Freud: Two Theories of Love*, New York, 1988.

has been treated like ποίησις. There are many kinds of creation: the productions of all the arts are creations, and their producers creators, but the word ποίησις has been marked off to stand for a single branch of creation, that in music and meter, "poetry." The same is true of Eros. Generically, it is every desire for good things and happiness, but those who turn to it in ways other than sexual, in money-making, or love of athletics, or of wisdom, are not said to love or be lovers. Those who assiduously pursue one special kind of love obtain the name of the whole.

Since men love the good as kindred to them (οἰκεῖον, 205e) rather than alien (ἀλλότριον),[98] they desire to possess it and possess it forever. So the object of Eros is to possess the good for oneself always, or forever (ἀεί, 206a, b). This is a considerable result; Diotima will infer from it that Eros is love of immortality (207a).

Diotima here also directly answers Aristophanes (205e; compare 211d, 212c): what lovers seek is not "their other half," reuniting the halves of a hermaphrodite, but only the good; they will reject what is evil even if it is as near to them as their hands and feet.

Diotima has defined Eros. Eros, the lover just insofar as he loves, is a relative term, to be defined by its object; that object is to possess the good for oneself forever. That the object of Eros is to possess the good for oneself forever, follows from the analysis of Eros in terms of βούλησις, rational wish, whose object is happiness, which consists in the possession of good things. Since everyone always wishes for happiness, everyone wishes always to have good things (205a) and everyone loves the same things always (205b). The ultimate object of desire has been identified with the object of rational wish, and it is common to all mankind. If one always wishes to possess good things, then, since one can never wish to cease to be happy, one's wish must be to possess good things always, that is, forever. If there is an apparent gap between Eros always wishing to possess good things and Eros wishing to possess good things always, Diotima's analysis has spanned it.[99]

If Eros, desire, is desire for good things and happiness (205d), then the ultimate object of Eros is not the apparent good but the real good. The notion of happiness is the key to the inference: for happiness implies well-

98. See *Lysis* 221e, 222c, *Charmides* 163c–d, *Republic* IX 586e. See also Aristotle *Nicomachean Ethics* X 1178a 5–8.

99. Dover (*Symposium*, p. 144) suggests that this conclusion "does not rest on reasoning at all," and goes on to question Plato's honesty in offering the argument. "Naturally, as long as the alternative possibilities of having good and having bad exist, we wish to have good, but it does not follow that we ourselves wish to exist forever." On the contrary, it does follow, insofar as we love, since the good wished for is happiness, as distinct from the object of some contingent desire.

being. So desire to possess what is really good for oneself implies wish for continued existence, and Eros, ever wishing to possess the good, wishes to possess the good forever. One may compare Eros to Spinoza's *conatus esse sui conservandi*: "Each thing endeavors, as far as possible, to persist in its own being,"[100] from which conatus both will and appetite spring.

Wish and What Is Primarily Valuable

Desire for a hot drink on a cold day is manifestly not the same as the wish for happiness, for if it were, then, by transitivity of identity, it would be the same as desire for a cold drink on a hot day, and a ham sandwich to go. The desire of a thirsty man for a cup of water, it may be urged, is not a desire for happiness any more than it is a desire for wisdom: it is a desire for water. But by Diotima's account the objects of desire are ranked in a hierarchy of purposes: the desire for water is implicated with the wish for happiness.

The ranking of purposes is analyzed in the *Lysis* (218d–220d), which develops a general theory of value, of what is lovable. Medicine is valuable ($\phi\iota\lambda o\varsigma$) to the body by reason of ($\delta\iota\alpha\ \tau\iota$) illness and for the sake of ($\varepsilon\nu\varepsilon\kappa\alpha\ \tau o\upsilon$) something else, namely, health. Health also is valuable, and if valuable, valuable for the sake of something else. We must necessarily go on proclaiming this, or arrive at a first principle ($\dot\alpha\varrho\chi\dot\eta$) that no longer refers to another valuable, but will reach that which is primarily valuable, for the sake of which we say that all other things are valuable (219c–d). This then is the source of value in other things, which are as it were images ($\varepsilon\iota\delta\omega\lambda\alpha$) of what is truly valuable, and deceive us in respect to what is primary and first. Socrates proceeds to illustrate. If a man loves his son above all else and learns that his son has drunk hemlock, he will value three gills of wine if he thinks it will save his son, and value a cup if it contains the wine. It isn't that he thinks the wine and the cup are equal in value to his son; on the contrary, the wine is valuable for curing the son, and the cup is valuable for holding the wine:

> All such concern as this is directed, not at things provided for the sake of something, but at that for the sake of which all such things are provided. We often say, no doubt, that we count silver and gold of great importance; but it is not true. Rather, we count of utmost importance that for the sake of which gold and everything is provided. . . . The same account holds for the valuable: in respect to everything we say is valuable for the sake of something else which is

100. *Ethics* III vi; cf. III ix and Scholium.

valuable, we appear to use only a word; what is really valuable is that by itself in which all these so-called valuable things terminate (219e–220b).

This should be compared to Aristotle's account of goodness at the beginning of the *Nicomachean Ethics*:

If, then, there is some end of the things we do, which we desire for its own sake (everything else being desired for the sake of this), and if we do not choose everything for the sake of something else (for at that rate the process would go on to infinity, so that our desire would be empty and vain), clearly this must be the good and the chief good. Will not the knowledge of it, then, have a great influence on life? Shall we not, like archers who have a mark to aim at, be more likely to hit upon what is right? If so, we must try, in outline at least, to determine what it is, and of which of the sciences or capacities it is the object (1.1094a.18–25, trans. W. D. Ross).

The *Lysis* offers a theory of value whose rudiments are found in other dialogues. In the *Laches*, Socrates is consulted about the educational value of learning to fight in armor. But the counsel (βουλή) is not about fighting in armor, any more than counsel about whether to apply salve to the eyes or a bit to a horse is about the salve or the bit instead of the eyes or the horse. "When someone considers something for the sake of something [ἕνεκά του], the counsel is really about that for the sake of which he inquired, not about what he inquired into for the sake of something else."[101] Fighting in armor is considered for the sake of the souls of the young men who are to learn it. In taking counsel for the sake of the soul, we must ask in what its excellence or virtue, its ἀρετή, consists.

If the aim of living is that our souls should be as good as possible, then the subject of our counsel defines the object of our wish. Our wish is for goodness of soul, virtue, however often our desires (*Meno* 77d–78a) or what seems good to us (*Gorgias* 467a–468d) runs counter to our wish. This account involves a peculiar priority. In Greek as in English, there is a distinction between virtuous actions and virtue as excellence of soul. It is often assumed that virtue, as an excellence of soul, is merely a disposition to perform virtuous actions, or behave virtuously. So before determining what virtue is, we must first find out what actions are virtuous: handsome is as handsome does. This precisely reverses the Socratic analysis, which implies that handsome does as handsome is. Actions in themselves are

101. *Laches* 185d.

neutral, neither good nor bad; they take their value from their object, that for the sake of which they are done. The *Laches* suggests that the worth of a practice such as fighting in armor must be estimated by reference to the soul and its excellence, and that courage is an excellence of soul. This is a reason for supposing that courage in souls is prior—ontologically, and in definition—to the paronymous courageousness of actions. It is misleading to say that courageous men are the kind of men who do courageous actions; on the contrary, courageous actions are the actions of courageous men. The issue is not one of statement equivalence, but of ontological and definitional priority. Issues of the value of actions are founded on moral psychology, and moral terms such as *courage* and *justice* and *temperance* and *virtue* are not in any primary sense dispositional predicates. To say that Nicias is courageous is not like saying that salt is soluble.

The claim that when one considers *a* for the sake of *b*, the counsel is about *b* and not about *a*, is a claim of priority further considered in the *Gorgias*, where βουλή, counsel, becomes βούλησις, rational wish.[102] Because the examples given in the *Gorgias* include medicine for the sake of health and sailing for the sake of wealth, it is easy to suppose that it is the relation of means to ends that is primarily in view. But the *Laches* implies that the principle is broader than that: eyes are not the aim or purpose of salve, nor horses of bits, nor souls of subjects of study, though salve may benefit the eyes, bits the horse or his rider, and study the soul. In general, means do not benefit ends, and ends are not benefited by means. Eyes, horses, and souls are not things at which action aims, but things for whose benefit action is done; as the *Lysis* suggests (219d), they move by being valued or loved. Aristotle may have had the *Lysis* in mind when he wrote, in book XII of the *Metaphysics*: "That a final cause may exist among unchangeable entities is shown by the distinction of its meanings. For the final cause is (a) some being for whose good an action is done, and (b) something at which the action aims; and of these the latter exists among unchangeable entities though the former does not" (XII 1072b 1–5, trans. Ross). The son poisoned by hemlock is plainly a final cause in the first sense; the wine as an antidote, and the cup that holds the wine, are valued for his sake. The *Lysis* treats the Primary Valuable as a final cause in an analogous though not thereby an identical way; it is the ultimate source of all goodness.

What are we to understand by the Primary Valuable? If we interpret the *Lysis* through the speech of Diotima in the *Symposium*, the first answer is that it is happiness, the object of βούλησις. If we ask why we do what

102. *Gorgias* 467d; cf. *Euthydemus* 279d–281d.

we do, what it is we really desire, the ultimate answer is happiness, and this answer is final in that we cannot sensibly say that we wish happiness for the sake of something else. But if the answer is final, it is also incomplete. If happiness is the aim of all our actions, in what does happiness consist?

If happiness consists in possession of good things, it consists in living well, and to live well is to live justly and temperately and wisely. In short, happiness consists in virtue, and the main purpose of Socrates' mission to Athens was to exhort his fellow citizens to pursue virtue. When Diotima comes to describe the lover's education of the beloved, it will involve discourses on virtue and the good man's character and pursuits (209b–c; compare 210a), and the guide in the Greater Mysteries will lead the lover to the contemplation of Beauty itself.

The distinction between desire and wish implies that we may desire what we do not wish for, that is, desire to possess what does not conduce to our own well-being. So the *Symposium* anticipates the *Republic*[103] and its distinction between necessary and unnecessary desires: necessary, those desires we cannot divert, and whose satisfaction is beneficial; unnecessary, those desires that can be got rid of, and whose presence in the soul is not good and in some cases is harmful. This account is ascetic, in that it implies rejection not only of vicious but of useless desires, and abstention from available pleasure. Alcibiades will later portray Socrates as unmoved by sexual desire and its pleasures, and accuse him of *hubris* because of it; in this Socrates represents the inner nature of Eros.

Of Human Bondage

Happiness consists in virtue, excellence of soul, and this is the root of the belief that human bondage is human ignorance. Diotima accepts an important premise for the Socratic conclusion, or paradox, that no one voluntarily does evil. All men wish for the good, though they differ in their ability to attain it, for many do not know where it is to be found (*Meno* 78b). Wrongdoing implies error, and error is involuntary. Precisely because the good man knows what evil is, he cannot do it, since his wish is for the good. Put briefly, he has the knowledge, but lacks the power. The bad man, on the other hand, cannot voluntarily do evil, because he does not know what it is; lacking knowledge, he acts at random.

Diotima's account of βούλησις leaves no place for the deliberate choice of evil recognized as such. For, by her account, knowingly to choose evil would be to choose to possess things one knows to be bad for oneself rather

103. *Republic* VIII 558d–559c; cf. 554a, 571b, *Phaedo* 64d–e, *Philebus* 62e.

than good for oneself, and this we are not constituted to do. This is an important premise for the Socratic conclusion, or paradox, that no one willingly does evil. Wrongdoing implies error, and error is involuntary. This is not meant to deny, but to explain, a familiar fact about human behavior, namely, that it is often self-destructive. Human bondage is ignorance of where one's own good lies. Compare Augustine and the pears:

> Your law, O Lord, punishes theft; and this law is so written in the hearts of men that not even the breaking of it blots it out: for no thief bears calmly being stolen from—, not even if he is rich and the other steals through want. Yet I chose to steal, and not because want drove me to it—unless a want of justice and contempt for it and an excess of iniquity. For I stole things which I already had in plenty and of better quality. Nor had I any desire to enjoy the things I stole, but only the taking of them and the sin. There was a pear tree near our vineyard, heavy with fruit, but fruit that was not particularly tempting either to look at or to taste. A group of young blackguards and I among them, went out to knock down the pears and carry them off late one night, for it was our bad habit to carry on our games in the streets till very late. We carried off an immense load of pears, not to eat—for we barely tasted them before throwing them to the hogs. Our only pleasure in doing it was that it was forbidden. Such was my heart, O God, such was my heart: yet in the depth of the abyss You had pity on it. Let that heart now tell You what it sought when I was thus evil for no object, having no cause for wrongdoing save my wrongness. The malice of the act was base and I loved it—that is to say I loved my own undoing. I loved the evil in me—not the thing for which I did the evil: my soul was depraved, and hurled itself down from security in You into utter destruction, seeking no profit from wickedness but only to be wicked.[104]

Diotima's reply to Augustine would be, first, "You contradict yourself," and second, "You boast." He boasts because he claims to have done what is impossible: to have loved evil and his own undoing. This false claim is supposed to follow because he willfully broke the law, a fact that in no way entails it. He contradicts himself because he claims to have stolen the pears for no reason, that he was evil for no object, but also claims to have taken pleasure in doing what was forbidden. In Platonic terms, the case he makes, at its strongest, is that stealing the pears was an apparent good that did not accord with the real good, the object of his wish. That is to

---

104. *Confessions* III iv, trans. Sheed.

say, his reason was overborne by disorderly and ungoverned passions: he was not master of himself, a fact explicable by bad character and bad education.

Augustine, on the other hand, would have insisted on the ability of men to deliberately choose evil recognized as such, to deliberately choose their own harm—and their own damnation. The voluntary theft of the pears represents the very substance of sin. To which the *Hippias Minor* makes the ironic reply that, if this is so, we are better men than we thought, since ignorance is worse than knowledge, and Augustine claims he knew what he was doing.

Behind Augustine's conception of sin lies a conception of man as an inherent rebel against the laws of God. Sin is a guilty act following on *mens rea*, a guilty mind, triggering criminal penalties attached to willful breach of legal rules. The Socratic conception of morality and of human moral psychology suggests the primacy of reasons to rules, of ideals to laws. An ideal may be more or less clearly understood, more or less fully attained; a law, and in particular a criminal law, is either known or unknown, kept or broken. No one can doubt that it is possible to break a law voluntarily, that is, willingly and wittingly; it is far less clear that one can voluntarily, willingly and wittingly, decline happiness and choose his own harm. We choose evil, and we choose to break the law; but if Socrates is right, we do not choose evil voluntarily, and we do choose voluntarily to break the law. Law is not the measure of good and evil, but measured by it.

The claim that all men wish for happiness, that the most virtuous men and women share this wish with the most depraved criminals and tyrants, that at the root of depravity there is a failure of intellect and understanding, contradicts the doctrine of original sin, at least as defended by Augustine. It also contradicts a modern variant found in psychoanalytic speculation, the notion of a death instinct. Freud in later life contrasted Eros with Thanatos, Eros a primary instinct toward life and community, and Thanatos a primary instinct toward death and destruction, one's own or another's. Freud first explicitly sponsored the notion of a death instinct in *Beyond the Pleasure Principle*, written just after the First World War, partly because of theoretical problems involved in the tendency to relive unpleasant experiences that Freud ascribed to neurotic compulsion,[105] but

105. A further reason for assuming Thanatos as an instinct or drive to self-destruction was Freud's program of reductive analysis for psychology, which he hoped to see explained in terms of biology and ultimately biochemistry; physiologically, anabolism is balanced by catabolism, a constant building up and wasting away of cells and tissues; one might then treat mental health, by analogy with metabolism, as a "vital balance" between life instincts and death instincts. But the analogy seems unhelpful to the cause of psychoanalysis. If psy-

partly also perhaps because of long-held theories about the instincts or drives. The result is a psychology whose explanatory apparatus depends upon a primary dualism, and it is doubtful that this pattern of explanation is satisfactory. Granting the undoubted fact of human cussedness, to claim that men are aggressive and self-destructive because of an instinct toward aggression and self-destruction is a level of explanation attained by Molière's doctor, who knew that opium is a soporific because it has dormative power. The same applies, *mutatis mutandis,* to doctrines of original sin and to theories, usually Manichaean in origin, of "radical evil." Concepts may be empty, in the sense that in application they cannot be falsified, and yet have practical consequences—compare astrology, anciently known as "judicial astronomy." The assumption that there is an innate human impulse toward destructiveness too easily suggests that cruelty and social oppression and war are in some strict sense incorrigible, and that the fundamental ordering principle among individuals, societies, and nations is and must necessarily be not rational persuasion but force. Civilization has then indeed its discontents: it becomes the lid on a cauldron, requiring the renunciation of putatively primary instincts. By their fruits you shall know them: both in terms of explanatory power and hope for human improvement, Diotima's assumption that all men wish for happiness and their own good, a good which in Socratic terms is implicated with justice and the common good, is perhaps to be preferred.

Abraham Lincoln and the Pig

Eros is of the good being his own forever; for men love the good as what is kindred and not alien, and they love it to be their own and to be their own forever (206a). It may help to understand this claim, as a proposition in moral psychology, by adverting to Abraham Lincoln and the pig.

Lincoln as a young lawyer rode circuit in Illinois from one county seat to another, following a tradition as old as the common law. He was traveling with another lawyer to the next county seat, on horseback because the spring rains had left the road so mired that it was impassible on wheels, and as they rode, as lawyers will, they argued. Lincoln maintained that all men act only to get pleasure and avoid pain, and do so because they are by nature so constituted that they cannot do otherwise. For Lincoln had read Jeremy Bentham's *Principles of Morals and Legislation,* a book

---

chical events either are or are nomologically dependent on physical events, if a thought either is or is a derivative of an enzyme, if the mind-body problem is to be resolved by monism or epiphenomenalism, as Freud seems to have supposed, the primary cure for mental disease or defect is to be sought in the pharmacy; the causal connection to this of induced recollection of putative past events, insight therapy, is conjectural at best.

closely studied, along with *A Fragment on Government,* by American public men in the thirties and forties of the last century: "Nature has placed mankind under the governance of two sovereign masters, pain and pleasure. It is for them alone to point out what we ought to do, as well as to determine what we shall do. . . . They govern us in all we do, in all we say, in all we think: every effort we can make to throw off our subjection, will but serve to demonstrate and confirm it."[106] Lincoln's companion argued, to the contrary, that men are capable of acting for the interests of others even at the cost of their own, and for motives other than pleasure.

They rounded a turn in the road, and found a large sow hopelessly mired in a wallow, unable to move and squealing piteously. Lincoln climbed off his horse, waded into the mudhole, grabbed the sow around the middle with his long arms, and deposited her on dry ground. He then remounted his horse, covered in mire from head to foot. His companion looked at him and laughed, "There, Lincoln, you've just refuted your theory by your actions." Lincoln replied, "No, I haven't. If I hadn't helped that sow, I'd have felt badly about it all day."

It is worth asking, from the point of view of the moral psychology of Diotima, why Lincoln's character was plainly better than his theory.

The *Symposium,* though its cast of characters and its theme connect it directly with the *Protagoras,* where hedonism as a moral theory is formulated for the first time, does not mention pleasure at all. There is no need. Pleasure is a concomitant of fulfillment of desire; given then that the satisfaction of any desire is pleasant, the claim that all desire is desire for pleasure is, in a sense, trivially true. But triviality becomes fallacy if hedonism, the doctrine that pleasure is the good, is offered as an explanation of human motives and actions: hedonism puts the cart before the horse, since pleasure is not an object of desire but a concomitant of its satisfaction. The contrast between desire and wish in the *Symposium* suggests that the primary task of moral psychology is not defined by the fact that the satisfaction of desire is pleasant, but by the question of what desires ought to be satisfied. Which is why, allowing that compassion is a desire and extends to the relief of animal suffering, Abraham Lincoln was mistaken about why he helped the pig.

If not hedonism, perhaps psychological egoism. Perhaps men are by nature so constituted that they act only for their own interest, and hedonism merely specifies that interest as pleasure. As to psychological egoism, it may seem, Bentham's doctrine and Diotima's coincide: Eros loves the good to be *his own* forever.

106. *Principles* I i.

Perhaps then one need only distinguish between the object of a desire and its ownership. If Jones desires that Smith should be fed, feeding Smith satisfies Jones's desire, as it also satisfies Smith's hunger. As there is trivial hedonism, so there is trivial egoism: in general satisfaction of a desire that someone else be benefited is, since desire arises out of one's own lack, a benefit to oneself. So in some sense psychological egoism is trivially true.

Diotima, however, is claiming more than this: desire is self-interested because happiness defines interest, and all men wish to be happy. So the question, What is in one's own interest? reduces to the question, In what does happiness consist?

Here the *Symposium* breaks new ground. Socrates does not in the early dialogues couch his moral theory in terms of happiness as an ultimate goal. He speaks rather of that in us which is benefited by justice and harmed by injustice, the soul, and he offers the Socratic Proportion: that virtue is to the soul as health is to the body. No doubt in the concept of psychical health there is an implicit claim about happiness, for happiness is not a feeling but a state of well-being; the *Symposium* develops what is already there. Aristotle, in the *Nicomachean Ethics,* will make the virtues means to happiness as an end, but the *Symposium,* true to its Socratic heritage, assumes that happiness consists in virtue and justice: Eros, as love of beauty, is love of goodness.

Virtue and justice imply concern for the good of others. Diotima will claim that the works of Eros issue in education; Socrates, in the *Euthydemus* (275a), says he desires that Cleinias should become as good as possible, and this, indeed, defined Socrates' peculiar mission to Athens: "I go about doing nothing but persuading you, young and told, to care not for the body or money in place of, or so much as, excellence of soul" (*Apology* 30a). If the pursuit of happiness is inherently self-regarding—in one's own interest—it is also inherently other-regarding—in the interest of others: concern for one's own good is implicated, not accidentally but essentially, with the common good. That implication is grounded on the Primary Valuable of the *Lysis,* the Form of Beauty in the *Symposium,* the Form of the Good in the *Republic.* Moral psychology has a metaphysical foundation; self-interest implies community, and community, universality. Egoism has as its contrast altruism: but that contrast is otiose if the good of the self is the good of others.

The Works of Eros: Begetting in Beauty (206b–207a)

Diotima's account of Eros now modulates into a new key. Eros is love of the beautiful. The beautiful at first was the object of desire, the apparent good. It has now become the real good, the object of rational wish. And it will end as the Idea of Beauty, an ontological first principle of both love and knowledge.[107] Agathon said much more than he knew when he claimed that Eros is love of the beautiful, and that there is no love of the ugly.

Diotima has now told who, or what, Eros is. He is an intermediate divinity, a δαίμων, the child of Poros and Penia, conceived on the birthday of Aphrodite; he is not merely sexual desire, nor even desire in all its forms, but wish for happiness, and therefore wish to possess good things for oneself forever.

Having said who Eros is, Diotima, following the plan first suggested by Agathon and ratified by Socrates, now describes his works. If Eros in himself is wish to possess good things for oneself forever, the works of Eros involve begetting or creating in beauty in order to obtain a kind of vicarious immortality. The desire to procreate and give birth is treated as the product of a desire shared by men with other animals for continued possession of the good.

Diotima's discussion of the works of Eros (206b–209e) is markedly rhetorical, sometimes to the point of parody. The style is characterized by strong and emphatic rhythms, though it avoids the jingles of isology and assonance (compare 185c). There is rhetorical use of metonymy, though now with a purpose (206d; compare 187e). There is much imprecision in the use of words having to do with reproduction: the various stages of fertility, arousal, intercourse, pregnancy, and birth are mixed together in a way that cannot be adequately represented in English; sometimes it seems things are born before they are begotten (206d.5, 209b.2, c.3). There is sophistic play at contradiction for the sake of emphasis—the object of Eros is now said to be, not the beautiful, but begetting in the beautiful (206d–e; compare 180a, 186a, 194e–195a). There is rhetorical overstatement, as when Diotima claims that erotic passion causes animals to sacrifice their lives for their offspring without remarking that it does not always cause this (207b). There is rhetorical overgeneralization, failure to distinguish cases, as when Diotima explains the fact that Alcestis died in behalf of Admetus and that Achilles died in addition to Patroclus as both equally the result of love of honor and remembrance (208c–209a), contradicting Phaedrus's rhetorical claim that the motive in each case was the courage born of love. It comes as no surprise when Socrates speaks

107. Cf. Aristotle *Nicomachean Ethics* VIII 1155b 23–26 (trans. W. D. Ross): "It is thought that each loves what is good for himself, and that the good is without qualification lovable, and what is good for each man is lovable for him; but each man loves not what is good for him but what seems good."

of Diotima as "most wise" and suggests at one point that she replies "as the accomplished sophists do" (208b–c).

The reason is that Diotima's speech is couched in a style suitable for an encomium. Socrates has already explained that one should tell the truth about what is praised, selecting what is most beautiful and putting it in the most suitable way (198d). Diotima is telling the truth about Eros, but in discussing his works she selects her truths and presents them in a style that imitates a sophistical display, an *epideixis*.

Imitation runs deeper than style: it is exhibited by content. Diotima's passage from Eros as desire for beauty to Eros as desire to procreate and give birth in the beautiful (206e) is a radical transition: desire to procreate is not the same as the rational wish for happiness, and if Eros implies rational wish for happiness, Eros is most assuredly not found in the animal kingdom, where Diotima will trace it. The immortality that Diotima claims to find in procreation is not the continuing existence of what is one and the same, but reproduction of something of the same kind, and this according to body and soul. That is, it is not immortality, but a kind of imitation of it. Diotima's sophistical style suits her subject matter.

Eros is love of immortality. We love only what we lack. Therefore, Eros cannot be immortal. This conclusion seems to contradict the attempts in the *Phaedo, Republic,* and *Phaedrus* to establish the immortality of the soul by proof, and Hackforth suggested that Plato had "lapsed into skepticism" on the subject of immortality when he wrote the *Symposium*.[108] The inference involves a logical mistake. If it is true that Eros is love of immortality, it is an immortality desired by the lover just insofar as he loves; this does not imply that the lover does not have an immortal soul, but only that he does not have it qua lover. Put otherwise, if there is an immortal principle in the lover, it is not in him by virtue of his love, which derives from his lack. The immortality that Eros desires is explicitly said to be immortality of the mortal nature, contrasted to the immortal nature (208b.4). Immortality of the mortal nature, procreation, is different in kind from the immortality of the soul that Plato was concerned to establish by proof. If the soul is immortal, as Socrates argues in the *Phaedo,* then, given Diotima's claim that the lover qua lover lacks immortality and desires to possess it, this must imply that love, if it is of the essence of the lover, is not of the essence of his soul. Mortality attaches to the lover, not essentially, but as a term in a relation. Eros is not Psyche, and it is a root of error to confound them.

---

108. R. Hackforth, "Immortality in Plato's *Symposium*," *Classical Review* 44 (1950), pp. 43*ff.*; cf. J. V. Luce, *Classical Review*, n.s. 2 (1952), pp. 137*ff.*

But in what sense is Eros love of immortality? Immortality, as it happens, is not the sort of thing that can be desired. To love is to desire that things not present be present in future (200a–e). Therefore, if Eros desires immortality with the good (207a), to wish to possess the good for oneself always is not the same as to desire to possess immortality: for the good can be possessed at present and still be desired, whereas immortality of the mortal nature, understood as existence in all subsequent time, cannot be possessed at present and still be desired. So if Eros is love of immortality, it can only be love of vicarious immortality—love not of possession of the beautiful, but of procreation in the beautiful. Procreation is an image or imitation of immortality, and not in the strict sense immortality at all.

Immortality and the Mortal Nature (207a–208b)

Diotima now proceeds to describe the reason for love and desire. The mortal nature seeks to be ever existent and immortal. It can achieve this only in begetting, leaving a new creature behind in place of the old that passes away. This process of continual generation occurs, not only in the species, but also within the individual; for our bodies and those aspects of our souls associated with our bodies are continually dying. It is only for a little time that an animal is said to live and be the same, and even though he is called the same, he is not so, for he does not possess the same properties; the new is constantly replacing what is continually being lost. This applies not only to the body but to the soul; habits, customs, opinions, desires, pleasures, pains—all are continually changing. Even our knowledge is continually coming to be and passing away, so that we are never the same persons in what we know. Every mortal thing is preserved, not by remaining forever the same, but by substituting another like it for what departs. It is in this way that mortal nature has a share in immortality—and mortal nature here clearly includes what Plato elsewhere refers to as mortal, not immortal, soul.[109]

The work of Eros is to create in the beautiful (ἐν τῷ καλῷ); by this device the mortal nature has a share in immortality. So beauty is indeed a birth goddess (206c–d), a necessary condition of begetting and thereby of immortality.

Reproduction aims at continuation of the species, not of the individual. Diotima anticipates Aristotle's account in the De anima:

109. See *Timaeus* 69c and A. E. Taylor, *Commentary on Plato's Timaeus*, Oxford, 1928, p. 498.

For any living thing which has reached its normal development and which is unmutilated, and whose mode of generation is not spontaneous, the most natural act is the production of another like itself, an animal producing an animal, a plant a plant, in order that, as far as its nature allows, it may partake in the eternal and divine. This is the goal towards which all things strive, that for the sake of which they do whatsoever their nature renders possible. The phrase "for the sake of which" is ambiguous; it may mean either (a) the end to achieve which, or (b) the being in whose interest the act is done. Since then no living thing is able to partake in what is eternal and divine by uninterrupted continuance (for nothing perishable can ever remain one and the same), it tries to achieve that end in the only way possible to it, and success is possible in varying degrees; so it remains not indeed as the self-same individual but continues its existence in something *like* itself—not numerically but specifically one.[110]

Aristotle's analysis is directed toward the nutritive soul, whose functions are nutrition and reproduction. Diotima's account assimilates nutrition to reproduction, hunger and thirst to sex.

Her analysis puts sexuality on a new basis; it is found to have a foundation in the life of men and other animals that is broader than itself, in that desire for sexual intercourse, like hunger and thirst, exists for the sake of immortality, that is, continued existence in time. It follows that sexuality is not to be understood primarily in terms of desire for sexual intercourse, or the emotions that attend on it and constitute romantic love, but in terms of offspring. Diotima adduces the fact that animals will sacrifice their lives for their young: this is not a deduction but a description of how men and other animals, in some cases, do in fact behave (compare 207c–d, 208b, 208c–d, 212a). So in the mortal nature, Eros, directed to the continued existence of the individual organism, has as its work the continued existence of the species, and may require sacrifice of the life of the individual organism—as is sometimes true not only in men but other animals. This is a biological image of that wish for happiness which issues in courage and friendship.

The begetting of children (206c) is the natural object of Eros in respect to the body (207c, 208b, e), since Eros aims at immortality. It is but a short step to infer that sexual intercourse that cannot issue in the begetting of children is unnatural, and Plato in fact reached this result for homosexuality in the *Republic* (III 403a–c) and *Laws* (VIII 838e; compare VIII

110. *De anima* II 415a 26–b 8 (trans. Smith); cf. *De generatione animalium* II i. See also *Metaphysics* XII 1072b 1*ff.*

841d, 836c–e, I 636e). The seeds of later Natural Law doctrines of sexuality, and their implicit asceticism, are found in the *Symposium*'s insistence that the natural object of sexuality is procreation.

Diotima's description of the mortal nature, in respect to body and soul, recalls the *Cratylus*: "Heraclitus says somewhere that all things change and nothing remains, and he likens things which are to the flow of a river, saying that you cannot step in the same river twice" (402a). The *Cratylus* (339d–440c) asserts the existence, among other characters, of Beauty itself, and analyzes it very much as Diotima does: it is always (ἀεί) of such sort as itself, ever the same and unchanging in that it does not depart from its own form; and the object of knowledge. The *Cratylus* further argues that the objects of knowledge must be unchanging. If all things change and nothing remains the same, there is no knowledge; for if the very character of knowledge changes, it would change into another character of knowledge and not be knowledge; there would then neither be knowing nor anything known. Therefore, if there is knowing, there is also always what is known—the Beautiful, the Good, and each of the things that are— and if this account is true, the account of Heraclitus that all things change must be false. Diotima's treatment of the ways or turnings (τρόποι) of the body, of hair, flesh, bone, and blood, and of the soul, its character, habits and opinions, desires, pleasures, pains and fears, as perpetually coming to be and passing away, appears to imply that Heraclitus's account is true. And Heraclitus's account would indeed be true if there were no Ideas: the samenesses and identities of the mortal world are formal and structural, products of the presence of common characters. The immortality achieved by the mortal nature in terms of persistence of species, Diotima argues, is that of sameness in kind, and this is the only kind of sameness the mortal nature admits. The very process of begetting cannot be understood without reference to Beauty itself.

Diotima is here speaking of the works of Eros in respect to the mortal nature, which aims at procreation because it is implicated with lack and futurity, and therefore with time, becoming new or young as it grows older.[111] Lack of an end in which process can terminate is inherent in an account of desire that makes its aim immortality in time, an aim that cannot in principle be attained. Eros, it will be recalled, is the lover qua lover, who lacks what he desires to possess.

Diotima's conclusion that we are never the same even in what we know (207e–208a) is indeed "much more extraordinary still." The claim is

---

111. 207d 7; cf. 208b 1. This is a basis for certain arguments in Hypotheses about Unity in the *Parmenides* (I.1.ix, I.2.x, I.3). In the *Timaeus* (38a), it is assumed that what moves becomes older and younger through time.

stated with great generality: not only are we not the same in the kinds of things we know from day to day, but not the same even in each single one of those things. Our knowledge from day to day is different, and differs even when it appears to be the same. This is knowledge, of course, which belongs to the mortal nature (compare 209a) and is infected with the perishability of its objects. The image or imitation of genuine immortality produces an image or imitation of genuine knowledge.

Creation in Respect to Body and Soul (208b–209e)

That Eros is love of immortality is shown by the love of honor among men, and the fact that they are willing to sacrifice their lives for fame. This is why Alcestis was willing to die for Admetus, Achilles for Patroclus, Cadmus for his children. Those pregnant of body express their love sexually, and seek immortality through begetting offspring; those pregnant in mind or soul leave behind them such children of the mind as Homer and Hesiod and other poets have done, or as lawgivers they beget the virtue and temperance that order cities rightly, or they reach out to a beautiful youth and take in hand his education by rearing friendship and virtue in common with him.

In discussing marriage regulations in the *Laws* (IV 721b–d), the Athenian in effect makes sexual reproduction a legal obligation: "It is a man's duty to marry between the ages of thirty and thirty-five, recognizing that it is in this way that the human race by nature has a certain share of immortality, which indeed everyone naturally desires; for the desire to become famous and not to lie nameless in the grave is for just that. The race of men is twin-born with all time, and journeys and shall journey with it to the end, and it is immortal in this way, by leaving children's children, and, being ever one and the same, it has a share of immortality by giving birth." To the immortality gained from perpetuation of the species and the memory of future generations, Diotima adds the immortality gained by generating φρόνησις, wisdom, intelligence, temperance, in soul or state. This activity is education, and the product of friendship.

Eros is directed more toward friendship than toward sexual intercourse. In the *Prior Analytics* (II 68a.40–b.8), Aristotle refers to an argument that justifies this result by proportion theory:

> If then every lover insofar as he loves would choose (a) that his beloved be so disposed as to gratify him and yet (c) that he not gratify him, rather than (d) that he gratify him and yet (b) that he not be so disposed as to gratify him, it is clear that (a), being so disposed, is

more to be chosen than (d), being gratified. Therefore, to be loved is more to be chosen than intercourse. Therefore, love [ἔρως] is more of friendship [φιλία] than intercourse; but if it is especially this, then this is its end [τέλος]. Therefore, either intercourse is not an end at all or it is so for the sake of being loved; so too with other desires (ἐπιθυμία] and arts.

Diotima's speech is distinguished by its excellence of structure, and in the course of her account she found opportunity to comment by implication on all of the speeches that have gone before. Contrary to Phaedrus (178a), Eros is not a god but an intermediate (202cff.), and the noble acts of Alcestis and Achilles (179b) are due to a desire for fame (208d). Contrary to Pausanias, who distinguished Vulgar from Heavenly Eros (180d–e), Eros is one, a single whole of varied parts (202b, 203cff.), though its works may concern either the body or the soul (208e–209e). Contrary to Eryximachus, Diotima does not locate Eros in all of nature, though she finds it, or an image of it, in animals other than man (207a–208b). Contrary to Aristophanes, Eros is not the desire for wholeness or completeness through another bodily half (192b, e), but only for one's own good (205e). Contrary to Agathon (197c), Eros is not beautiful nor divine (201e, 202bff., 204c), though it is love of the beautiful, and Socrates explicitly approves (199c) of Agathon's distinction (195a) between who Eros is and his works, a distinction crucial to the structure of Diotima's speech.

If Diotima offers rhetoric of a sophistical tinge, she also offers an analysis of the human condition—that is to say, the mortal condition—in terms of a deep and incongruous longing. We aim at immortality, and undertake to achieve it by producing children or getting fame, producing poems, laws, education. However well we succeed, we fail of our aim. There is a difference between desire for continued existence with the good and desire for immortality, and vicarious immortality is not immortality at all, but only an image of it. The restless heart is restless still.

The Ladder of Love (209e–210e)

The structure of Diotima's speech may be likened to a triangle. The base of that triangle is the general analysis of Eros as desire for what is beautiful, and thereby, as wish for the good to be its own forever (201d–206a). This defines who, or what, Eros is. One leg of the triangle is Diotima's analysis of the works of Eros as implying production or creation. The other leg is the ascent to apprehension of an ultimate principle, Beauty itself, on which all other beautiful things depend.

It is important to see that this triangular structure is also in some sense dynamic. Because Eros has as its aim possession of the good forever, it is love of immortality; this it can achieve only vicariously, through procreation. But vicarious immortality, precisely because it is vicarious, is not genuine immortality after all; if Eros were exhausted in it, desire would be empty and vain, and happiness unobtainable. So the ends achieved in procreation are inadequate to the nature of Eros, and what has gone before points beyond itself to what is to follow.

What follows stands to what has gone before as *explanans* to *explanandum*: it is "the final and completed revelation for the sake of which [ἕνεκα] these others exist" (210a), a revelation that leads to the apprehension of Beauty itself, and perhaps a kind of immortality in likeness to the divine.[112] That is, procreation in respect to body and soul exists for the sake of what is to be revealed in the Greater Mysteries—exists, that is, for the sake of Beauty itself (210e, 211c). This is the language of teleology, final causation.

It has been suggested that in the opening words of this section, Plato intimates that what is to follow goes beyond the teaching of the historical Socrates, that the revelation of the transcendental Form of Beauty is peculiarly Plato's own. But it is unnecessary to refer outside the dialogue for what can be sufficiently explained within it. Diotima's words have an obvious dramatic function, to emphasize the importance of the account that follows, and Socrates has already expressed repeated ignorance and surprise at Diotima's teaching.[113] The issue of historicity is otiose.

Diotima describes the ascent of the lover to Beauty itself as a progress of Eros up an ordered ladder of objects, rising to the apprehension of an ultimate first principle, Beauty itself, on which all other beautiful things depend. If the works of love imply begetting in the beautiful, they imply the apprehension of Beauty itself; for beauty is prior to begetting in beauty (212a). The aim of procreation is immortality, and at the end of the ascent the lover qua lover will achieve such immortality as the mortal nature admits.

The ascent of the lover begins with beauty in respect to the body, that form of beauty which provokes desire for procreation through sexual intercourse: if his guide guides him rightly (210a), his love is first directed to one single body; the beloved becomes a bridge over which desire is directed to the ultimate object of desire, Beauty itself. Realizing that the beauty of any one body is akin to that of any other, the lover recognizes

---

112. 212a; cf. *Republic* VI 490a–b, *Timaeus* 90b–c, *Theaetetus* 178b.
113. 208b–c; cf. 201a–202a, 202b–d, 204a–b, c–d, 205a–b, 206b, 206c–207a, 207c.

that beauty, insofar as it attaches to visible form, is one and the same in—Diotima actually uses the word ἐπί, on—all bodies, and it is therefore unreasonable to value highly the beauty of any single thing. Socrates is here speaking of beauty of appearance (210b.2), the ἄνθος, or bloom (compare 210b.8); the beauty of this individual beautiful body attaches to all bodies insofar as they are beautiful, and apprehension of this beauty is prior to the desire to beget in what is beautiful. The ascent of the lover begins by detaching Eros from the particular and concrete, so that the lover comes to recognize and prefer beauty as a universal, present in many things. Eros is indeed a philosopher; there is a contemplative element, an apprehension of beauty as a universal, implicit even in sexual passion.

Begetting in the beautiful in respect to the body has been distinguished from begetting in the beautiful in respect to the soul (206b–c, 207d–e, 208e–209a). The lover in his ascent to Beauty itself will next come to cherish beauty of soul above bodily beauty.[114] At this level and its congener, love of the beauty of laws and institutions, knowledge of Beauty itself has not yet come.

From beauty of soul it is but a short step to the beauty of laws and institutions, whose beauty is akin; so in the *Republic*, the same principles provide both soul and state with their beauty and proper order.[115] Diotima supposes, as the Greeks did generally, that character and custom insofar as they are good evince an aesthetic element, an element intensified at the next level, where the lover comes to contemplate the beauty and order of the sciences, among them, importantly, we must assume, mathematics and proportion theory.[116]

The lover who was drawn to beget in the beautiful according to the soul became a poet or lawgiver or educator (209a–e); his attention is now drawn to that beauty on which education depends. In contemplating the beauty of the sciences, the lover is impelled toward the ocean of beauty made manifest in reasoning, that is, in dialectic and philosophy.[117] At this level he must remain until he has gathered strength to attain to the knowledge of Beauty itself, the goal of all his efforts, that for the sake of which all his former labors exist.

114. This is the level attained by those who have passed through primary education in the *Republic* (III 402c*ff.*): to them, the most beautiful spectacle is the coincidence of a beautiful body and a noble soul, and this is the object of their love; but it is not beauty of body they care for so much as beauty of soul.
115. Cf. *Republic* II 368e*ff.*, IV 435e*ff.*, VIII 544d*ff.*
116. In the advanced educational program in *Republic* VII, the sciences are identified as arithmetic, geometry, stereometry or solid geometry, astronomy, and harmonics. All of these sciences were unified by proportion theory.
117. Compare the distinction between the sciences and dialectic in *Republic* VII.

Diotima's language may be understood to present in a temporal sequence of before and after an order of priority that is in some sense logical, in that it is defined in terms of universality or kinship, and analogy. The beauty that attaches to one body attaches to all, for the beauty of all bodies is akin (ἀδελφόν, 210b.1). Beauty of laws and institutions is all kindred (συγγενές, 210c.5) to itself, and by comparison, bodily beauty is a small thing. The beauty of the sciences is superior to the beauty of any one given thing by reason of their universality—the beautiful in its multitude.

Beauty in respect to the body is all akin; beauty in respect of laws and institutions, and presumably therefore also of soul, is also kindred. What Diotima does not say is that beauty in respect to the body is akin or kindred to beauty in respect to the soul. Indeed, there is good reason to deny this: for beauty of body is necessary for procreation in respect to the body, that is, the begetting of children; beauty of soul is necessary for procreation in respect to the soul, that is, of poems, laws and education. It is evident that, according to the analysis of the *Symposium*, beauty of body and beauty of soul are different kinds of beauty. Beauty of soul is more to be valued than beauty of body (210b), and bodily beauty by comparison to it is a small thing (210c–d). But the comparison here is one of kind, not of degree. The two kinds of beauty are analogous, in the way that children are analogous to poems or laws in respect to procreation (208e–209e).

The finest achievement of modern aesthetic theory has been the discovery of a unit of measure of beauty. This is the millihelen: that quantum of beauty required to launch one ship. But the millihelen is an inappropriate measure of beauty in the ascent passage of the *Symposium*, for application of a measure implies invariance in what is measured, and beauty of body and beauty of soul are of different kinds. So there is no number of millihelens by which Socrates' soul is prettier than Helen of Troy's body; if they differ in beauty, the difference is other than can be expressed by an arithmetical ratio. It is the difference between what is truly beautiful and what merely seems so, as though one were to intend to trade gold for bronze (219a).

But though different in kind, one kind being superior in value to the other, beauty of body and beauty of soul are the same in that all beautiful things partake of Beauty itself, a single character or Form or Idea that is universal, shared by many things. Beauty of body and beauty of soul do not share identical predicates, but partake of the same Idea. Because Beauty is a cause, beauty of body and beauty of soul are beautiful by reason of their relation to that cause, though beauty of body is inferior in kind to beauty of soul. They are similar by reason of their relation to one Idea, and different by reason of the difference in their manner of participation. That is, they are derivatively beautiful. Beauty itself is beautiful in the primary sense, in that it is the source of beauty in other things and excludes all ugliness.

To this it will be objected that bodies, souls, and indeed Beauty itself all have the same predicate. But, it will be said, if ". . . is beautiful" can be predicated of bodies and souls and Beauty, they must all be the same, not different, in kind. Millihelen ho!

But what are we to understand by ". . . is beautiful," or the "predicate" of being beautiful?

One thing we might understand is that, in English or in Greek, we may apply the same form of words or linguistic formula to them. This, of course, is not only true but trivially true. It does not contradict the claim that beauty of soul and beauty of body are different in kind, though both are beautiful. The form of words is the same—the things are homonymous—but the conditions under which the form of words is applied are different in kind. For if one were to render an account of what beauty of body consists in, it would have reference to shape and color, but beauty of soul to wisdom and temperance; so the accounts differ, though the form of words is the same. The uses are not radically equivocal, as pen is in "pig pen" and "fountain pen," because they introduce the same Idea, Beauty itself. But they are not univocal either, because the kinds of things to which they are applied, and the conditions under which they may be properly applied, are different—so different, indeed, that there is no ground for assertion of similarity except by reference to the Idea of which they in different ways partake. Compare ". . . is healthy" as applied to climates, complexions, and people, or ". . . is wet" as applied to water and the clothes in the wash. We deal here with what has been called equivocity by reference.[118]

118. See Joseph Owens, *The Doctrine of Being in the Aristotelian Metaphysics,* 2d ed., Toronto, 1963, chap. 3: "The Aristotelian Equivocals." See also J. L. Austin, *Philosophical Papers,* Oxford, 1963, pp. 37–42. Equivocity by reference is not paronymy, since there need be no difference in ending; it is not univocity, because definitions are not the same; and it is only in a qualified sense equivocity, in that the definitions introduce the same form; neither is it some form of "family resemblance." The phrase "focal meaning" introduces a metaphor, rather than clarifying the use, which Aristotle supposed had reference to causes: issues of meaning tack on in complex ways to the structure of the world. G. E. Moore once denied in conversation that water is wet, and his dialectical instincts were sound. If water is wet, and goodness is equivocal by reference, the naturalistic fallacy isn't a fallacy.

The Ascent to Beauty Itself (210e–212a)

It is Beauty itself that is the supreme object of desire—eternal, free from relativity and change, absolute in its simplicity and grandeur. It is revealed to the lover "suddenly," "in an instant," in an act of intellectual intuition, as the sacred objects of the mystery religions were suddenly revealed to the eyes of the worshippers in a blaze of light. As in the mysteries, the culmination is described as a marriage, the sacred marriage of Eleusinia, the marriage of the soul and Beauty. In the *Republic* (VI 490a–b), the offspring of this marriage is said to be intelligence and truth; in the *Symposium* (212a), intellectual intuition—grasping or touching—leads to the begetting of true virtue, got by contemplation of what is. The lover in his quest for beauty ascends *there*, to another world, to *that*—the use is repeated and emphatic—and in describing the nature or essence of Beauty found there, the prose suddenly bursts into dithyrambs, in the manner of a choric ode (211a–b). This is a metaphysical description that is also a hymn. Plato's style quickens under the impulse of certain ideas; it is impossible to preserve in translation the pounding beat of his rhythms, the beat of the dance.

The lover climbs as by a ladder in his ascent to Beauty. Eros is a philosopher, and the ultimate object of rational wish is not a matter of choice. It will be observed that Beauty itself is a universal, not in the sense that it is a predicate applying to many subjects, but as that for the sake of which all other things are valued as beautiful. And as it is an ultimate object of desire, so also is it an ultimate object of knowledge. As Aristotle was later to remark: "There is something which moves without being moved, being eternal, substance, and actuality. And the object of desire and the object of thought move in this way; they move without being moved. The primary objects of desire and of thought are the same. For the apparent good is the object of appetite, and the real good is the primary object of rational wish."[119]

It is characteristic of a ladder that one leaves the lower rungs behind as one climbs. But one does not stop loving the beauty of bodies solely by reason of the fact that one has come to love the beauty of souls; or the beauty of souls solely because one has come to love the beauty of laws and institutions, which are directed to beauty of soul; or the beauty of the sciences, especially mathematics and proportion theory, whose principles are also principles of justice and beauty of soul, solely because one has come to love Beauty itself. Plato here, as in the analysis of society in *Re-*

119. *Metaphysics* XII 1072a 25–28, trans. W. D. Ross.

public II, the account of the decline of the just state in *Republic* VIII and IX, and the origins of the world order in the *Timaeus,* presents as a temporal sequence what is in fact an order of natural priority.

The Idea of Beauty

The transcendental Idea of Beauty, knowledge of which is the lover's goal, is distinct from the things of this world:

First, in respect to changelessness. Beauty itself admits of neither generation nor destruction, growth nor diminution (211a.1–2). Since it is not in anything other than itself (211a.8), it does not admit of local motion; since it suffers nothing (211b.5), it is not affected by what comes to be or passes away. The analysis here derives directly from the *Cratylus* (439d–440b): the object of knowledge is unchanging, and it is an Idea. This became the basis of an Academic argument known to Aristotle, that something is known when particular things have perished.[120] Alexander gives it as follows.[121] The "Argument from Thinking" for the existence of Ideas is the following sort: if when we think man or foot or animal, we both think something among things that are and nothing among things that are particular (for the same thought remains when those things have perished), it is clear that there is something besides particulars and sensibles, which we think when those things both are and are not; for we do not then think something that is not; but this is the Form and Idea. This is a variant of the "Argument from the Sciences":[122] If medicine is not knowledge of this given health but simply of health, something will be Health itself; and if geometry is not knowledge of this given equal and that given diameter, but of what is strictly equal and strictly diameter, something will be Equal itself and Diameter itself; but those things are Ideas. These arguments, deriving ultimately from the *Cratylus* and the *Symposium* itself, cast their implication backwards: Diotima's earlier claim that in the mortal nature knowledge comes to be and passes away (207e–208a) implies that the object of mortal knowledge is not to be understood to be Ideas, with their attendant universality and necessity, but particulars and sensibles.

Second, in respect to purity. Beauty itself is in no sense qualified by its own opposite, ugliness: it is not beautiful at one time or place but ugly at another, or beautiful relative to one thing but not to another, or beautiful to one man but not to another (211a.2–5). This is part of what is meant by saying that it is pure and unalloyed and unmixed (211e.1). The *Symposium* here may be compared to the doctrine of the Two Worlds of Knowl-

---

120. *Metaphysics* I 990b 14–15, XIII 1079b 10–11.
121. In *Metaphysics* 81.25–82.1, Hayduck. Cf. Asclepius, in *Metaphysics,* 72.2–7, Hayduck.
122. Alexander, in *Metaphysics,* 79.11–15.

edge and Belief in the *Republic* (V 475e–476a, 479a–d, VII 523a–524c),
and the second argument to prove that Knowledge Is Recollection in the
Phaedo (74a–c), whose main premise is that there exists a Form of Equality: "We say, I suppose, that there is something equal—I do not mean as
stick is equal to stick or stone to stone or anything of that sort, but something else over and beyond all these things—the equal itself." Equality
and sensible equals are different sorts of things, for sensible equals sometimes appear equal to one thing but not to another, whereas things which
are just equal never appear to be unequal, nor Equality to be Inequality;
therefore, Equality and sensible equals differ in that equality cannot be
qualified by inequality, whereas sensible equals may also be unequal.

Third, in respect to separation, Beauty itself will not appear beautiful
as a face does, or hands or parts of the body, or as discourse or knowledge,
or as what is somewhere in something other than itself is beautiful (211a–
b). In the *Phaedo* (102d, 103b) the largeness in us is distinguished from
largeness in the nature of things, and in the *Timaeus* (52a–c) it is to be
argued that what truly is cannot be in space; it belongs to an image, and
only to an image, to be *in* something other than itself, and *of* something
other than itself; an Idea neither receives anything into itself from elsewhere, nor itself enters into anything anywhere. Beauty itself exists alone
by itself, single in nature forever (211b.1; compare 211e.1, 4). Other
things are beautiful by having a share of it; they are later referred to as
images or insubstantial forms of Beauty (εἴδωλα, 212a.4), and though the
things that partake of it come to be and pass away, Beauty itself is not
affected (211b.2–5). The claim that one mark of being is power to act or
be acted upon is not true of the Form of Beauty, any more than it is true
of Aristotle's God.[123]

Beauty and Goodness

The theory of Forms or Ideas is both a theory of meaning and a theory
of the structure of the world; as such, it performs many different functions in Plato's dialogues. For example, the theory is directly connected
with the "What is it?" question. In the *Euthyphro*, Socrates asks what Ho-
liness is in order to obtain a standard by which to judge whether Euthyphro's action in prosecuting his father for murder in behalf of a hired
man is, as he claims and his father and other relatives deny, holy: the Form
is here used as a criterion for detecting its instances. In the *Meno*, Socrates
asks what virtue is in order to determine whether it is taught, or acquired

---

123. Compare Aristotle's description of God as ἀπαθὲς καὶ ἀναλλοίωτον, impassive and
unalterable (*Metaphysics* XII 1073a 12).

by nature, or present in men in some other way; the Form is here used, not to identify its instances, but to determine its relation to other attributes, such as teachability.

The *Symposium* offers still a different function for the Form of Beauty. First it is a terminus of wish and desire: the whole appetitive life of men, and their emotional life insofar as it is appetitive, is founded on and rooted in Beauty itself. But the Form is also a terminus of knowledge: the ascent to Beauty implies passage through the sciences.

Beauty is treated as equivalent to Goodness, and the ascent passage of the *Symposium* looks forward to the *Republic* and the comparison of the Good to the Sun in book VI. That the Good is there an Idea or Form is clear (508e.3, 517a.1, 534c.1); as such, it is intelligible and can be known (517c, 504d.3, 518c–d, 534c, e), grasped by λόγος (511b, 534c), and distinguished from other Forms (534b); and as a Form, it is a thing which is (507b; compare 532b), and at the same level as the Beautiful (507b; compare 532b). It is to the intelligible world as the sun is to the sensible world: as the sun is the source of light by which the eye sees and objects are visible, so the Good is the source of intelligence and intelligibility. It is a first principle of the sciences, as Beauty is in the *Symposium*. Since Beauty and Goodness are first principles of explanation, it must follow that not all things that are can be purposively or teleologically explained. That is, Beauty and Goodness are not equivalent to Being, but beyond Being, surpassing it in dignity and power. The *Republic* and *Symposium* are on this point consistent with the doctrine of Necessity in the *Timaeus* (compare *Republic* II 479b).

The ultimate object of wish and desire in the *Symposium* is identical with the ultimate object of knowledge. Beauty as it presents itself to sense, the ἄνθος or bloom on a lovely body, is the sensuous aspect of goodness.

Contemplation

The guide in the ascent, when he guides rightly, leads the lover to contemplation of Beauty itself.

The centrality of contemplation in the life of men is probably in origin a Pythagorean doctrine. There was a tradition, to which Diotima has already implicitly referred (205d), about how Pythagoras,[124] when asked who he was, replied that he was a philosopher, and compared human life to a festival. Some come to the fair to buy and sell; they are the businessmen, the money-makers. Some come to compete in games that will bring

124. Diogenes Laertius VIII 8, on the authority of Sosicrates, perhaps relying in Heraclides of Pontus. See also Cicero *Tusculan Disputations* V 3 and Iamblichus *Vita Pythagorae* 58.

them victory and honor; they are the athletes. But the best come as θεαταί, spectators, to watch and contemplate. So similarly in life, some seek gain, others fame, but philosophers seek truth and reality. Aristotle preserved the heritage of this tradition in contrasting the three lives of enjoyment, politics, and contemplation.[125]

If contemplation is allied to intellectual intuition, the description of Socrates at Potidaea (220c–d) implies that it also involved hard thought: he stood for twenty-four hours, from dawn to dawn, "thinking something over and considering it," and "when he found no solution he didn't leave but stood there inquiring into it," and then he offered a prayer to the sun and left. His state of mind is not prayer but explicitly contrasted to prayer;[126] nor is it trance-like, for the verbs used to describe it imply ratiocination. It is well to recall that Pythagoras, if he identified philosophy with contemplation, included in it the doing of mathematics: the pleasantness of contemplation, and its connection with beauty, included the deductive satisfactions of proof. The upward path to Beauty in the *Symposium* represents the alternative movement of mind, the ascent to first principles. If it includes an emotional response that may fairly be called adoration (211d–e), its essence is cognition.[127]

It is possible to supplement this account. Aristotle distinguishes two

125. *Nicomachean Ethics* I 1095b 17–22. In this he was following the *Republic* (IX 581c; cf. *Phaedo* 68c, 82c).

126. Neither is it, at least on this evidence, mystical. The word derives from μύω, to shut the mouth, to shut the eyes—the Indo-European root occurs in English *mouse*. Slang, as often, preserves an archaic root in the expression "to keep mum," that is, to keep one's mouth shut, and in the pleasant oxymoron "mum's the word." Mysticism suggests secret doctrines, that is, doctrines that ought not or cannot be communicated to others. The speech of Diotima, on the contrary, is born not of secrecy but of the intent to communicate, and contemplation involves intellectual apprehension of a first principle that is taken to be explanatory of the structure of the world; it is, that is to say, inherently rational.

It follows that the *Symposium* provides no evidence of secret or esoteric Platonic doctrines. To the degree that this claim has ever had a rational as distinct from a cabalistic basis, it derives from Aristotle, whose testimony about Plato has now been shown to derive primarily from his own interpretation of Plato's *Parmenides*. See R. E. Allen, *Plato's Parmenides*, Minneapolis, Minn., 1983.

127. One may recall the remark of that radical empiricist, William James: "Looking back on my own experiences, they all converge towards a kind of insight to which I cannot help ascribing some metaphysical significance. The keynote of it is invariably a reconciliation. It is as if the opposites of the world, whose contradictoriness and conflict make all our difficulties and troubles, were melted into a unity. Not only do they, as contrasted species, belong to one and the same genus, but one of the species, the nobler and better one, is itself the genus, and so soaks up and absorbs its opposite into itself. This is a dark saying, I know, when thus expressed in terms of common logic, but I cannot wholly escape from its authority" (*The Varieties of Religious Experience* [1902], London, 1952, p. 379).

concepts of truth, combination and contact, whose opposites are, respectively, falsehood and ignorance. Negation cannot be identified with falsehood because "this depends, on the side of objects, on their being combined or separated, so that he who thinks the separated to be separated and the combined to be combined has the truth, while he whose thought is in a state contrary to that of the objects is in error."[128] But if truth may consist in combination and separation, and its opposite in falsehood, it is otherwise with that truth which consists not in combination and separation but in contact:

> But with regard to *incomposites,* what is being or not being, and truth or falsity? A thing of this sort is not composite, so as to 'be' when it is compounded and not to 'be' if it is separated, like, "that the wood is white" or "that the diagonal is incommensurable"; nor will truth and falsity still be present in the same way as in the previous cases. In fact, as truth is not the same in these cases, so also being is not the same; but (a) truth or falsity is as follows—contact and assertion are truth (assertion not being the same as affirmation), and ignorance is non-contact. For it is not possible to be in *error* regarding what a thing is, save in an accidental sense . . . it is not possible to be in error, but only to know them or not to know them. But we do inquire what they are, viz. whether they are of such and such a nature or not. (b) As regards the 'being' that answers to truth and the 'non-being' that answers to falsity, in one case there is truth if the subject and attribute are really combined, and falsity if they are not combined; in the other case, if the object is existent it exists in a particular way, and if it does not exist in this way it does not exist at all. And truth means knowing these objects, and falsity does not exist, nor error, but only ignorance—and not an ignorance which is like blindness; for blindness is akin to a total absence of the faculty of thinking.[129]

The source of this is *Republic* V: the opposite of truth and reality is not falsehood but ignorance, and ignorance corresponds to not-being, lack of any object for the mind to grasp. So in the *Parmenides* (132b–c) it is assumed that a thought, to be a thought, must be of something which is. Thought, insofar as it is true or false, involves combination and issues in statements; but combination presupposes contact with the nature of

128. *Metaphysics* IX 1051a 34–b 5 (trans. W. D. Ross); cf. *Sophist* 163b–d.
129. *Metaphysics* IX 1051b 18–1052a 4 (trans. W. D. Ross).

things that are, and implies intellectual intuition, that intuition which is of the essence of contemplation, and which must ultimately touch the principle or principles on which all else depends, Beauty itself and Goodness.

Virtue and Contemplation

Perhaps there is a paradox within the structure of Diotima's speech itself. What is primarily valuable is happiness; happiness consists in living justly and temperately, but also in the contemplation of a transcendent Idea, Beauty itself. But living justly and temperately do not seem at all the same as the contemplation of Beauty.

The paradox is more apparent than real. On the side of objects, justice and temperance are parts of virtue. Virtue—$\dot\alpha\varrho\varepsilon\tau\dot\eta$ is the abstract noun of which $\dot\alpha\gamma\alpha\theta\dot o\varsigma$ is the adjective—is goodness; and Beauty and Goodness are equivalent.

But then, the contemplation of Beauty and Goodness, as distinct from Beauty and Goodness, is surely a state of mind, whereas the practice of justice or temperance or courage is a matter of action and conduct. No doubt it is tempting to think of justice and temperance and courage as dispositional predicates, as solubility is a dispositional predicate of salt; Socrates, however, treats the virtues as attributes of soul intimately connected with wisdom. The connection between virtue and contemplation may be taken as internal, as Aristotle afterward claimed in a passage that is a precipitate of Diotima's account of the ascent to Beauty:

> If happiness is activity in accordance with virtue, it is reasonable that it should be in accordance with the highest virtue; and this will be that of the best thing in us. Whether it be reason or something else that is this element which is thought to be our natural ruler and guide and to take thought of things noble and divine, whether it be itself also divine or only the most divine element in us, the activity of this in accordance with its proper virtue will be perfect happiness. That this activity is contemplative we have already said.[130]

And again:

> Now he who exercises his reason and cultivates it seems to be both in the best state of mind and most dear to the gods. For if the gods have any care for human affairs, as they are thought to have, it would be reasonable both that they should delight in that which was best and most akin to them (i.e. reason) and that they should reward those

130. *Nicomachean Ethics* X 1177a 11*ff*. (trans. W. D. Ross).

who love and honour this most, as caring for things that are dear to them and acting both rightly and nobly. And that all these attributes belong most of all to the philosopher is manifest. He, therefore, is dearest to the gods. And he who is that will presumably also be happiest; so that in this way too the philosopher will more than any other be happy.[131]

Aristotle, speaking in his own voice, is often Plato's most helpful commentator.

Diotima suggests that the man who has laid hold of or touched (ἐφάπτειν) Beauty itself comes to possess true virtue and is beloved of god, and "he, if any man does, becomes immortal."[132] To be immortal is to be divine, and the philosophical life implies an imitation of the divine nature, so that, as one approximates to the nature of god, one approximates to the nature of the immortal. The ultimate fulfillment of human nature is intellectual; human happiness consists in rationality, and it is a law of the intellect that like knows like.[133]

Recollection

It may perhaps be asked how the lover, ignorant of beauty, is able to ascend, or why he is not satisfied with the state he is in. The *Meno*, the *Phaedo*, and the *Phaedrus* suppose that knowledge is recollection; but here, in the ascent passage of the *Symposium*, there is only reference to a guide (210a). Perhaps that guide is the educator to whom Diotima has already referred (209b–c). But Diotima must ultimately refer to "that by which it is necessary to contemplate" Beauty itself, to "seeing the Beautiful with that by which it is visible" (212a), that is, to the eye of the soul (compare *Republic* VII 533d). We shall then understand that, as in the *Phaedo* (74d–e, 76d–e) perception provokes recollection, so the sight of physical beauty reminds the lover of the nature of Beauty itself. Diotima, in her account of

---

131. *Nicomachean Ethics* X 1179a 22–32.

132. 212a; cf. *Republic* VI 490b. See also *Timaeus* 90b–c (trans. F. M. Cornford): "Now if a man is engrossed in appetites and ambitions and spends all his pains upon these, all his thoughts must needs be mortal and, so far as that is possible, he cannot fall short of becoming mortal altogether, since he has nourished the growth of his mortality. But if his heart has been set on the love of learning and true wisdom and he has exercised that part of himself above all, he is surely bound to have thoughts immortal and divine, if he shall lay hold upon truth, nor can he fail to possess immortality in the fullest measure human nature admits; and because he is always devoutly cherishing the divine part and maintaining the guardian genius that dwells with him in good estate, he must needs be happy above all." See also *Theaetetus* 176b.

133. See *Timaeus* 37a–c, *Phaedo* 78bff., *Republic* X 611e. See also A. J. Festugière, *Contemplation et vie contemplative selon Platon*, Paris, 1936, pp. 110–122.

Beauty itself, has in fact provided the premise that in the *Phaedo* (72e–73b, 74a–77a) is understood to imply that knowledge is recollection and that the soul is immortal.

Given that this is so, Beauty in the *Symposium* and the Good of *Republic* VI may be compared to the God of Augustine's *Confessions*: "I would not have sought Thee had I not already found Thee." Aspiration presupposes implicit knowledge of what is aspired to; what the lover seeks is already within him, guiding the search, and the guide who leads him upward is ultimately the active principle of his own rationality. This is a claim in metaphysics and epistemology, but perhaps it is also a religious claim as well, one that recalls Augustine: "Our hearts are restless till they rest in Thee."

The apprehension of Beauty itself presupposes that Beauty itself exists. If at one level the *proton philon* of the *Lysis*, what is primarily valuable, consists in happiness, and happiness in the contemplation of Beauty itself, then Beauty itself, that in which all derivative images of beauty participate, is the ontological condition of all value. In the *Lysis* (211c), Socrates suggests that "when a cause is destroyed, it is surely impossible for that of which it is the cause to continue to exist." What is primarily valuable is a necessary condition for the existence of other things insofar as they are valuable. One may compare Aristotle (*Metaphysics* V 1019a.1*ff.*): "Some things are called prior and posterior . . . in respect of nature and substance, that is, those which can be without other things, while the others cannot be without them—a distinction that Plato first used."

The Descent of Eros

The wish to contemplate beauty is universal among men, but often thwarted. The failure of most people to attain their own good is the result of ignorance, and of something more. In the *Phaedrus* (248a–b), souls in their passion to attain the heights and follow the gods come into conflict with one another; their wings are broken in the struggle and they fall to earth to feed upon the food of semblance.

In his reflections on dialectic in the *Phaedrus*, Socrates considers the relationship between the two doctrines of Eros he had earlier explained. After a recantation of the view of Eros given in his first speech, he turns to a second.

Socrates' first speech had defined Eros as a species of ὕβρις, wantonness: "When irrational desire, pursuing the enjoyment of beauty, had gained the mastery over judgment that prompts to right conduct, and has acquired from other desires akin to it fresh strength to strain toward bodily beauty, that very strength provides it with its name: it is the strong passion called Love" (*Phaedrus* 238b–c). But in his second speech, Socrates refers to this love as sinister (*Phaedrus* 266a).

The notion of a sinister love is relevant beyond its immediate application. The speech of Lysias (230e–234c), where lust is extolled as a proper basis for human relationships, is an example of it, and ranging beyond the *Phaedrus*, *Republic* VIII and IX may be taken as a description of the downward passage of Eros. The progressive perversion and corruption of the philosophical nature is there analyzed as a social condition, a degeneracy of constitution; but to each kind of constitution there is a corresponding human character.[34] Corruption introduces into that character the seeds of its own destruction, and unless corrected, both state and individual tend to sink to governance by their lowest elements. In the individual, this implies the tyranny of a single master passion, a passion that enslaves other impulses and inverts the natural order of the soul. That tyrannical master passion is "an Eros" and a kind of madness.[135]

By contrast with a sinister love, divine love reminds the lover of something seen before: "When one who is fresh from the mystery (of the vision of the Ideas), and saw much of the vision, beholds a god-like face or bodily form that truly expresses beauty, first there comes upon him a shuddering and a measure of that awe which the vision inspired, and then reverence as at the sight of a god; and but for fear of being deemed a very madman he would sacrifice to his beloved, as to a holy image of deity."[136] Human love derives from recollection of the Ideas.

Eros and Psyche

F. M. Cornford supposed that the ascent of the lover from the physical world to Beauty itself shows that Eros is a spiritual impulse that is one and continuous throughout the process of ascent, a moving fund of psychical energy operating at a deeper level of the soul than the tripartite psychology of *Republic* IV:

> We are now to learn that the three impulses which shape three types of life are not ultimately distinct and irreducible factors, residing in three separate parts of a composite soul, of some in the soul, some in the body. They are manifestations of a single force or fund of energy, called Eros, directed through divergent channels toward various ends. This conception makes possible a sublimation of desire; the energy can be redirected from one channel to another. The flow

134. *Republic* VIII 544d*ff.*
135. *Republic* IX 572e, 573b, d; cf. *Laws* VIII 837a.
136. *Phaedrus* 251a (translation after R. Hackforth).

can be diverted upwards or downwards. The downward process is analysed in the eighth and ninth books of the *Republic*. It leads to the hell of sensuality in the tyrannical man. The upward process is indicated in the *Symposium*.[137]

Cornford supports his interpretation by referring to a passage of the *Republic* in which the movement of desire is likened to the flow of a stream:

> From this conception of a common fund of moving force Plato elsewhere draws an inference, based on experience. The amount of energy directed into one channel is withdrawn from the others, as if only a limited quantity were available. In the *Republic* (588b) the soul is imaged as a composite creature, part man, part lion, part many-headed monster. One who praises injustice is saying that it is profitable to feed and strengthen the multifarious monster and to starve and enfeeble the man, so as to leave him at the mercy of the other two. Again (485), where the language of Eros is used to define the philosophic nature by its essential passion for truth, the metaphor of channels is used. "When a person's desires are set strongly in one direction, we know that they flow with corresponding feebleness in every other, like a stream whose waters have been diverted into a different channel. Accordingly when the flow of desires has set towards knowledge in all its forms, a man's desire will be turned to the pleasures which the soul has by itself and will abandon the pleasures of the body, if his love of wisdom be not feigned."[138]

The hydraulic metaphor, as it happens, is one that Freud also used to characterize libido, though the senses of Eros and libido are exactly opposite. Eros is not something that originates in the basement of the human soul—the metaphor again is Freud's—and, deflected from earth by repression, undertakes to gain an (illusory) heaven by sublimation.[139] Its proper nature is expressed only in possession of the highest object to which human nature can attain, the contemplation of Beauty itself:

> To return to the theory of Eros: the energy which carries the soul in this highest flight is the same that is manifested at lower levels in the instinct that perpetuates the race and in every form of worldly ambition. It is the energy of life itself, the moving force of the soul; and

---

137. "The Doctrine of Eros in Plato's *Symposium*," *The Unwritten Philosophy*, Cambridge, 1952, pp. 70–71.
138. Ibid., p. 73.
139. See John Gould, *The Development of Plato's Ethics*, Cambridge, 1955, p. 89.

the soul was defined by Plato precisely as the one thing that has the power of self-motion. The Platonic doctrine of Eros has been compared, and even identified, with modern theories of sublimation. But the ultimate standpoints of Plato and Freud seem to be diametrically opposed. Modern science is dominated by the concept of evolution, the upward development from the rude and primitive instincts of our alleged animal ancestry to the higher manifestations of rational life. The conception is not foreign to Greek thought. The earliest philosophical school had taught that man had developed from a fish-like creature, spawned in the slime warmed by the heat of the sun. But Plato had deliberately rejected this system of thought. Man is for him the plant whose roots are not in earth but in the heavens. In the myth of transmigration the lower animals are deformed and degraded types, in which the soul which has not been true to its celestial affinity may be imprisoned to work out the penalty of its fall. The self-moving energy of the human soul resides properly in the highest part, the immortal nature. It does not rise from beneath but rather sinks from above when the spirit is ensnared in the flesh. So, when the energy is withdrawn from the lower channels, it is gathered up into its original source. This is indeed a conversion or transfiguration; but not a sublimation of desire that has hitherto existed only in the lower forms. A force that was in origin spiritual, after an incidental and temporary declension, becomes purely spiritual again.[140]

Since Plato believed, at least by the time he wrote the *Phaedrus*, that soul is self-moving motion, Cornford is suggesting that Eros and Psyche are one: "In the *Phaedrus* . . . the emphasis falls at first on the moving power of the soul in the living creature. The soul is defined as the only thing capable of moving itself, and hence the source and fountain of all motion in the universe. The whole context seems to imply (though this is not explicitly stated) that the moving force in the soul is desire, Eros; for desire is the type of motion which reaches forward to its object, and is not pushed from behind by an antecedent mechanical cause."[141] It is perhaps odd to think of desire being a kind of motion at all, let alone self-moving motion, but Cornford is drawing on a tradition also represented by Léon Robin:

Love was conceived in the *Symposium* as an impulse which is always either in action or ready for action; for love always desires something other than what it has: it is ceaselessly in chase, ceaselessly moving

140. Cornford, "Doctrine," pp. 78–79.
141. *Principium Sapientiae*, Cambridge, 1954, p. 80.

forward. Thus love is mover and moved; itself, but at the same time all the rest, soul as well as body, since it is only through love that both flesh and the spirit have a share in immortality through generation. Now this double desire is transferred to the soul in the *Phaedrus*. The desire to make itself immortal, to perpetuate itself in other souls or bodies is, according to the *Symposium,* the fundamental expression of love; in the *Phaedrus* it is transformed into an essential immortality of the soul, without which even love itself would be unintelligible. Thus it is the soul which moves itself, and everything else. But this movement is love: the soul loves itself, and it is this which causes it to accomplish its celestial rotations, moved by the desire to contemplate those true realities the vision of which provides sustenance for what is best in it. Again, the soul governs and administers everything deprived of soul; it is thus the desire by which it moves everything to which movement is communicated. . . . Finally, it is this desire which, awakened in the soul by Anamnesis, arouses an enthusiasm from which will spring the philosophical love from which the soul will draw the force that will lead it to its natural place.[142]

It will be evident that both Cornford and Robin, like Plotinus,[143] treat Eros as a substance in its own right, an *οὐσία*. Once this is done, it is but a short step to suppose that it is identical with soul, and its identification with self-moving motion in the *Phaedrus* appears to follow as of course.

It seems evident that Eros cannot be identified with self-moving motion. For if Eros were a motion, it could not be self-moving: arising in lack, ending with fulfillment, the child of both Poros and Penia, it is motion *a quo* and *ad quem*. Eros cannot be identified with soul, conceived as self-moving motion, because soul is immortal and Eros implies lack of immortality.

Nor can Eros be said to be moved by its objects. Eros involves futurity: the object of desire is not a presently existing thing, but a future state of affairs involving possession. The thirsty man desires, not water, but to possess water. Since desire implies lack of possession, the object of desire does not exist when desire exists. So the object of desire is peculiarly evanescent: when desire is, it is not; and when desire is not, it is not. Insofar as desire implies possession of an unpossessed object, its object is, and is necessarily, nonexistent. What is nonexistent cannot move anything, either as efficient or as final cause.

If Eros is not a motion, neither is it a "force" nor a "moving fund of

142. *Phèdre,* Paris, 1933, pp. cxxxviii–ix.
143. See *The Myth of Poros and Penia* (203a–e): Plotinus and Ficino, pp. 120–121.

energy." The hydraulic metaphor for desire, as a stream capable of being diverted into other channels, is helpful precisely because it states a common-sense truth: that human beings must often choose between gratifying contending kinds of desires, and their choices shape their character. Because desire is a relative, desire is not a substance, as Plotinus had it, nor a force nor a fund of energy, as Cornford had it, nor the soul, as Robin had it; these are metaphors that merely obscure. The ascent to Beauty is, and is explicitly said to be (210a), that of the lover. If we choose to describe this as the ascent of Eros, we do so by virtue of the logical import of a literary fiction, namely, Diotima's personification of Eros; Eros is the lover qua lover, the lover just insofar as he loves. The lover insofar as he loves is neither a motion nor a force nor a fund of energy; and since he is not, qua lover, immortal, neither is he his soul.

Eros and Agape

Since the object of Eros is happiness, and since happiness consists in justice and virtue, and ultimately in the contemplation of Beauty and Goodness as universal principles of the world order, it must often be the case that desire arises for the sake of, and has as its object, benefit to others. But in recent Protestant theology, it has become almost a truism that Eros is to be contrasted with Agape, a form of love that is peculiarly and specifically Christian. Here is Karl Barth on Agape: "Christian love turns to the other precisely for the sake of the other. It does not desire it for itself. It loves it simply because it is there as the other, with all its value or lack of value. . . . In Christian love the loving subject gives to the other, the object of love, that which it has, which is its own, which belongs to it. It does so irrespective of the right or claim it may have to it, or the further use that one might make of it."[144] Barth contrasts this with another kind of love, which "does not have its origin in self-denial, but in a distinctively uncritical intensification and strengthening of natural self-assertion. . . . This is the reason for its interest in the other. It needs it because of its intrinsic value and in pursuance of an end" (p. 174). This is pagan Eros, the basis of the sin of pride. It is to be contrasted with Christian love, "the love which seeks and attains its end as the self-giving of the one who loves to the object of his love" (p. 175). Eros and Agape are radically distinct: "We have to do here with two movements in opposite directions, so that there can be no harmony but only conflict between them. The first type

144. *Church Dogmatics: A Selection,* trans. G. W. Bromiley, New York, 1962, p. 173. The same position is put at greater length by Anders Nygren, *Eros and Agape,* trans. P. S. Watson, New York, 1969.

cannot pass over or be transformed into the second, nor the second in the first" (p. 176). Barth proceeds to back this with a philological claim:

> It is immediately apparent that the New Testament consistently avoids the use of the verb ἐρᾶν and the substantive ἔρως—the terms which in classical Greek plainly describe this other grasping, taking, possessing and enjoying love. . . . The reader who meets the concept of love in these pages is obviously not even to be reminded of this other love. Apart from an occasional use of φιλεῖν with its emphasis on feeling the normal term for love in the New Testament is ἀγαπᾶν, with the substantive ἀγάπη, which is unknown in classical Greek and only sparing used in Hellenistic. It is only in New Testament usage that this word has acquired the well-known meaning and content of a love opposed to ἔρως. In itself it is rather colorless. It has something of the sense of the English 'like.'

The noun ἀγάπη is in fact a late back-formation, first found in the Septuagint, from the verb ἀγαπάω, which in classical Greek means to delight in, to greet with affection, thus making its application to sexual intercourse in the Septuagint intelligible; it becomes the ordinary word for love in New Greek.[145] Barth is quite right in claiming that ἔρως and ἐρᾶν, in ordinary classical Greek usually used of sexual love, do not occur in the New Testament; this is a dialect shift characteristic of New Greek. Barth's inference from it, that "the reader is not even to be reminded of this other love," is inadequate even as an argument from silence.

The translation offered by the Authorized Version of ἀγάπη, for example by St. Paul in I Corinthians xiii, is charity, and charity is not a form of altruistic desire opposed to selfish desire, but a virtue like faith and hope.[146] Augustine goes to the heart of the matter, with a comment which shows that Barth's philological misunderstanding is not new:

> He who resolves to love God, and to love his neighbor as himself, not according to man but according to God, is on account of this love said to be of good will; and this is in Scripture more commonly called charity, but it is also, even in the same books, called love. . . . Some are of opinion that charity or regard (*dilectio*) is one thing, love (*amor*) another. They say *dilectio* is used of a good affection, *amor* of an evil

145. C. D. Buck, *A Dictionary of Selected Synonyms in the Principal Indo-European Languages*, Chicago, 1949, 16.27.2.

146. Or, as Aquinas describes it, a theological virtue: *Summa Theologiae*, part I, question lxii, article 1.

one. But it is very certain that even secular literature knows no distinction.

The right will is, therefore, well-directed love, and the wrong will is ill-directed love. Love, then, yearning to love what is loved, is desire; and having and enjoying it, is joy; fleeing what is opposed to it, is fear; and feeling what is opposed to it, when it has befallen it, is sadness. Now these motions are evil if the love is evil; good if the love is good.[147]

Having offered the outlines of a psychology of the emotions based on love or desire, Augustine goes on to contrast charity with the sin of pride: "For 'pride is the beginning of sin.' And what is pride but the craving for undue exaltation? And this is undue exaltation, when the soul abandons Him to whom it ought to cleave as its end, and becomes a kind of end in itself. This happens when it becomes its own satisfaction. And it does so when it falls away from the unchangeable good that ought to satisfy it more than itself."[148] Barth in effect makes Eros the sin of pride, "a distinctively uncritical intensification and strengthening of natural self-assertion." Eros is the love characteristic of the natural man without the grace of God, the love characteristic of nothingness and sin.

This account of Eros and Agape is confused at every level. Philologically, it rests on an argument from silence that ignores dialect changes. Conceptually, it ignores the fact that Agape has as its classical equivalent Philia, friendship. As an account of Plato, it neglects the fact that concern for others is an element in the analysis of Eros itself, insofar as Eros is directed toward happiness; it makes Eros selfish or self-interested[149] at the expense of ignoring happiness as consisting in justice and friendship, the works of Eros as issuing in creation not only according to the body but the soul, and the termination of Eros in contemplation of the *summum bonum*. Socrates, on grounds of justice, laid down his life for his city, and thereby for its citizens: Eros is not distinct from Agape as egoistic desire is distinct from altruistic, or selfishness from unselfishness, or self-love from benevolence. To project these distinctions onto Eros is to distort not only the *Symposium* but the whole tradition of Socratic and Platonic moral psychology.

One may also ask whether Barth's concept of Agape, love purely for the sake of the other without regard to the value or worth of that other, is not also confused. Theologically, it is based on conviction of man's utter

147. *City of God* XIV 7 (trans. Dods).
148. Ibid., XIV 13.
149. For Plato's views on selfishness in contrast to justice, see *Laws* V 731d–732a.

sinfulness and nothingness. The greatness of God and the nothingness of man are taken to imply that God's grace is sovereignly independent of man's will or his works: if justification is by faith alone, then salvation must result from an act of grace having nothing to do with human desert or merit. To this Calvin added the corollary of predestination: that God in his sovereignty ordains men in their nothingness, some to salvation and eternal life, others to reprobation and eternal damnation, for no other reason than that He wills it. Salvation, then, comes by a free act of grace that is as incomprehensible as it is inexplicable. Barth's account of Agape, of a love that takes no account of the worth of its object, has its roots in the doctrine that men in their nothingness are worthy to be damned. Yet this can scarcely be true, if their own willful irrationality is imitated by their god.

The contrast drawn between Eros and Agape in recent neo-orthodox theology is tendentious and misleading: concern for others without concern for oneself is not only psychologically but morally absurd. As Erwin Goodenough once remarked, Agape without Eros is a paper flower. No doubt there is a difference between Christian and Platonic accounts of love. Augustine in the *Confessions* (VII ix) remarks that he has read in the works of the Platonists that there is a light that enlightens every man who comes into the world, but nowhere had he read that the Word became flesh and dwelt among us. For Christianity, the Incarnation is the seal, not the symbol, of divine love: "Herein is love, not that we loved God, but that he loved us, and sent his Son to be the propitiation for our sins" (I John iv.10). In the *Symposium*, we love Beauty itself, the summum bonum, the ontological condition of all loving; but there is no indication that Beauty loves us back.[150] The notion that God loves us back has an ethical consequence, for it is supposed that God's love for us is the foundation of our obligation to love our neighbor: charity or benevolence has its source in grace. Diotima supposes that it has its source in nature—our own nature, directed toward friendship.

Socrates' Peroration (212b–c)

Socrates now affirms his approval of Diotima's account; he has praised Eros with a difference, and Phaedrus, the master of ceremonies, may not

150. This is not to deny that Plato has a theory of providence. In *Laws* X, arguing with the atheists, Plato holds that there are gods, that they have care for human affairs, and that they cannot be bribed by prayers and sacrifices; this recapitulates questions raised by the speech of Adeimantus in book II of the *Republic*. But the providence of the gods reduces to the claim that the universe is ordered and directed to the good of the whole. Here, as everywhere in Plato, what is good for each individual is essentially implicated with the common good.

recognize it as an encomium (compare 198cff.). Nor is it given the tumultuous applause Agathon's account received (198a).

Aristophanes tries to interrupt, presumably to defend himself against Socrates' criticism (205e–206a). But the comic poet is eclipsed by Alcibiades, whose arrival provides comic relief which is also wholly serious. Both Beauty itself and this glorious embodiment of Dionysus and Aphrodite appear ἐξαίφνης, suddenly—as Socrates will appear to Alcibiades (213c).

Aristophanes Redivivus

The speech of Aristophanes defined Eros in terms of love for unique individuals, and the speech of Alcibiades, in its praise of Socrates, will provide an example of that love. Gregory Vlastos reproaches Socrates and Diotima, whose account he identifies with Plato's, for not agreeing:

> We are to love the persons so far, and only insofar, as they are good and beautiful. Now since all too few human beings are masterworks of excellence, and not even the best of those we have the chance to love are wholly free of streaks of the ugly, the mean, the commonplace, the ridiculous, if our love of them is to be only for their virtue, the individual, in the uniqueness and integrity of his or her individuality, will never be an object of our love. This seems to me the cardinal flaw in Plato's theory. It does not provide for love of whole persons, but only for love of that abstract version of persons which consists of the complex of their best qualities. This is the reason why personal affection ranks so low in Plato's *scala amoris*. . . . The high climactic moment of fulfillment—the peak achievement for which all lesser loves are to be 'used as steps'—is the one farthest removed from affection for concrete human beings.[151]

Diotima would reply that love of individual human beings, if it is genuinely to be love, must be grounded in love of Beauty itself, and that Goodness or Beauty is a third term in any love-relation that is real and true.

Martha Nussbaum, repeating Vlastos's words, finds it all a bit mysterious—what do uniqueness and individuality come to?—yet decides that there must be, after all, something in what Vlastos says. She suggests that while Socrates and Diotima have described one kind of love, Plato, as author of the *Symposium*, has described two kinds of love, between which he means for his readers to choose. There is the love of unique individuals that Aristophanes has described and Alcibiades will manifest, and on the

---

151. *Platonic Studies*, Princeton, N.J., 1973, p. 31. Compare Dover, *Symposium*, p. 113.

other hand the love of Beauty. Plato means for us to understand that to choose one is to give up the other, so that to choose Beauty is to lose some beauty. The choice is inherently tragic—or should one say "existential," as inherently irrational?—and it is our choice:

> But what, then, becomes of us, the audience, when we are confronted with the illumination of this true tragedy and forced to see everything? We are, Alcibiades tells us, the jury (219c). And we are also the accused. As we watch the trial of Socrates for the contemptuous overweening (*huperephanias,* 219c.5) of reason, which is at the same time the trial of Alcibiades for the contemptuous overweening of the body, we see what neither of them fully see—the overweening of both. And we see that it is the way we must go if we are to follow either one or the other. But so much light can turn to stone.[152]

It is flattering to be told that we may see what neither Socrates nor Alcibiades see, but the account does not inspire confidence by reason of inaccuracy. It is not we but the company who are addressed as the jury; no text suggests that we are also the accused; Socrates is not on trial for the contemptuous overweening of reason, whatever that might be, nor Alcibiades for the contemptuous overweening of the body either; light does not turn things to stone.

Inexactness of statement, here and elsewhere, is matched by inexact analysis. Socrates and Diotima, it will be recalled, argue that the object of love is the beautiful, and that the lover is not beautiful. One might attempt to formalize this as: For all y and all x, if y loves x, x is beautiful, and, For all y and all x, if y loves x, y is not beautiful. To the latter one may object: "we do not understand how he has reached the conclusion that y lacks beauty. We thought he was talking about people. We had a situation where some y—let us say Alcibiades—is in love with beautiful Agathon. He wants to possess this beautiful person, and yet he is aware that he does not possess him. . . . So there is a beautiful person whom he both loves and lacks. This does not, however, show that he himself lacks beauty, even given the earlier premises of the argument. He may be quite beautiful, for all we know."[153] If Plato were as slipshod in argument as this, why bother to read him? The gloss confuses Alcibiades as lover, who as such lacks beauty, with Alcibiades himself, who may be as pretty as you please: Eros is the lover qua lover, not the lover considered apart from his loving. Confusion over relative terms leads to further confusion: "So far there is some beauty

152. *The Fragility of Goodness,* Cambridge, 1986, p. 198.
153. Ibid., p. 178.

loved by the lover: Alcibiades loves the beauty of Agathon. From this it follows only that Alcibiades lacks *that* beauty—not that he lacks *all* beauty . . . : if Alcibiades is *kalon* in physical appearance, can he not still love and lack the beautiful soul of Socrates? What we now see is that Socrates' argument depends on a strong hidden assumption: that all beauty, *qua* beauty, is uniform. All manifestations of the *kalon* must be sufficiently like one another that if you lack one kind it is natural to conclude that you lack them all."[154] That is, if you lack one kind of beauty, you lack all kinds of beauty, because all kinds of beauty are one kind of beauty: so if you lack the beauty of a rosebud, you're not a pretty fellow. This is an astonishing piece of reasoning, a specimen of the here's-your-hat-what's-your-hurry? school of Plato criticism: it's not supposed to make sense. Instead of retracing one's steps to see what went wrong, one may rush to a conclusion:

> It is a startling and powerful vision. Just try to think it seriously: this body of this wonderful beautiful person is *exactly* the same in quality as that person's mind and inner life. Both, in turn, the same in quality as the value of Athenian democracy; of Pythagorean geometry; of Eudoxian astronomy. What would it be like to look at a body and see in it exactly the same shade and tone of goodness and beauty as a mathematical proof—*exactly* the same, differing only in amount and in location, so that the choice between making love with a person and contemplating the proof presented itself as a choice of having n measures of water and n + 100? . . . These proposals are so bold as to be pretty well incomprehensible from the ordinary point of view.[155]

The White Queen, as a result of practice, sometimes believed six impossible things before breakfast. Perhaps you can too. While you are trying, reflect on this implication: "The lover, seeing a flat uniform landscape of value, with no jagged promontories or deep valleys, will have few motivations for moving here rather than there on that landscape. A contemplative life is a natural choice."[156] As natural a choice as any other, no doubt, for in such a universe any choice would be a matter of indifference—if one can still choose when moral nihilism is bounded by ennui. But one might not seem quite convinced that a contemplative life is a natural choice even so: "Socrates is put before us as an example of a man in the process of making himself self-sufficient—put before us, in our still

154. Ibid., pp. 178–179.
155. Ibid., pp. 180–181.
156. Ibid., p. 181.

unregenerate state, as a troublesome question mark and a challenge. Is this the life we want for ourselves? Is that the way we want, or need, to see and hear? We are not allowed to have the cozy thought that the transformed person will be just like us, only happier. Socrates is weird."[157] A man responsible for a body of thought which has moved the world is thus dismissed in a single three-word sentence.

Interlude: The Arrival of Alcibiades (212c–215a)

The action now changes with dramatic swiftness. Alcibiades comes, supported by a flute girl, crowned with ivy and violets and fillets of ribbons, drunk, the very embodiment of Dionysus. He has come to crown the head of Agathon as victor in the tragic competition, but takes back some of the fillets and places them on Socrates' head, as ever victorious in speech over all mankind. Agathon had earlier suggested to Socrates that Dionysus would decide which of them was wiser, but the argument itself has decided, and the representative of Dionysus here symbolically ratifies the decision.

Alcibiades was born about 450 B.C., the son of Cleinias, an Athenian general and statesman of great distinction, and raised in the house of Pericles, who was his guardian. While still very young, his fortune, his magnificent presence, his intelligence, and his dazzling talents made him a leader of Athens. He was mainly responsible for moving in the Assembly the expedition against Sicily in 415 B.C., and so for the disaster that followed. Alcibiades was himself one of the generals of the expedition, recalled from Sicily for trial on a capital charge of impiety. He was accused of taking part in the mutilation of the herms, the square pillars, surmounted by a head, that guarded many doorways in Athens including the entrance to the Acropolis, some weeks before the expedition sailed; this was an act of sacrilege, and of extreme ill omen.[158] Alcibiades was also accused, perhaps with more foundation (see 217e, 218b), of having engaged in drunken mockery of the Eleusinian Mysteries. Called home for trial, he deserted to Sparta, where he betrayed many of Athens's military secrets. He was able to return to Athens in 407 but was forced again to

157. Ibid., p. 184.
158. Most modern historians think that the charge was false, since Alcibiades must have known such an act would endanger his own foreign policy, and that not only the accusation but the actual mutilation of the herms may have been engineered by his political opponents in order to discredit him. But Alcibiades' contemporaries were not so sure: he was a conflicted man. His references to Socrates' head and its crowning (213e) recall his reputed dealings with other heads, and suggest his ambivalence toward Socrates.

withdraw, and was murdered in Phrygia in 404 at the behest of the Thirty Tyrants, Critias and Charmides among them. It was a brilliant, star-crossed, wasted life, which Plato described in the *Republic* (VI 494b–d): immense talents corrupted by boundless ambition to manage affairs, fed by the flattery of the mob and unaccompanied by the hard work of reflection.[159]

Aristophanes, in introducing his own speech, had said that he would speak about the human condition, about how human nature is constituted. The thematic role of Aristophanes, the comic poet whose chief business concerns Dionysus and Aphrodite, wine and sex, is now taken over by Alcibiades—drunk, lascivious, and very funny—and Alcibiades sums up in his own person the human condition insofar as it is not liberated by understanding of the aims and purposes of human life. Alcibiades can represent the human condition because here, at this party, he is a kind of exemplar of it. He has, or seems to have, everything the human heart could desire: wealth, noble birth, beauty, political power. And yet, Plato's readers knew he was not enviable but tragic. He hasn't failed yet, as he attends this dinner party in the year 416 B.C., but he is going to fail soon, and the source of his failure, if the *Symposium* is any guide, is that he values and passionately loves the wrong things—even in his relation to Socrates.

It is a scene heavy with drunken humor, but Alcibiades is quite serious in saying he can praise no one, whether god or man, but Socrates; and Eryximachus, the physician of the body who abhors drunkenness and who defined the rules by which the previous speeches were conducted, accedes. Socrates, not Eros, shall be the subject of Alcibiades' praise.[160] Socrates, concerned for truth, is invited to interrupt if Alcibiades says anything false. He will not interrupt, and by his silence warrants the factual truth of Alcibiades' account.

159. For Thucydides' comments on the character of Alcibiades, see VI 15–16 (also 89); on the mutilation of the hermes, VI 27; on Alcibiades accused of parody of the Mysteries, VI 28; on the politicization of Alcibiades' case, his being refused right of immediate trial because of his enemies' fear of the army's support for him, VI 29. The Sicilian Expedition left in midsummer (VI 30), although the Assembly authorizing it met in early spring (para. 8).

Plutarch's *Life of Alcibiades* also contains useful information. It lays particular emphasis on Alcibiades' hatred of the flute and contempt for flute players—an interesting gloss on the emotional ambivalence implied in Alcibiades' comparison of Socrates to Marsyas.

160. R. G. Bury, following Schleiermacher, found in this the key to the meaning of the *Symposium*: "It is in the portrait of the ideal Socrates that the main object of the dialogue is to be sought" (*Symposium*, p. lxv). This is exactly wrong: the ultimate object of Eros is the contemplation of a first principle, and the object of the dialogue is to show it. Alcibiades will praise Socrates as wise; Socrates, being a philosopher, is not wise but a lover of wisdom, and Alcibiades therefore confuses love with its object. This is equivalent to confusing Socrates with Beauty itself, in a manner akin to idolatry.

The Speech of Alcibiades (215a–222b)

Here now is the final, remarkable act of the *Symposium.* It is an account of one of the most remarkable love stories in all literature, told by one of the principals. Alcibiades portrays himself a lover scorned—this is Socrates' *hubris,* his refusal to render to Alcibiades' youthful bloom the sexual tribute that belonged to it by right. But this is no story of unrequited love, for Socrates loves Alcibiades back, and says so (213c–d). In the *Gorgias,* arguing with Callicles, he compares his love of Alcibiades to his love of philosophy (481d): but the son of Cleinias has different arguments for different occasions, and philosophy has ever the same ones (482a–b). As for himself, "better that a whole multitude of people disagree and contradict me, than that I, but one man, should contradict and be at discord with myself " (482c). Socrates later predicts that Callicles and Alcibiades will share the same fate at the hands of the city they both want to dominate and lead (519a–b).

So in this strange love affair, Alcibiades and Socrates return each other's love. But the main expression of Alcibiades' love is in respect to the body, and Socrates' is in respect to the soul and its education. Socrates' aim is to create in a beautiful medium, the soul, and the ascetic analysis of sexuality conjoined to this makes sexual intercourse impossible. Alcibiades, in the homosexual quest he has embarked on, cannot expect to create anything at all. Given that Socrates' love for Alcibiades is real, it cannot be sexual; given that Alcibiades' love for Socrates is sexual, it cannot be real. Alcibiades, who offers likenesses or images to discuss Socrates instead of Eros, himself offers a mere image of love. Alcibiades portrays himself as a lover scorned by Socrates. But Socrates is in fact the true lover, who loves what is really beautiful and good, the proper object of love, instead of what only seems so. Real love seeks contemplation of Beauty, not sexual intercourse. It is Alcibiades, in fact, who is guilty of *hubris.*

In the *Protagoras,* Socrates was introduced fresh from pursuit of the vernal beauty of Alcibiades: he was the lover, the pursuer. It turns out now that Socrates was in fact the beloved, the pursued; it is Alcibiades who is the lover, the pursuer.

Alcibiades' speech in its major headings summarizes the portrait of Socrates given at the beginning of the dialogue. Socrates is a figure of paradox: the lover unmoved by sex, the drinker who cannot be made drunk, a man unconquered by Aphrodite and untouched by Dionysus. And he is persuaded that the highest happiness for a man is contemplation.

R. G. Bury, after a careful analysis of the relation of the speech of Alcibiades to what has gone before, remarks:

Alcibiades, describing Socrates, uses phrases which definitely echo the language or repeat the thought of the earlier encomiasts. When one considers the number of these "responsions" and the natural way in which they are introduced, one is struck at once both with the elaborate technique of Plato and, still more, with the higher art which so skillfully conceals that technique. For all its appearance of spontaneity, a careful analysis and comparison prove that the encomium by Alcibiades is a very carefully wrought piece of work in which every phrase has significance, every turn of expression its bearing on the literary effect of the dialogue as a whole. . . . The speech of Aristophanes contains references, more or less frequent, to sentiments and sayings expressed by every one of the previous speakers. It is chiefly in his description of himself that Alcibiades echoes the language of the first five speakers, and in his description of Socrates that he echoes the language of Socrates.[161]

Socrates was put to death in 399 B.C. on a charge of impiety, and the *Symposium* brings together two figures who influenced, each in his own way, the outcome of the trial. Aristophanes is the chief of the "Old Accusers," and the *Clouds* contributed to the prejudice against Socrates by portraying him as a sophist (*Apology* 18b–c, 19b–c). But the heart of the charge of impiety, confirmed by the controversy over the verdict afterward, was corrupting the youth. An example of that corruption was Socrates' relation to Critias and Charmides, two of the Thirty Tyrants, who had Alcibiades killed and would have killed Socrates if their government had lasted. But the palmary example was Socrates' relation to Alcibiades—Alcibiades, widely believed guilty of sacrilege, who led Athens into the stunning reversal of the Sicilian Expedition, who betrayed Athens to Sparta. Plato has now shown, out of Alcibiades' own mouth and in language which recalls that of Socrates in his speech of defense in the *Apology*, the nature of the relation between Socrates and Alcibiades. He has also shown the inner connection between Alcibiades and Aristophanes.

The importance of the speech of Alcibiades is indicated by the fact that the narrative form of the dialogue, from its very beginning, has been shaped by it. For if one asks why Aristodemus is introduced as narrator instead of Socrates, the answer is that Socrates could not have narrated the scene with Alcibiades. Alcibiades is concerned to praise Socrates rather than Eros. It would have been an affront to modesty, indecorous, to have Socrates narrate such praise of himself. This also helps explain

161. *Symposium*, lxii–lxiii.

the introduction of Diotima, for Socrates could scarcely be made to offer an encomium of Eros which, when Alcibiades praises him, turns out to fit Socrates himself. The speech of Alcibiades is integral to the narrative structure of the *Symposium,* and this implies that it is integral to the meaning of the *Symposium.*

It is certain that Alcibiades' relation to Socrates was used, perhaps not explicitly but by implication, against Socrates at his trial. When Anytus and Meletus charged Socrates with corrupting the youth, they expected his judges to remember, not only Critias and Charmides, who became members of the Thirty Tyrants in 404 B.C., but Alcibiades. It becomes the more important, then, to consider what Alcibiades says. First, there was never a sexual relation between Socrates and Alcibiades, and this because Socrates refused it; again, the high distinction accorded Alcibiades as a soldier in service to Athens might better have been awarded to Socrates; again, their relation, though intimate, was distinguished by the fact that Alcibiades precisely did not follow Socrates, but went another way: the charge against Socrates of corrupting the youth is met by Alcibiades' remark that he was drawn away from Socrates though being "worsted by the honors of the multitude."[162] It is Athens, not Socrates, that corrupted Alcibiades, who explicitly says that he would have lived differently if he had lived by Socrates' precepts. No doubt Socrates was hard to know: on the outside a Silenus, an ugly satyr, on the inside he contained a golden image of divinity. By an irony, the Athenians not only did not know Socrates, they did not know themselves, or that they corrupted the youth. It is an ironical enough comment on the trial. Alcibiades is Aristophanes in action, the old accuser and the old accusation.

That the reader is meant to be reminded of Socrates' trial by Alcibiades' speech is further shown by language that echoes the speech of the *Apology.* Alcibiades addresses the company as jurymen and judges, issues a mock charge against Socrates for ὕβρις, outrage, a recognized head of fault in Athenian law, and asks the jurors for their vote (219c).

Plato's portrait of Socrates in the *Symposium* is a powerful defense of Socrates. Socrates himself could not have been made to say these things, but they needed to be said; Plato gets them said by the device of having Alcibiades himself say them—and letting Aristodemus narrate what he said.

Alcibiades undertakes to praise, not Eros, as previous speakers had done, but Socrates; and he praises Socrates not only for his temperance and courage, especially courage in battle, but for his wisdom. This intro-

162. 216b. Cf. *Republic* VI 491b–492d, 494a–495b.

duces fundamental incongruity into the speech of Alcibiades, for Socrates
has said over and again that he is not wise, except in the love-matters he
learned from Diotima. If wisdom implies possession of knowledge, then
Alcibiades is confused. He has identified the object of love with someone
who lacks that object, identified wisdom with the philosopher who loves
wisdom and does not possess it. In short, Alcibiades has done exactly what
Agathon did: he has confused love with the object of love, desire with
what is preeminently desirable—"this genuine divinity, this wonderful
man" (219c). In the intensity of the love of Alcibiades for Socrates, a human being is elevated to the status of an ultimate object of desire. This is
an emotional mistake that ultimately rests on an intellectual mistake: Alcibiades has confused a human being with goodness itself. The passion
he feels is appropriate to the ultimate object of desire, Beauty itself, not
to a lover of wisdom who lacks what he loves. In treating as ultimate a
person who points beyond himself, Alcibiades is worshipping a kind of
graven image.

Nor is Alcibiades happy. He is tortured, divided against himself, and
his very comparisons show it. There is beauty in his comparison of Socrates to the statues of Silenus that contain the image of a god; but silenes
are very like satyrs, and Alcibiades also compares Socrates and his words
to the satyr Marsyas and his music. Marsyas challenged Apollo himself,
and when he lost, he was flayed alive for his *hubris,* and his hide stretched
into a wineskin (*Euthydemus* 285d). It is an ugly, angry image; but then,
Alcibiades, the passionate lover, also sometimes wishes Socrates dead
(216b–c). *Odi et amo.*

Indeed, his very praise of Socrates is close to condemnation. He turns
to Socrates and says, "You are outrageous [ὑβριστής], are you not?" (215b;
compare 221e). In context, this is something more than an affectionate
jibe. ὕβρις was a recognized head of fault in Athenian law, involving in-
terference with someone else's rights ranging from insolence to wanton
violence, and partaking of both crime and tort. When Pausanias wants to
praise the best kind of Eros, the heavenly Eros, he says it is without ὕβρις,
without lust or lewdness, but also without outrage. Alcibiades charges Socrates with ὕβρις because Socrates refused to give in to sexual seduction,
and if the charge anticipates the *Apology,* the charge of *hubris* is also implied in Alcibiades' comparison of Socrates to Marsyas.

This theme knits the end of the *Symposium* to the beginning. In the beginning, Agathon, ever courteous, invited Socrates to lie next to him so
that he might absorb Socrates' wisdom by proximity, as by a wick. Socrates,
equally courteous, disclaimed his own wisdom by comparison to Agathon's, whose victory in dramatic competition had shown his wisdom to

the whole of Athens. Agathon replies to Socrates with the exact words Alcibiades will use: "You are outrageous [ὑβριστής], Socrates" (175e), and suggests that Dionysus will be the judge of their contending claims. That is, Dionysus will judge between Agathon's claim that Socrates is wiser and Socrates' claim that Agathon is wiser.

The presence of Dionysus at this drinking party is recalled again with the introduction of Aristophanes, whose whole business as a comic poet has to do with wine and sex (177e). But the decision between Agathon and Socrates is made not by Dionysus, but by the argument begun in the *elenchus* of Agathon and carried through in the speech of Diotima: Agathon is not wise because he quite literally, by his own admission, does not know what he is talking about; Socrates is not wise—as Diotima directly says (210a) and Socrates throughout has protested—because he is a philosopher, a lover of wisdom, and can love only what he lacks. Now comes Alcibiades, a symbolic representation of Dionysus himself, very nearly the god's epiphany, offering praise of Socrates which from the point of view of either Dionysus or Aphrodite amounts to condemnation. He loves him, he has been enslaved by him, he would like to see him dead. The epiphany of the wine-god is a servant; the surrogate of a chthonian deity has been bitten by a snake.[163]

The *hubris* of Socrates in refusing sexual seduction is something more than what Alcibiades describes as temperance, self-control. If Eros is wish for happiness and implies desire for generation according to body or soul, much sexual desire is not Eros. Specifically, Alcibiades' desire for sexual intercourse with Socrates was not Eros, because it was sterile. The Eros praised by the others at the banquet, the Eros of romantic love, is at best an image, an εἴδωλον, of genuine Eros, exemplified in the philosopher and embodied in Socrates. The *hubris* of Socrates consists in a principled disdain. If Eros is wish for what is truly good, then asceticism in respect to desire and especially sexuality, that most tempting and troubling of all desires, is implied in the *Symposium* and at the core of its moral psychology.

Socrates Replies (222c–223b)

Socrates now suggests that Alcibiades' frankness in praising him instead of Eros is a form of erotic concealment, meant to put Socrates and Agathon at odds. He turns Alcibiades' comparison of him to Silenus back on itself by comparing Alcibiades' speech to a satyr play. Then, in the final

163. Dionysus was represented crowned with snakes: Euripides, *Bacchae* 99–104. Alcibiades enters crowned with fillets of ribbons.

by-play with Agathon, Socrates, the unseduced beloved, is transformed once again into a lover, and by a neat piece of reasoning and the promise of an encomium, leads Agathon to lie beside him.

Conclusion (223b–d)

Beauty itself had appeared to the soul of the lover suddenly; Alcibiades had appeared to the company suddenly, and Socrates to Alcibiades suddenly, and now a mob of revelers appears at the doors suddenly. Their arrival marks the end of discourse.

The *Symposium* ends in impassive calm. Socrates has vanquished the wine-god.

TRANSLATION

Prologue: Apollodorus to a Companion
(172a–174a)

172a APOLLODORUS. I think I'm not unprepared in what you ask about. In fact, I happened to be coming into town the other day from my home in Phalerum, when someone I know caught sight of me from behind and called to me at a distance with a playful summons—"Hey there, you Phalarian," he said, "Apollodorus! Won't you wait up?" So I stopped and waited.

b And he said, "Why really, Apollodorus, I was just looking for you a little while ago, because I wish to learn all about the meeting of Agathon and Socrates and Alcibiades and the others, the time they were together at the banquet, and what the speeches were about love. Someone else heard it from Phoenix, son of Philippus, and related it to me, and he said you knew too; but he had nothing clear to say. So please relate it to me; for it's very right of you, after all, to report the discussions of your friend. But first tell me," he said, "were you present at this gathering yourself?"

And I said, "It seems he related nothing clear to you at all, if c you think the meeting occurred so recently that I was present too."

"Yes, I did think that," he said.

"How so, Glaucon?"[164] I said. "Don't you know that Agathon

---

164. Perhaps Glaucon, son of Ariston, Plato's elder brother and a leading speaker in the *Republic*; but if so, and if he, like Apollodorus, was only a child when the banquet occurred in 416 B.C. (173a), he must have been very close in age to Plato, for Plato was then about twelve years old.

hasn't lived here for many years, whereas it's not even three years
173a   yet that I've associated with Socrates and made it my care each
day to know what he says or does? Before that I ran round every
which way and thought I was doing something when I was more
wretched than anybody, no less than you are right now, thinking
one must do anything else at all except pursue wisdom."

"Don't jest," he said. "Tell me when this meeting took place."

"We were still children," I said. "It was when Agathon won
with his first tragedy, the day after he and his chorus celebrated
their victory feast."

"Quite a while ago, it seems," he said. "But who told you?
Socrates himself?"

b   "No indeed," I replied. "It was the same person who told Phoenix, a certain Aristodemus of Cydathenaeum, a little fellow, always barefoot. He was present at the meeting, and he was I think
one of Socrates' most devoted lovers[165] at the time. But of course
I afterwards also asked Socrates about some of the things I heard
from him, and he agreed it was as Aristodemus related it."

"Then why not relate it to me?" he said. "The road into town
is surely well suited for talking and listening."

Well, we walked on together and discussed it, so as I said to
c   begin with, I'm not unprepared. If I'm obliged then to relate it
to you as well, it must be done. And anyway, when I talk about
philosophy myself or listen to others do so, quite apart from
thinking I'm benefited, it's extraordinary how much I enjoy it;
but when I hear other kinds of talk, especially from you rich
businessmen, I feel irritation myself and pity for you and your
friends, because you think you're doing something and you're
d   accomplishing nothing. On the other hand, maybe you'll believe
I'm unfortunate too, and I think you're right. But I don't just
think it about you, I well know it.

COMPANION. You're always the same, Apollodorus; you're always
speaking ill of yourself and others, and I think you believe that
everyone without exception, beginning with yourself, is wretched
except Socrates. I don't know where you ever got the name of
being soft! For you're always like this in argument, provoked at
yourself and everyone else except Socrates.

165. ἐραστής, 173b2. Note that there is here no sexual implication in the word,
which might be translated "admirer" or perhaps even "disciple" (cf. 218c, 219c–d),
though its use is proleptic for the discussion of Eros to follow. See also, for example,
Protagoras 317c.7, Euthydemus 276d.2.

e APOLLODORUS. Dear friend, is it then really so clear that in thinking this way both about myself and the rest of you, I've gone crazy and lost my wits?

COMPANION. It's not worth quarreling about that now, Apollodorus; please don't do other than what I asked of you, but relate what the speeches were.

174a APOLLODORUS. Well, they were something like this—. No, I'll start at the beginning, and try to relate it to you just as he did.

Aristodemus's Prologue (174a–175e)

Aristodemus said Socrates met him bathed and anointed and with slippers on his feet, which he seldom wore; and he asked Socrates where he was going so beautifully dressed.

To a banquet at Agathon's, he replied. I stayed away from his victory feast yesterday because I was afraid of the crowd; but I agreed to be present today. So that's why I got dressed up, to be beautiful when going to beauty. But how about you? he said.
b   Would you be willing to go to a banquet uninvited?

Aristodemus said he replied, Whatever you say.

Then come along, he said, so that we may also spoil the proverb by changing it to mean that "the good go of their own accord to the feasts of the Good."[166] Homer, indeed, comes close not only to spoiling that proverb but to committing outrage on it, for he makes Agamemnon a surpassingly good soldier but Menelaus a
c   "soft warrior,"[167] and then makes Menelaus go uninvited to the feast when Agamemnon was offering a sacrifice and entertaining—a worse man going to the feast of the better.

Aristodemus said that when he heard this he said, But maybe I won't fit your version but Homer's, Socrates, an inferior going uninvited to the feast of a wise man. So consider what defense you're going to make for bringing me, because I won't agree that
d   I came uninvited, but that I was invited by you.

"When two go together,"[168] he said. We'll take counsel about what to say on the way. But let's go.

166. Socrates here puns on Agathon's name—Good.

167. *Iliad* xvii 587: Apollo's taunt to Hector. Socrates' misuse of the passage is very much in the sophistic manner. Cf. *Republic* III 411b.

168. Socrates allusively quotes *Iliad* x 224, "When two go together, one of them knows before the other" (cf. *Protagoras* 348d). Two heads are better than one.

After some such discussion as this, he said, off they went. Well,
Socrates turned his thought inward as they proceeded along the
road, and fell behind; when Aristodemus waited for him, he bid
him go on ahead. He found the door open when he reached
Agathon's house, and he said it put him in a ridiculous position:
for one of the servants inside immediately met him and took him
to where the others were reclining, and he found them just about
to dine. Well, as soon as Agathon saw him, he said, Hello, Aristodemus, you're just in time to join us; if you've come for something else, put it aside for another time, because I looked for you
yesterday to invite you and couldn't find you. But how is it you
don't bring Socrates for us?

I looked around, Aristodemus said, and Socrates was nowhere
to be seen following, so I said that I had myself come with Socrates, because he invited me here to dine.

It's good of you to come, said Agathon. But where is he?

He was right behind me just now. I wonder where he is myself.

Aristodemus said that Agathon said to a servant, Won't you go
find Socrates and bring him in? And you, Aristodemus, he said,
please recline here by Eryximachus.

He said the servant washed him[169] so that he might lie down;
another servant came and announced, Socrates is here. He's withdrawn to the porch next door, he's standing there, and he won't
come when I call.

That's strange, Agathon said. Keep calling him and don't give
up.

And Aristodemus said he said, No, let him be. That's his way;
he sometimes stops and stands wherever he happens to be. He'll
be along presently, I think. Don't disturb him, but let him be.

He said that Agathon said, Then we must do so, if you think
it best. But servants, serve dinner to the rest of us. You always
put out whatever you wish in any case, when there's no one su-
pervising you—which I've never yet done—so now assume that
you've invited me with these others to dine as your guests, and
serve us so that we may praise you.

After this they dined, he said, but Socrates didn't come in.
Well, Agathon several times suggested they send for Socrates, but
Aristodemus wouldn't allow it. Then after a little while Socrates
came, having spent the time in his accustomed way, when they

169. That is, his feet and perhaps his hands, a gesture of customary hospitality.

were right in the middle of dinner. Well, Agathon—for he happened to recline last and by himself—said, Come here, Socrates,
and recline by me, so that in touching you I'll get the benefit of
d   the wisdom that came to you on the porch. For you've clearly
found it and you've got it; otherwise, you wouldn't have left.

Socrates sat down and said, It would indeed be well, Agathon,
if wisdom were the sort of thing that might flow from the fuller
of us into the emptier if only we touch each other, as water flows
through a woolen thread from a fuller into an emptier cup.[170] If
e   wisdom is that way too, I value the place beside you very much
indeed; for I think I will be filled from you with wisdom of great
beauty. My own wisdom is a worthless thing, as disputable as a
dream, but yours is bright and full of promise, that wisdom
which, young as you are, shone out from you in such manifest
splendor the other day, with more than thirty thousand Greeks
to witness.

You're outrageous, Socrates, Agathon replied. You and I will
adjudicate our claims about wisdom a little later, using Dionysus
as judge. But now please first turn to your dinner.

Eryximachus Proposes Speeches in Praise of Eros
(176a–178a)

176a   After this, he said, when Socrates had lain down and dined
along with the others, they offered their libations and sang a
hymn to the god and did the other customary things, and turned
to the drinking. So Pausanias, Aristodemus said, led off with
some such speech as this: Very well, gentlemen, he said, how shall
we drink most at our ease? I tell you, I'm really quite uncom-
fortable from yesterday's bout and I need some relief—I think
b   most of you do too; for you were there yesterday—so consider
how we may drink most at our ease.

So Aristophanes replied, You're quite right, Pausanias, about
being in every way prepared to take it easy in our drinking; in
fact, I'm among those who got a dipping yesterday myself.

Aristodemus said that when Eryximachus, son of Acumenus,

170. The reference is to wicking. "Two cups, one empty the other full, are placed
in contact: a woollen thread, with one end inserted in the full cup, the other hanging
into the empty cup, serves by the law of capillarity to convey the fluid from the one
to the other." Bury, *Symposium,* on this passage.

heard this, he said, Fine. But I still need to hear from one more
of you: How is Agathon's strength for drinking?

I myself have no strength at all, he replied.

c   Well, that's a stroke of luck for the rest us, he said—me and
Aristodemus and Phaedrus and the others here—if you, the most
able drinkers, have now given up; for we're never up to it. I leave
Socrates out of account; he's sufficient either way, so whatever
we do will suit him. Well, since I think no one here is eager to
drink a lot of wine, perhaps I'd be less displeasing in telling you
what sort of thing being drunk is. For I think it has become very

d   clear to me from the art of medicine that drunkenness is hard
on people. I would not myself be willing to drink deeply if I could
help it, nor would I advise it for someone else, especially if still
hungover from the previous day.

Aristodemus said that Phaedrus of Myrrhinus interrupted and
said, Why really, I'm accustomed to obey you, especially in whatever you say about medicine, and the rest will now do so too, if
they're well advised.

e   Hearing this, everyone agreed that the gathering should not
be a drunken affair, but they would drink only for enjoyment.

Then, said Eryximachus, since it's been decided that each of
us should drink only as much as he wishes, nothing compulsory,
I next suggest that the flute-girl who just came in be let go;[171]
she can play to herself or to the women within the house if she
wishes, while we continue our present gathering through conversation. As to the sort of conversation, I'm willing to make a
proposal to you, if you wish.

177a   They all said that they did indeed wish, and bid him make his
proposal.

So Eryximachus said, The beginning of what I have to say fits
Euripides' Melanippe, for "mine is not the tale"[172] I'm about to
tell. It belongs to Phaedrus here. Phaedrus often complains to
me and says, "Isn't it terrible, Erixymachus, that the poets make
hymns and paeans for other gods, yet not a single one of them,

b   despite their number, has ever offered an encomium to Eros, a

171. The flute, or αὐλός (actually, a single- or double-reed instrument and strictly
not a flute but more like a clarinet or an oboe), had a shrill, piercing tone, and was
especially associated with Dionysus, as the lyre was with Apollo. In the *Republic* (III
399d–e; cf. *Laws* VII 812c–813a), αὐλός-players and αὐλός-makers are to be excluded from the Ideal State: Apollo and his instruments are to be preferred to
Marsyas and his.

172. Euripides, fr. 488 (Nauck): "Mine is not the tale; my mother taught me."

god so venerable and so great? Or if you wish, take our worthy
sophists: they write prose elegies of Heracles and others as the
excellent Prodicus did, and maybe that's not so very surprising,
but I once came upon a book by a wise man in which salt was
most astonishingly eulogized for its usefulness, and you see other
c   such stuff given lengthy praise—much ado over things like that,
and yet no one ever down to the present day has ventured worthily to hymn Eros. So neglected is so great a god!"

   I think Phaedrus was right about this. So I not only want to
make a contribution of my own and gratify him, but at the same
time I also think it's presently fitting for those of us here present
d   to adorn the god. So if you agree too, this would be a sufficient
topic for our conversation: I think each of us should make as
beautiful a speech as he can in praise of Eros, from left to right
starting with Phaedrus, since he lies first and at the same time is
father of the discourse.

   No one will vote against you, Eryximachus, said Socrates. For
I who claim to know nothing except the things of love[173] could
scarcely decline, and neither can Agathon and Pausanias, nor
e   Aristophanes, whose whole occupation concerns Dionysus and
Aphrodite, wine and sex; nor anyone else among those I see here.
And yet it isn't fair to those of us who lie last; if those ahead
speak sufficiently and beautifully, it will do for us too. Let Phaedrus begin and offer his encomium to Eros, and good luck to
him.

   Well, all the others therefore agreed and bid him do as Socrates
178a   suggested. Aristodemus did not quite remember all of what each
of them said, nor do I in turn remember everything that he said;
but I'll tell you what he especially remembered in the speech of
each, and which seemed to me worthy of mention.

The Speech of Phaedrus (178a–180b)

First of all, as I say,[174] he said Phaedrus led off with something
like this: Eros is a great god, wonderful among gods and men in
many other ways, but not least in respect to his birth.
b   For the god is held in honor as eldest among them, said he.

173. A claim Socrates is able to make, though he is otherwise ignorant, because
he has been instructed by Diotima.
174. 177d–e.

An indication of this is that Eros has no parents, nor does anyone, layman or poet, claim he does. Hesiod says that first Chaos came to be, "But then broad-bosomed Earth, ever safe abode for all, and Eros."[175] Acusilaus agrees with Hesiod too that next after Chaos this pair was born, Earth and Eros. And Parmenides says of the birth that "very first of all gods she devised Eros." So it is

c   agreed in many places that Eros is eldest among them.[176]

Being eldest, he is cause to us of greatest goods. For I cannot say what good is greater, from youth on, than a worthy lover, and for a lover, a worthy beloved. For those who intend to live beautifully must be led through the whole of life by what neither kinship nor honors nor wealth nor aught else can instill so beau-

d   tifully as Eros. What do I mean by this? Shame for things ugly, ambition for things beautiful; for without these, neither city nor private person can do great and beautiful deeds. I say then that a man in love, if discovered doing something shameful, or suffering it from another and failing through cowardice to defend himself, would not be so pained at being seen by his father or

e   friends or anyone else as by his beloved. We see this same thing too in the beloved, that it is especially before his lovers that he feels shame when seen in something shameful. If then there were some device so that a city or an army might be made up of lovers and their beloveds, it is not possible that they could govern their own affairs better than by abstaining from all things shameful and vying for honor among themselves; fighting side by side, men of this sort would be victorious even if they were but few against

179a   nearly all mankind. For a man in love would surely not let himself be seen by his beloved, beyond all others, deserting his post or throwing down his arms; he would choose to die many times before that. And again, as to deserting his beloved or not helping him in danger—no one is so bad that Eros would not inspire him to virtue so as to be equal to him who is by nature best. What

b   Homer said is absolutely true, that god "breathes valor" into certain of the heroes, a thing that Eros provides to lovers from his own resources.

175. *Theogony* 116ff., 120. Phaedrus truncates the passage.
176. Aristotle relies on this passage at *Metaphysics* I 984b 23–31. The cosmological implication that "among existing things there must be from the first a cause which will move things and bring them together," and the connection of this claim with Empedocles, are his own, but they are anticipated in the speech of Eryximachus, for example at 186d–e.

And again, only lovers are willing to die in behalf of others—
not only men but women too. Of that, Alcestis, daughter of Pelias,
provides sufficient proof to the Greeks in behalf of this argument. She alone was willing to die in behalf of her husband,
although he had both father and mother. Due to Eros, she so
c   much surpassed them in friendship that she made them appear
alien to their own son and related to him only in name.[177] When
she did this, the deed seemed not only to men but also to gods
so beautifully done that, although many have done many beautiful deeds, those whom the gods have rewarded by sending their
souls back from the Place of the Dead are easily numbered; yet
hers they sent back in admiration of her deed. So even the gods
d   especially honor zeal and virtue concerning Eros. But Orpheus,
son of Oeagrus, they sent back from the Place of the Dead empty-
handed, showing him an appearance of the wife he'd come for
but not giving her, because they thought he was soft due to being
a musician, and didn't dare die for the sake of Eros as Alcestis
had, but contrived to go to the Place of the Dead alive.[178] For this
reason, then, they punished him and caused his death at the
hands of women. In contrast, they honored Achilles, son of The-
e   tis, and sent him to the Isles of the Blest, because when he learned
from his mother that he would die if he killed Hector but that if

177. Admetus was fated to die. Apollo, by making the Fates drunk, persuaded
them to promise that Admetus might live if someone else were willing to die in his
place. No one would consent to do so, including his aged parents, except Alcestis,
his wife.

178. Orpheus was the great musician, charming trees, wild beasts and even
stones with his song. His wife, Eurydice, was killed by the bite of a snake, and
Orpheus journeyed alive—this is why Phaedrus claims he was a coward—to the
Underworld to bring her back.

> Or bid the soul of Orpheus sing
> Such notes as warbled to the string
> Drew Iron tears down Pluto's cheek,
> And made Hell grant what Love did seek.
> (Milton, *Il Penseroso*, lines 104–108)

But Eurydice was released on the condition that Orpheus not turn and look back
at her during the ascent. He did look back, and lost her forever. He was afterward
torn to pieces by Maenads, and his severed head floated down the stream, still
singing.

> What could the Muse herself that Orpheus bore,
> The Muse herself, for her inchanting son
> Whom universal nature did lament,
> When by the rout that made the hideous roar,
> His gory visage down the stream was sent,
> Down the swift Hebrus to the Lesbian shore.
> (*Lycidas*, lines 58–64)

180a he did not he would go home and live out a long life, he dared choose to help his lover Patroclus and avenge him, not only dying in behalf of but also in addition to the slain.[179] This is why the gods in high admiration surpassingly honored him, because he counted his lover so important. Aeschylus talks nonsense in claiming that Achilles was the lover of Patroclus, when he was not only more beautiful than Patroclus but doubtless than all the other heroes too, and still beardless, since he was very much younger, as Homer tells.[180] For though the gods really do honor this virtue

b of Eros in highest degree, they marvel and admire and reward it still more when the beloved cherishes the lover than when the lover cherishes the beloved. For lover is more divine than beloved: the god is in him and he is inspired. That is also why they honored Achilles more than Alcestis, and sent him to the Isles of the Blest.

Thus then I claim that Eros is eldest and most honored of gods, and most authoritative in respect to possession of virtue and happiness for men both living and dead.

The Speech of Pausanias (180c–185c)

c Phaedrus gave some such speech as this, Aristodemus said, and after Phaedrus there were some others he didn't remember very well. Passing them by, he related the speech of Pausanias, who said:

Phaedrus, I don't think the plan before us, being thus enjoined simply to offer an encomium to Eros, is a good one. It would be fine if Eros were one, but as it is he is not one. Since he is not one, it is more correct to be told in advance what sort of Eros

d ought to be praised. So I'll undertake to correct this, first by describing the Eros that ought to be praised, and next by worthily praising the god. For we all know there is no Aphrodite, no sex, without Eros. If then there were but one Aphrodite, Eros would be one, but since in fact there are two, Eros is necessarily also two.

How are there not two goddesses? The one, surely, is elder, the motherless daughter of Uranus, whom we therefore name Our-

179. Cf. 208d 2, 3.
180. *Iliad* xi 786. Homer does not in fact represent the relation of Achilles to Patroclus as homosexual.

ania, Heavenly. The other is younger, the daughter of Zeus and
e   Dione,[181] whom we call Pandemus, Popular or Vulgar. Necessarily
then it is also right to call the Eros who is partner to this one
vulgar, but to the other heavenly. One must of course praise all
gods, but one must also try to say what province falls to the lot
of each. For every action is as follows: in and of itself it is neither
beautiful nor ugly. For example, none of the things we are doing
181a   now, drinking or singing or conversing, is in itself beautiful; it
turns out that way according to how it is done. If done beautifully
and correctly, it becomes beautiful; if incorrectly, ugly. Thus,
then, not all loving and Eros are beautiful nor worthy of an encomium, but only the Eros that turns us toward loving beautifully.
    Now, the Eros of Vulgar Aphrodite is truly vulgar, and works
b   at random; this is the Eros of common sorts of men. First, such
men love women no less than boys; next, they love their bodies
rather than their souls; again, they love the stupidest they can
find, looking only to the act, careless of whether or not it is done
beautifully. Whence then it follows that they do whatever they
happen to do, good or the opposite alike. For this Eros derives
c   from the goddess who is younger by far than the other, and has
a share of both male and female in her birth.
    But the Eros of the Heavenly Aphrodite, first, does not partake
of female but only of male—it is the Eros for boys—and next is
elder, and without share of outrage or wantonness. This is why
those inspired by this Eros turn to the male, delighting in what
is by nature stronger and possessed of more intelligence. One
might recognize those moved purely by this Eros even in the love
d   of boys itself: for they do not love boys except when they begin
to get intelligence, that is, when they are on the verge of getting
a beard. Those who begin to love them at this point, I think, are

181. Heavenly Aphrodite, Aphrodite Ourania, is the daughter of Uranus; more
precisely, she sprang from the severed member of Uranus, who had been castrated
by his son Cronus, as it floated in the sea and gathered foam (ἀφϱός; cf. *Cratylus*
406b–c) about it. This is a story that Plato particularly condemned as false to the
nature of divinity: *Euthyphro* 6a–b, *Republic* II 377e–378a. Popular Aphrodite, Aphrodite Pandemus, is identified by Pausanias as the daughter of Zeus and Dione;
Dione is simply the feminine form of Zeus (genitive, Διός); in Homer she consorted
with Zeus to become the mother of Aphrodite, but there is a later tradition in which
she is, by Ares, the mother of Eros. (See H. J. Rose, *A Handbook of Greek Mythology,*
New York, 1959, pp. 22, 53.) Pausanias, with his two Aphrodites and two Erotes,
exploits in the sophistic manner a characteristic inconsistency in the mythological
tradition, and uses it to imply a distinction between good Eros and an Eros that isn't
as good, and which, after an apotropaic compliment, he treats as bad.

prepared to be with them through the whole of life and pass
their lives in common, rather than deceiving them by catching
them in the thoughtlessness of youth and then contemptuously
e abandoning them and running off to someone else. There ought
to be a law against loving boys,[182] so that great effort is not wasted
where the outcome is unclear; for what a boy will be when he
grows up is unclear, and how he will turn out in respect to virtue
and vice both of body and soul. Now, good men lay down this
law for themselves voluntarily, but vulgar lovers ought also be
compelled to do the same, just as we compel them, so far as we
182a can, not to make love to free-born women. For it is they in fact
who have caused reproach, so that some people even venture to
say it is shameful to gratify lovers; they look to them in saying
this, seeing their impropriety and injustice, since surely what is
done in a lawful and orderly way could not justly bear reproach.

Again, the law and custom in other cities concerning Eros are
easy to know, for they are simply defined; but here and in Sparta
b they are complex. In Elis and Boeotia, and where there is no skill
in speaking, it is simply given as law that gratification of lovers
is beautiful, and no one, young or old, would claim it is shameful
or ugly—in order, I suppose, not to have the trouble of trying to
persuade the young by speech, because they cannot speak. But
in Ionia and many other places ruled by barbarians, it is held
shameful.[183] Yes, it is actually held to be shameful by the barbar-
c ians, along with philosophy and the love of exercise, due to their
tyranny; for it is not, I think, to the advantage of rulers to have
great thoughts engendered in those ruled, nor strong friendships
and associations, which Eros above all others is especially wont to
instill. Tyrants, in fact, have here learned this by actual deeds;
for the Eros of Aristogiton and the friendship of Harmodius,
steadfastly abiding, overthrew their rule.[184] Thus, where it is set-

182. Pausanias now means children, where before he meant adolescents; the
verbal confusion is an index of his precision of thought.
183. Pausanias's suggestion that Ionia is under barbarian rule suggests a date
after the King's Peace in 387 B.C. Since not only the dramatic but the narrative date
of the *Symposium* is before the death of Socrates in 399, this appears to be deliberate
anachronism.
184. Aristogiton and Harmodius were Athenian tyrannicides; they attempted to
kill the tyrant Hippias, succeeded in killing his brother, Hipparchus, and were ex-
ecuted in 514 B.C. The tyranny was overthrown a few years later, and they were
honored and called Liberators. Simonides composed a poem to them, statues of
them were erected in the Agora, and their descendents were given the right to public
subsistence, meals in the Prytaneum—an honor Socrates suggested as a counter-
penalty at his trial.

tled that it is shameful to gratify lovers, it is settled by the badness
d of those who settled it, by the overreaching of the rulers, by the
cowardice of the ruled; but where it is acknowledged simply and
without qualification, it is due to the laziness of soul of those who
settled it. But the law here is much more beautiful than that and,
as I said, not easy to comprehend.

Bear in mind that it is held to be more beautiful to love openly
than in secret, and especially to love the most noble and best even
if they are uglier than others; and again, that the encouragement
everyone gives to the lover is astonishing and not as if he were
doing something shameful, and that it is regarded as beautiful
to capture and shameful to fail, and that relative to the attempt
e to capture, law and custom have given liberty to the lover to be
praised for doing quite extraordinary deeds, deeds which, if anyone dared do them in pursuit of anything else at all, wishing to
183a accomplish anything except this, would issue in greatest blame
for philosophy.[185]

For if anyone, wishing to get money or obtain office or some
other position of power from someone, were willing to do the
sorts of things lovers do for their beloveds, making supplications
and prayers in their entreaties, swearing oaths, sleeping on doorsteps, willing to do slavish acts of a sort not even a slave would
do, he would be prevented from acting this way both by his
b friends and his enemies, these rebuking him for his flattery and
servility, those admonishing him and ashamed for them. Yet people are charmed by the lover who does all this, and the law allows
it without reproach, as though he were doing something quite
beautiful. But the strangest thing, as most people say, is that only
to the lover is forgiveness granted by the gods for breach of
oaths—for they deny that a sexual vow is a vow. So both gods
c and men have granted full liberty to the lover, as the law here
declares.

For this reason, then, one might suppose that loving and the
friendship got from lovers would be acknowledged in this city as
quite beautiful. But when fathers set tutors over those loved and

185. φιλοσοφίας, 183a.1, obelized by Burnet and excluded by Bury and Dover,
following Schleiermacher, but read by all major manuscripts and supported by
184c.8–d.1; cf. 182c.1. The *Symposium* has been a much emended text, but a con-
servative hand is perhaps more than usually justified; the speakers are sometimes
drunk not only on wine but on their own rhetoric, and this is specifically true of
Pausanias.

forbid them to talk with their lovers, and the tutor is so ordered, while companions of his own age also rebuke him if they see
d   anything of that sort going on, and their elders do not in turn prevent the rebuke or criticize it as ill founded—looking to these things, one might believe again in turn that this sort of thing is here regarded as most shameful.

But the fact, I think, is this: it is not simply good in and of itself, nor yet ugly and shameful, but as I said to begin with, beautiful if done beautifully, shameful if done shamefully. Shamefully in gratifying a base lover basely, but beautifully in gratifying a worthy lover beautifully. The vulgar lover, who loves the body
e   more than the soul, is base; he is inconstant because the thing he loves is inconstant. For as soon as the bloom of the body he once loved fades, "he takes off and flies," many speeches and promises disdained. But the lover of a worthy character abides through life, for he is joined to what is constant.

184a   Our law and custom therefore wishes to test them beautifully and well, those to be gratified, those to be shunned. For this reason, then, it commands pursuit to these, flight to those, organizing a competition to test of which sort the lover is and of which sort the beloved. It is due to this cause, first, that the law deems quick capture shameful, in order that time may pass— which indeed seems to be an excellent test for most things—and
b   next deems it shameful to be captured by money or political power, or if he cowers when ill treated and is not staunch, or if when offered favors of money or political success he does not despise them; for none of these seems abiding or constant, quite apart from the fact that a noble friendship does not naturally result from them.

One way then is left in our law, if beloved intends to gratify lover beautifully. For it is law among us that, just as it is not
c   flattery or in any way subject to reproach for lovers to be willing to submit to every kind of slavery for their beloved, so also there is only one kind of voluntary slavery not subject to reproach: that involving virtue. For it is held by us that if someone is willing to serve someone in the belief that through him he will become better, in respect either to some kind of wisdom or to any other part of virtue whatever, this voluntary servitude is on the contrary not shameful, nor is it flattery.[186]

186. Cf. *Euthydemus* 282b—if wisdom can be taught.

One must then combine these two laws, the law concerning
d pederasty and the law concerning philosophy and the rest of
virtue, if it is to result that it is good for the beloved to gratify a
lover. For when lover and beloved come together in the same
place, each governed by his own law, the one would serve justly
in serving in any way at all the beloved who has gratified him;
the other would submit justly, on the other hand, in submitting
in any way at all to one who makes him wise and good. The one
e is able to contribute intelligence and the rest of virtue, the other
needs to possess it in respect to education and the rest of wisdom:
only at that point, when these laws combine in the same place,
does it happen that it is beautiful for the beloved to gratify the
lover, but elsewhere not at all.

In such a case, there is no shame even in being deceived and
seduced, but in all other cases it bears shame whether seduced
185a or not. For if one gratified a lover for money because he was rich,
and was deceived and got no money because the lover turned out
to be poor, it would be no less shameful; for it is thought such a
man shows himself for what he is, that he would submit to anyone
in anything for money, and this is not beautiful. By the same
account, even if one gratified someone because he was good,
intending that he himself might be better through the friendship
of a lover, and was deceived when he turned out to be bad and
b not to possess virtue, the deception is nevertheless good; for it is
again thought that he has made clear exactly what he is, that he
would eagerly do everything for everyone for the sake of virtue
and his own improvement, and this in turn is of all things most
beautiful. So it is in every way beautiful to provide gratification
for the sake of virtue. This is the Eros of the Heavenly Goddess,
and heavenly himself, and of great worth both to city and to
private citizens, compelling the lover to be much concerned for
c his own virtue, and the beloved too. Lovers of the other sort all
belong to the other goddess, the vulgar one.

This is what I have to offer you just on the spot, Phaedrus, he
said, about Eros.

First Interlude: Aristophanes and His Hiccups
(185c–e)

Pausanias paused—for the wise men teach me to speak in equal
measures like this—and Aristodemus said that Aristophanes was

supposed to speak, but he came down with hiccups from being
full or something else and wasn't able to speak. He said—Eryxi-
d   machus, the doctor, was lying right below him—"Eryximachus,
you must either stop my hiccups or speak for me until I can stop
them on my own."

And Eryximachus said, "Why, I'll do both. I'll take your turn
speaking, and you take mine when you stop. But while I'm speaking, if you'll hold your breath a long time the hiccups will stop.
If not, gargle with water. But if they're perhaps very strong, get
e   something to tickle your nose, and sneeze; if you do this once or
twice, even if they're very strong, they'll stop."

"On with your speech," said Aristophanes. "I'll do it."

The Speech of Eryximachus (185e–188e)

So Eryximachus said, Well, since Pausanias began his speech
186a   beautifully but didn't end it satisfactorily, it seems it's up to me
to try to bring the account to a conclusion. He did well, I think,
to divide Eros in two. But Eros exists in the souls of men not only
toward beautiful people, but also toward many other things and
in other things—in the bodies of all animals, in what grows in
the earth, and in general in all that is. I think I have seen from
b   medicine, our art,[187] how great and wonderful is the god, how
he extends over everything both human and divine. I will start
then from medicine in my speech, so that we may also venerate
the art.

For the nature of bodies has this twofold Eros; the health and
sickness of the body are admittedly different and unlike, and
what is unlike desires and loves unlike things. So the Eros in the
healthy body is one thing, that in the diseased body another. As
Pausanias just now said, it is beautiful to gratify what is good for
c   men but shameful to gratify the intemperate; so also among bodies themselves it is beautiful to gratify what is good and healthy
for each body, and it must be done, and this has the name of
medicine, but it is shameful to gratify what is bad and diseased,
and it must not be gratified if one intends to be a real practitioner.

For medicine, to speak summarily, is knowledge of the things

187. Eryximachus speaks as an Asclepiad, a member of the guild of physicians
whose founder was Asclepius (cf. 186e), hero and god of healing. In the *Iliad* Asclepius is a mortal; to Hesiod and Pindar, he was the son of Apollo.

of love belonging to the body relative to filling and emptying,[188] and he who diagnoses the beautiful and shameful Eros in these

d   things is the genuine physician, and he effects change so that the body possesses one Eros instead of the other. He who knows how to instill Eros where it is not present but ought to be, and to remove it where it is present and ought not to be, is the good practitioner: for it is necessary to be able to make the most inimical elements in the body friendly and love each other. But the most inimical are the most opposite: cold to hot, bitter to sweet,

e   dry to wet, all such as that; it is by knowing how to instill Eros and unanimity that our progenitor Asclepius, as these poets here say[189] and I myself believe, established our art.

So all medicine, as I said, is governed by this god, as are gym-

187a nastics and agriculture. It is also obvious to anyone who pays the slightest attention that music is in this respect the same, as Heraclitus also perhaps meant to say, though his actual words don't put it well. He says that the One, "being at variance with itself, is drawn together with itself, like the attunement[190] of bow and lyre."[191] But it is utterly absurd to say that attunement is at variance, or derives from things still at variance.[192] Perhaps he meant to say instead that it has come to be from things formerly at

b   variance, namely, the high and the low, when they afterward are brought into agreement by the art of music. Surely attunement could not derive from continuing discord of high and low. For attunement is concord, and concord a kind of agreement—it is

188. Dover quotes Hippocrates, *De flatibus* I, "Emptying cures fullness, filling emptiness, and rest exertion," because a medical condition is cured by its opposite.

189. The reference is presumably to Aristophanes and Agathon.

190. ἁρμονίαν. It is important to bear in mind F. M. Cornford's remark (*The Unwritten Philosophy*, Cambridge, 1950, p. 19): "Tradition, truly as I believe, reports that Pythagoras declared the soul to be, or to contain, a harmony—or rather a *harmonia*. For in Greek the word *harmonia* does not mean 'harmony,' if 'harmony' conveys to us the concord of several sounds. The Greeks called that *symphonia*. *Harmonia* meant originally the orderly adjustment of parts in a complex fabric; then, in particular, the tuning of a musical instrument; and finally the musical scale, composed of several notes yielded by the tuned strings. What we call the 'modes' would be the Greek *harmoniai*." The closest analogue to a mode, in our music, is the difference between major and minor.

191. The reference is presumably to Heraclitus, Diel-Kranz, *Fragmente der Vorsokratiker* B 51: "They do not understand how being at variance with itself, it is drawn together with itself: a back-stretched [or backward-turning] attunement, like a bow or a lyre." As the bow is drawn, its tips are drawn together; Eryximachus interprets so as to avoid the apparent paradox Heraclitus intended, namely, that the world-process is a dynamic equilibrium of opposite tensions.

192. Eryximachus has himself already said almost exactly this at 186d–e.

impossible for agreement to derive from things at variance so long as they are at variance; on the other hand, it is impossible to attune what is at variance and does not agree—just as rhythm too derives from the quicker and slower, which had before been
c   at variance but afterward come to agree. Music here, like medicine there, puts agreement into all these things, implanting Eros and unanimity with each other. And music in turn is knowledge of the things of love concerning attunement and rhythm. It is not hard to diagnose the things of love in the very constitution of attunement and rhythm, nor is the twofold Eros there yet.[193]

But when one needs to apply rhythm and attunement to men,
d   either in composing, which is called musical composition, or in correct use of melodies and meters once composed, which is called education and culture—here there is indeed difficulty, and need for a good practitioner. For the same account recurs: one must gratify orderly men, and those not yet orderly in such a way that they may become more orderly, and watch out for their Eros, and this is the beautiful, heavenly Eros of the Heavenly Muse.

e   But as for the Vulgar Eros of the many-tuned Muse Polyhmnia,[194] one must apply it with caution to those to whom one applies it, in order to harvest its pleasure but plant no intemperance, just as in our own art it is an important task to make proper use of desires involving the art of cookery, so that its pleasure is harvested without disease. In music and medicine and all other things, human and divine, one must, so far as practicable, watch out for each kind of Eros; for both are present.

188a   Indeed, even the constitution of the seasons of the year is filled with them both, and whenever the things I was just now mentioning, hot and cold and wet and dry, attain orderly Eros relative to each other and receive mixture and attunement in a temperate way, it comes bearing prosperity and health to men and to the other animals and plants, and does no injustice;[195] but when the Eros, accompanied by outrage and wantonness, gains mastery of

193. Or perhaps, reading πως for Badham's πω, "the twofold Eros is in no sense there." See David Konstan and Elisabeth Young-Bruehl, "Eryximachus's Speech in the *Symposium*," *Apeiron* 1985, p. 41.

194. A pointless substitution for the Aphrodite Pandemus of Pausanias, as the "Heavenly Muse" was for the Heavenly Aphrodite: sophistical metonymy.

195. Perhaps an echo of the single surviving fragment of Anaximander, in which the opposites pay penalty to each other in the cycle of days and seasons, according to the assessment of Time, for their injustice, that is, their encroachment on the proper provinces of one another.

the seasons of the year, it destroys many things and does injustice.

b   For plagues like to arise from such things as these, and many other unusual diseases both in beasts and plants; in fact, frost and hail and blight arise from mutual overreaching and disorder among things of love such as these, knowledge of which, as it concerns motions of stars and seasons of years, is called astronomy. Still further, all sacrifices and the objects of the seer's art—

c   that is, the mutual intercourse of gods and men—have to do with nothing other than protection and cure of Eros. For all kinds of impiety, concerning parents both living and dead and concerning the gods, like to arise if one does not gratify the orderly Eros and honor and revere him in every action, but instead gratifies the other Eros. The seer's art has therefore been ordained to oversee these kinds of Eros and heal them, and the seer's art,

d   again, is a craftsman of friendship between gods and men, by knowing which things of love among men tend toward piety and what is religiously right.

So all Eros has, in summary, very great power, or rather all power, but it is the Eros fulfilled in good things accompanied by temperance and justice, both among us and among gods, that has the greatest power and provides all happiness to us and enables us to associate with each other and be friends, even with the gods, who are stronger than we are.

e   Well, perhaps I too have left out many things in praising Eros, but at least not willingly. If I did leave something out, it's your job, Aristophanes, to fill it in. Or if you intend to offer some other kind of encomium to the god, please do so, because your hiccups have stopped.

Second Interlude: Aristophanes Recovered from His Hiccups (189a–c)

189a   Well, Aristodemus said that Aristophanes took over and said, Yes, the hiccups did indeed stop, though not before I applied the sneeze, so I wonder if the more orderly element of the body doesn't desire the sorts of noises and tickles a sneeze is. Because it stopped right away, when I applied the sneeze to it.

And Eryximachus said, My dear Aristophanes, look what you're doing. You make jokes just when you're going to speak, and you compel me to become a guardian of your own speech, to see that

you don't say something ridiculous, when you could have spoken
in peace.

b   Aristophanes laughed and said, You're right, Eryximachus. Let
me unsay what was said. Please relax your guard, because I'm
worried about what I'm going to say, not lest I say something
ridiculous—that would be gain, and native to my Muse—but lest
it make me a butt of ridicule.

Having let fly with this, Aristophanes, he replied, do you think
you'll escape? Pay attention and speak as if you'll be called to
c   account for it. Perhaps, however, if I think fit, I'll let you off.

The Speech of Aristophanes (189c–193e)

Why really, Eryximachus, said Aristophanes, I intend to say
something a bit different from what you and Pausanias said. For
I think people do not fully perceive the power of Eros, since if
they did, they'd build him their greatest temples and altars and
offer their greatest sacrifices, whereas now they do nothing of
the kind, though it very much needs doing. For he is the most
d   philanthropic of gods, a helper of human beings and a physician
for those ills whose cure would be greatest happiness for the
human race. So I will try to describe to you his power, and you
will teach others.

You must first learn human nature and its condition. For our
ancient nature was not what it is now, but of another kind. In the
first place, there were three sexes among men, not two as now,
e   male and female, but a third sex in addition, being both of them
in common, whose name still remains though the thing itself has
vanished; for one sex was then derived in common from both
male and female, androgynous both in form and name, though
the name is now applied only in reproach.

Again, the form of each human being as a whole was round,
with back and sides forming a circle, but it had four arms and
an equal number of legs, and two faces exactly alike on a cylin-
190a   drical neck; there was a single head for both faces, which faced
in opposite directions, and four ears and two sets of pudenda,
and one can imagine all the rest from this. It also traveled upright
just as now, in whatever direction it wished; and whenever they
took off in a swift run, they brought their legs around straight
and somersaulted as tumblers do, and then, with eight limbs to
support them, they rolled in a swift circle.

b   The reason there were three sexes of this sort was that the male
originally was the offspring of the Sun, the female of the Earth,
and what has a share of both of the Moon, because the Moon also
has share of both. They were spherical both in themselves and in
their gait because they were like their parents. Well, they were
terrible in strength and force, and they had high thoughts and
conspired against the gods, and what Homer told of Ephialtes and
Otus[196] is told also of them: they tried to storm Heaven in order
to displace the gods.

c   Well, Zeus and the other gods took counsel about what they
ought to do, and were at a loss, for they didn't see how they could
kill them, as they did the Giants, whose race they wiped out with
the thunderbolt—because the honors and sacrifices they received
from human beings would disappear—nor yet could they allow
them to act so outrageously. After thinking about it very hard indeed, Zeus said, "I believe I've got a device by which men may
continue to exist and yet stop their intemperance, namely, by be-

d   coming weaker. I'll now cut each of them in two," he said, "and
they'll be weaker and at the same time more useful to us by having
increased in number, and they'll walk upright on two legs. But if
they still seem to act so outrageously and are unwilling to keep
quiet," he said, "I'll cut them in two again, so that they'll have to
get around on one leg, hopping."

So saying, he cut human beings in two the way people slice

e   serviceberries[197] to preserve them by drying, or as they cut eggs
with a hair; he ordered Apollo to turn around the face and the
half-neck of whoever he'd cut to where the cut was made, so that
the man would be more orderly by contemplating his own division,
and he bid Apollo heal the other wounds. Apollo turned the face
around and drew together from all sides the skin on what is now
called the belly, as purses are closed by a drawstring, and, tying it
off in the middle of the belly, he made a single mouth which peo-

191a   ple call the navel. And he smoothed out most of the other wrinkles
and carefully shaped the chest with a tool of the sort shoemakers
use to smooth out wrinkles in the leather on a last; but he left a
few wrinkles around the belly and the navel, as a reminder of the
ancient suffering. Now when their nature was divided in two, each

196. Who planned to overthrow the gods by piling Mount Ossa on Olympus and
Pelion on Ossa, to climb the sky (*Odyssey* xi 307–320). Apollo destroyed them.

197. The European *Sorbus domestica*, of the apple family; it resembles the mountain ash, but with larger leaves and fruit, which is edible.

half in longing rushed to the other half of itself and they threw
b   their arms around each other and intertwined them, desiring to
grow together into one, dying of hunger and inactivity too because
they were unwilling to do anything apart from one another.
Whenever any of the halves died and the other was left, the one
left sought out another and embraced it, whether it met half of a
whole woman—what we now call a woman—or of a man. And so
they perished.

But Zeus took pity and provided another device, turning their
pudenda to the front—for up till then they had those on the out-
c   side too, and they used to beget and bear children not in each
other but in the earth, like locusts—well, he turned them to the
front and so caused them to beget in each other, in the female
through the male, for this reason: so that if male met female, they
might in their embrace beget and their race continue to exist,
while at the same time if male met male, there'd at least be satiety
from their intercourse and they'd be relieved and go back to work
and look after the other concerns of life. So Eros for each other
d   is inborn in people from as long ago as that, and he unites their
ancient nature, undertaking to make one from two, and to heal
human nature.

Each of us then is but the token of a human being, sliced like a
flatfish, two from one; each then ever seeks his matching token.[198]
Men sectioned from the common sex, then called androgynous,
e   are woman-lovers; the majority of adulterers are from this sex,
while on the other hand women from this sex are man-lovers and
adulteresses. Women sectioned from a woman pay scant heed to
men, but are turned rather toward women, and lesbians come
from this sex. Those sectioned from a male pursue the masculine;
because they are slices of the male, they like men while still boys,
192a delighting to lie with men and be embraced by them. These are
the most noble boys and youths because they are by nature most
manly.[199] Some say they're most shameless, but they're wrong: they

198. σύμβολον. Corresponding pieces of a knucklebone or other object which con-
tracting parties broke between them, each party keeping one piece to match in order
to have proof of the identity of the presenter of the other. The indenture, at common
law, originally an irregularly torn parchment, had an equivalent use.

199. This and what follows is ironical and sarcastic: "Since it is a taunt in Old
Comedy (e.g., Aristophanes *Knights* 875–880, Plato Comicus, fr. 186) that eminent
politicians in their youth submitted shamelessly (or for money) to homosexual im-
portunities, and this taunt, characteristic of the cynical attitudes of comedy (cf. Dover
Greek Homosexuality, p. 147f.), must have been familiar to Plato, he means Aristophanes to be speaking tongue-in-cheek." Dover, *Symposium*, on this passage.

don't do it out of shamelessness but out of boldness and courage
and masculinity, cleaving to what is like themselves. A great proof:
actually, it is only men of this sort who, when they grow up, enter
b on political affairs. When they reach manhood they love boys, and
by nature pay no heed to marriage and the getting of children
except as compelled to it by custom and law; it suffices them to
live out their lives unmarried, with one another. So this sort becomes wholly a lover of boys or a boy who loves having lovers, ever
cleaving to what is akin.

When the lover of boys and any every other lover meets his own
particular half, they are then marvelously struck by friendship
c and kinship and Eros, and scarcely willing to be separated from
each other even for a little time. These are the people who pass
their whole lives with each other, but who can't even say what they
wish for themselves by being with each other. No one can think it
is for the sake of sexual intercourse that the one so eagerly delights
in being with the other. Instead, the soul of each clearly wishes for
d something else it can't put into words; it divines what it wishes,
and obscurely hints at it.

Suppose Hephaestus with his tools stood over them as they lay
together and asked, "What is it you people wish in being at each
other's side?" And suppose if they were perplexed he further
asked, "Is this your desire—to be in the same place with each other
as much as possible, so that you're not parted from each other
night and day? Because if that's what you want, I will fuse and
e weld you into the same thing, so that from being two you become
one and, as one, share a life in common as long as you live[200] and
when you die, even there in the Place of the Dead you'll again be
one instead of two, and share being dead in common. See if it is
this you love, and if it will suffice for you should it happen."

We know that not a single lover on hearing this would refuse it
nor appear to wish for anything else; he'd simply think he'd heard
what he desired all along, namely, to join and be fused with his
beloved, to become one from two. The cause is that this was our
ancient nature, and we were wholes. Eros then is a name for the
193a desire and pursuit of wholeness. And as I say, before we were one,
but now we have been dispersed by the god due to our injustice

200. Aristotle refers to this passage at *Politics* II 1262b 11*ff.*, where he refers to
"the erotic discourses."

as the Arcadians were dispersed by the Spartans.[201] So there is fear
that if we should not be well ordered toward the gods, we shall be
split in two again and go around like the people molded in profile
on tombstones, sawed in half through the nose, born like split
dice.[202]

b
This is why all men should urge each other in all things to worship the gods, so we may escape this and meet with that, because
Eros is our guide and general. Let no one act to the contrary—
whoever acts to the contrary is hated by the gods—for by becoming friends and reconciled to the god we shall discover and meet
with our own beloved, which few now do.

And Eryximachus must not interrupt me and poke fun at this
account on the ground that I only mean Pausanias and Agathon—
c
perhaps they really are of this kind and are both masculine in
nature—but I'm saying about everyone, men and women alike,
that this is how our race would become happy, if we should fulfill
our love and each meet with his own beloved, returning to his
ancient nature.

If this is best, then necessarily what is nearest to it under present
circumstances is also best: that is, to meet a beloved who is naturally likeminded and congenial. In singing praises to the god re-
d
sponsible for it we would rightly hymn Eros, who at present brings
us the greatest benefits and leads us into what is properly our own,
and provides greatest hope in future that if we offer reverence to
the gods, he will restore us to our ancient nature, and heal us, and
make us blessed and happy.

There, Eryximachus, he said. That's my speech about Eros, of
a different kind than yours. As I begged you, don't poke fun at
it, so that we may also hear what each of the remaining speakers
e
will say—or rather, what each of the two will say: for only Agathon
and Socrates are left.[203]

201. The reference is almost certainly to the Spartan dispersion of the Mantineans
in 385 B.C. The city was razed and the inhabitants dispersed to separate villages. Since
the narrative date of the *Symposium* is before the death of Socrates in 399, this again
(cf. 182b) is an anachronism.
202. Dice were split as tallies, that is, as σύμβολα. Cf. 191d.
203. Since Aristodemus, the narrator, is lying next to Eryximachus (175a), he
would have been next to speak. But he was skipped over when Eryximachus took
Aristophanes' turn, and Aristophanes, following the order originally laid down, now
looks to Eryximachus's right, to Agathon and Socrates.

Third Interlude: Socrates and Agathon
(193e–194e)

Aristodemus said that Eryximachus said, Why, I'll obey you, for
I certainly enjoyed your speech. And if I were not aware that Socrates and Agathon are clever about the things of love, I'd very
much fear they'd be at a loss for words, because of the many and
varied things already said; but as it is, I'm nonetheless confident.

194a   So Socrates said, Yes, Eryximachus, because you yourself competed so well; but if you were where I now am, or rather perhaps
where I'll be once Agathon also speaks, you'd be very afraid and
quite as bewildered as I am now.

You mean to cast a spell on me, Socrates, said Agathon, so that
I'll be thrown into confusion by thinking my theater has great expectation I'll speak well.

I would be forgetful indeed, Agathon, said Socrates, if, after
b   seeing your courage and self-confidence in going up on the stage
with the actors and looking out on so great an audience, about to
exhibit your own play and in no way at all disconcerted, I now
thought you'd be thrown into confusion because of a few people
like us.

Really, Socrates? said Agathon. You surely don't believe I'm so
full of theater that I don't even know that to a person of good
sense, a few intelligent men are more formidable than many
fools?[204]

c   No, Agathon, I said, I'd hardly do well to think you capable of
anything boorish; I well know that if you met someone whom you
believed wise, you'd give heed to them rather than the multitude.
But maybe we're not they—for after all, we were also there, and
among the multitude—but still, if you met others who are wise,
you'd perhaps feel shame before them, if you thought you were
perhaps doing something shameful. Do you agree?

You're right, he said.

d   But wouldn't you feel shame before the multitude if you thought
you were doing something shameful?

Aristodemus said Phaedrus interrupted and said, My dear Aga-

---

204. See Aristotle *Eudemian Ethics* III 1232b 6*ff.* (trans. Solomon): "The magnan-
imous man would consider rather what one good man thinks than many ordinary
men, as Antiphon after his condemnation said to Agathon when he praised his defense of himself."

thon, if you answer Socrates it will no longer make the slightest difference to him how anything else turns out here, if only he has someone to converse with, especially someone handsome. But though I enjoy hearing Socrates converse, I am necessarily concerned about the encomium of Eros, and I have to exact a speech from each one of you; so the two of you may talk this way only after rendering what is due the god.

e   Why, you're right, Phaedrus, said Agathon, and nothing prevents my speaking; for it will be possible to converse often with Socrates later.

The Speech of Agathon (194e–197e)

I wish first then to say how I must speak, and then to speak. For all who spoke before seem to me not to offer encomium to the god, but to felicitate men for the good things of which the god is to them cause; but of what sort he himself is who gave them, no

195a   one has spoken. There is one right way to praise anyone in anything, namely, to describe in speech the nature of the subject of the speech, and the nature of that of which he is the cause. It is right then for us to praise Eros this way too, first his nature, then his gifts.

I say then that though all gods are happy, Eros, if it is meet and right to say so, is happiest among them, because he is most beautiful and best. He is most beautiful for these reasons: first, Phaedrus, he is youngest of gods. He himself provides a great proof

b   of this account, fleeing old age by flight, though it is clearly quick; at any rate, it comes on us quicker than it should. But Eros by nature hates it and will not go anywhere near it. But he is ever with the young, and he is young; for the ancient account is sound, that "like ever draws near to like." And though I agree with Phaedrus in many other things, I do not agree in this, that Eros is older than Cronos and Iapetus;[205] I claim on the contrary that he is

c   youngest among gods, and ever young, and the ancient affairs of the gods that Hesiod and Parmenides tell, if they were telling the

205. Cf. 178b. Cronus castrated Uranus, his father (cf. 180d), and was put in bonds and fettered by Zeus, his son. Iapetus was a Titan, father of Prometheus and one of the first inhabitants of earth, blasted by Zeus with the thunderbolt (cf. 190c). "Older than Cronus and Iapetus" was a proverbial expression for being really out of date; it is a jibe at Phaedrus, and a conclusion that necessarily follows from his claim that Eros is eldest among gods.

truth, have taken place through Necessity and not through Eros;
for there would have been no castrations and fetterings of each
other nor all that other violence if Eros had been present among
them, but friendship and peace, as there now is since Eros rules
the gods as king.

      He is young, then, and in addition to being young, delicate.
d There is need of a poet such as Homer to show a god's delicacy.
Homer says that Ate, goddess of delusion, is also delicate—her feet
at any rate are delicate—for he says,[206]

> her feet are delicate; for she steps not
> on the ground, but walks upon the heads of men.

So she shows her delicacy, I think, by a pretty proof, because she
walks not on what is hard but on what is soft. But we may also use
e the same proof to show that Eros is delicate: he does not walk on
earth, nor on heads, which are after all not very soft anyway, but
he walks and dwells in the softest things there are. For he makes
his home in the characters and souls of gods and men, though not
in every soul one after another; on the contrary, any soul he comes
upon that is hard in character he leaves, but the soft he dwells in.
So ever touching with his feet and in every way the most soft of
196a softest things, he is necessarily most delicate. He is youngest, then,
and most delicate, and in addition his shape is most supple. For
he could not twine himself round in every direction and through
every soul and yet escape notice when first entering and departing,
if he were hard. His gracefulness, which everyone agrees Eros surpassingly possesses, is a great proof of his well-proportioned and
supple form, for awkwardness and Eros are ever at war with one
another. The god's dwelling among flowers signifies beauty of
b color, for Eros does not pitch his seat in a body or soul or anything
else from which the bloom is faded and gone. But where a place
is well flowered and fragrant, there he takes his seat and abides.

      Concerning the beauty of the god, then, this is sufficient, and
more still remains; but one must next speak about the virtue of
Eros. What is most important is that Eros neither does injustice
to god or man nor suffers injustice from god or man. For if affected by anything, he is himself not affected by violence—vio-
c lence does not touch Eros, nor does he act violently when he acts—
for everyone willingly serves Eros in everything, and what is will-

206. *Iliad* xix 92–93.

ingly agreed by willing parties, "the Laws, kings of our city," hold to be just.[207]

In addition to justice, he partakes of temperance in fullest measure. For it is agreed that temperance is mastery of pleasures and desires, and no pleasure is stronger than Eros; but if weaker, they are mastered by Eros and he masters them, and, as mastering pleasures and desires, Eros would be surpassingly temperate.[208]

d   Again, in respect to courage, "not even Ares withstands"[209] Eros. For Ares does not possess Eros, but Eros Ares—an Eros for Aphrodite, as the story goes[210]—and the possessor is stronger than the possessed. But, mastering him who is most courageous among others, he would be most courageous of all.

Let this be said of the justice and temperance and courage of the god, but it remains to speak of his wisdom: as far as possible, one must leave nothing out. First of all, then, in order that I may in turn honor my own art as Eryximachus honored his, the god e is a poet so wise that he also makes others poets; all whom Eros touches, at any rate, become poets, "even if he was without music before."[211] So we may fittingly use this as proof that Eros is a poet who is, in sum, good in respect to all creation over which the Muses preside; for one could not give someone else or teach another what one neither has nor knows.

197a   Again, who will deny that the creation of all animals is the wisdom of Eros, by whom all animals are born and begotten? But do we not also know in the craftsmanship of the arts that he of whom this god becomes teacher turns out to be notable and illustrious, but he whom Eros leaves untouched remains in the shade? Yes, and surely Apollo invented the arts of archery and medicine and prophecy under the guidance of Eros and desire, so that even he b would be a pupil of Eros, along with the Muses of music and poetry, and Hephaestus in metalworking, and Athena in weaving, and Zeus "in guiding of gods and men." Whence it is then that

207. An early statement of "volunti non fit injuria" as a legal principle—voluntary assumption of risk.
208. Bury compares *Euthydemus* 276c*ff.*, Aristotle *De sophisticis elenchis* 165b 32*ff.* Having identified Eros as mastery of pleasures and desires, Agathon proceeds to identify Eros with the strongest desire.
209. Sophocles, fr. 235, said of Necessity, not Eros.
210. *Odyssey* viii 266*ff.* Aphrodite and Ares were lovers. Hephaestus, her husband, set a trap with chains to catch them in bed, and did catch them, and summoned the other gods to witness their crime. But the gods laughed and envied Ares, chains and all.
211. From Euripides, fr. 663, also quoted in Aristophanes *Wasps* 1074.

the affairs of the gods were arranged when Eros was born among them, Eros for beauty, obviously—for there is no Eros of ugliness—though before that, as I said to begin with, many terrible things occurred among the gods, as is told, through the sovereignty of Necessity. But since this god was born, all good things have come to be from love of beautiful things, both for gods and men.

c   So it seems to me, Phaedrus, that Eros, being himself first, as most beautiful and best, is, next, cause of other such things in others. I am moved to speak in verse, though it is he who composes it:

> Peace among men, waveless calm at sea,
> Rest from winds, slumber for our grief.

d   He empties us of estrangement but fills us with kinship, causing us to come together in all such gatherings as these, in festivals, in dances, in sacrifices a leader; he introduces gentleness, but banishes rudeness; giving of goodwill, ungiving of ill will; gracious, good; gazed upon by the wise, delighted in by the gods; coveted by those without portion, possessed by those of good fortune; father of delicacy, of luxury, of charm, of graciousness, of desire, of longing; caring for good things, uncaring for bad things; in labor,

e   in fear, in longing, in discourse a guide, defender, comrade in arms and best savior; beauty and good order of all gods and men, leader most beautiful and best, whom every man must follow chanting beautifully, sharing the song that he sings, touching with magic power the thought of all gods and men.[212]

There is my speech, Phaedrus, he said. Let it be dedicated to the god. It has a share, some of it, of play, but also of measured seriousness so far as I can provide it.

Fourth Interlude: Two Kinds of Encomium
(198a–199c)

198a   Aristodemus said that after Agathon spoke, everyone in the company applauded, because the young man's speech did so much credit both to himself and to the god. Then, he said, Soc-

---

212. Dover (*Symposium*, p. 124) has analyzed the rhythms of this passage and shown that it consists in metrical units characteristic of Greek lyric poetry.

rates glanced at Eryximachus and said, Well, son of Acumenus, do you think I've been troubled all this while by a groundless fear? Was I not prophetic when I said just now that Agathon would speak wonderfully and I would be at a loss?

You were prophetic in the one thing, I think, said Eryximachus—that Agathon would speak well. But as to you being at a loss, I doubt it.

b   And how am I not to be at a loss, dear friend, said Socrates, both I and anyone else who intends to speak after so beautiful and varied a speech? The other parts were wonderful, but not equal to the end: who could fail to be astonished at hearing the beauty of its words and phrases? Since I realize I will not be able to say anything nearly as beautiful as this myself, I'd leave and run away
c   for very shame if I could. Actually, the speech reminded me of Gorgias, so that I experienced exactly what Homer described: I was afraid that Agathon at the conclusion of his speech would send up the head of Gorgias, formidable in speaking, against my speech, and turn me to mute stone.[213] And then I realized how ridiculous I was to agree to take turns with you in offering an
d   encomium to Eros, to claim I was clever in the things of love when actually I knew nothing about how one should offer any sort of encomium at all. For in my foolishness I supposed one should tell the truth about each thing praised, and this should be the basis for picking out from that the most beautiful things and putting them in the most suitable way; I was overly confident that I would speak well because I knew the truth about how to praise things. But it turns out, it seems, that fine praise is not this at all, but
e   consists in ascribing the highest and most beautiful attributes to a thing whether it has them or not; it really doesn't matter if it's false.[214] For it was earlier proposed, it seems, not that each of us should offer an encomium of Eros, but that each of us should seem to offer an encomium to him. That's why, I suppose, you stir up every kind of story and apply it to Eros, and claim he is of such sort and cause of such great things, so that he may appear as beau-
199a   tiful and good as possible; and clearly to those who do not know him—not, surely, to those who do—your praise is beautiful and impressive. But I really didn't know the manner of praise, and not knowing, I agreed with you to take my turn in praising too. So,

213. *Odyssey* xi 632–635. Socrates puns on Gorgon/Gorgias: according to Pindar, the sight of the head of the Gorgon Medusa turned men to stone.
214. Cf. *Menexenus* 234c–235c, *Phaedrus* 272a.

"the tongue swore, but not the mind."[215] But let it go. For I don't any longer offer encomium in this manner—indeed, I cannot—

b but I'm nevertheless willing to tell you the truth in my own way if you wish, though not in competition with your speeches so that I may not incur your laughter. Consider then, Phaedrus,[216] whether there is really any need for a speech of this kind, to hear the truth spoken about Eros in such words and arrangement of phrases as may happen to occur.[217]

Well, Aristodemus said that Phaedrus and the others bid him speak in whatever way he thought he should.

Why then, Phaedrus, Socrates said, please let me ask Agathon just a few small questions still, so that I may speak thus after getting his agreement.

c Why, I do permit it, said Phaedrus. Ask your questions.

The Speech of Socrates (199c–212c):
The Elenchus of Agathon (199c–201c)

After this, then, Aristodemus said, Socrates began somewhat as follows:

Really, my dear Agathon, I thought you introduced your speech beautifully when you said it would first be necessary to show of what sort Eros is, and his works afterward. I like that beginning very much. Come then, since you've explained of what sort Eros is so beautifully and imposingly in other respects, tell me this too:

d is Eros of such sort as to be love of something or of nothing? I'm not asking if he is of some mother or father—the question whether Eros is love of mother or father would be absurd—but as if I were asking about father by itself, Is father father of something or not? You would doubtless tell me, if you wished to answer properly, that father is father of son or daughter. Not so?

Of course, said Agathon.

And so similarly for mother?

He agreed to that too.

e Then answer still a bit further, said Socrates, so that you may

215. Euripides *Hippolytus* 612.

216. Socrates turns to Phaedrus because he is acting as master of ceremonies (194d), and Agathon addressed his speech to him (195a).

217. Socrates throughout this passage parallels the introduction to his speech of defense in the *Apology* (17b–c), anticipating the many parallels to the *Apology* in the speech of Alcibiades.

better understand what I mean. Suppose I asked, Really? Is
brother, what this is by itself, brother of something or not?

It is, he said.

Namely, of brother or sister?

He agreed.

Then try and tell about Eros as well, he said. Is Eros love of
nothing, or of something?

Of something, surely.

200a   Keep in mind what that something is. But tell me this: Does Eros
of that of which he is love desire it, or not?

Of course, he said.

Does he have the very thing he desires and loves and then desire
and love it, or does he not have it?

It seems likely he does not have it, he said.

But consider whether it isn't necessarily so, instead of only likely,
said Socrates, that what desires, desires what it lacks, or does not
b   desire if it does not lack? For that seems remarkably necessary to
me, Agathon. How about you?

I think so too, he said.

Excellent. Then could anyone, being large, wish to be large or,
being strong, strong?

Impossible, from what has been agreed.

No, for he surely could not lack these things, which he is.

True.

For if being strong he could wish to be strong, said Socrates,
and being quick, quick, and being healthy, healthy—for one perhaps might suppose in these and all such cases that those who are
c   of this sort and have these things also desire the things they have,
and I mention this so that we may not be misled—for in these
cases, if you think about it, Agathon, he necessarily at present has
each of the things he has, whether he wishes or not, and who could
possibly desire that? Whenever someone says, "Being healthy I
also wish to be healthy, being wealthy I also wish to be wealthy,
and I desire the very things I have," we'd say to him, Sir, being in
d   possession of wealth and health and strength, you wish also to
possess them in future, since at least at present you have them
whether you wish or not. So when you say, "I desire things that
are present," consider whether you mean anything except, "I wish
things now present also to remain present in future." Can he do
other than agree?

He said Agathon assented.

So Socrates said, Then this is to love that which is not yet at hand for him and what he does not yet have, namely, that these things be preserved and present to him in future.

e   Of course, he said.

And so he and everyone else who desires, desires that which is not at hand and which is not present, and what he does not have, and what he himself is not, and what he lacks—desire and Eros are of such things as these.

Of course, he said.

Come then, said Socrates. Let us recapitulate what has been said. Is it not that Eros in the first place is *of* something, and next, of those things of which a lack is present to it?

201a   Yes, he said.

Then next recall of what things you said Eros is in your speech. If you wish, I'll remind you. I think you said something to the effect that affairs are arranged by the gods by reason of love of beautiful things; for there would be no love of the ugly.[218] Didn't you say something like that?

I did, said Agathon.

Yes, my friend, and very properly too, said Socrates. And if this is so, would Eros be anything except love of beauty, but not of ugliness?

He agreed.

b   Now, it is agreed that he loves what he lacks and does not have?

Yes, he said.

So Eros lacks and does not have beauty.

Necessarily, he said.

Really? Do you say that what lacks beauty and in no way possesses beauty is beautiful?

Of course not.

Then do you still agree that Eros is beautiful, if these things are so?

And Agathon said, Very likely I didn't know what I was talking about then, Socrates.

c   And yet you spoke so beautifully, Agathon. But a small point still: don't you think good things are also beautiful?

I do.

So if Eros is lack of beautiful things, and good things are beautiful, he would also lack good things.

218. Socrates recalls Agathon's remark at 197b.

He said, I cannot contradict you, Socrates. Let it be as you say. My beloved Agathon, it is the truth you cannot contradict, since it's surely not hard to contradict Socrates.

The Speech of Diotima (201d–212a): Eros as Intermediate (201d–202d)

d   And now I'll let you[219] go. But the account of Eros I once heard from a Mantinaean woman, Diotima, who was wise in this and many other things—she once caused the Athenians, when they offered sacrifices before the Plague,[220] a ten-year delay in the onset of the disease, and it was she who instructed me in the things of love—well, the account she used to give I will myself try to describe to you[221] on my own, from the agreements which Agathon and I have reached, as best I can.

It is necessary then, Agathon, as you explained, first to recount
e   who Eros is and of what sort, and his works afterwards.[222] Now, I think I can most easily recount it as she used to do in examining me. For I used to say pretty much the same sort of thing to her that Agathon was saying now to me, that Eros would be a great god, but of beautiful things; but she refuted me by these arguments I offered him, that Eros by my account would be neither beautiful nor good.

And I said, How do you mean, Diotima? Eros then is ugly and bad?

And she said, Hush, don't blaspheme! Or do you suppose that whatever is not beautiful is necessarily ugly?
202a   Yes, of course.

And not wise, ignorant? Are you not aware that there is something intermediate between wisdom and ignorance?

What is it?

Don't you know, she said, that right opinion without ability to render an account is not knowledge—for how could an unaccountable thing be knowledge?—nor is it ignorance—for how

219. Singular, addressed to Agathon.
220. In 430 B.C. See Thucydides II 47.
221. Plural. Socrates is now addressing the company.
222. Socrates loosely repeats Agathon's formula at 195a, but with significant emphasis on who Eros is (τίς ἐστιν).

could what meets with what is be ignorance? Right opinion is surely that sort of thing, intermediate between wisdom and ignorance.

True, I said.

b   Then don't compel what is not beautiful to be ugly, nor what is not good to be bad. So too for Eros, since you yourself agree that he is neither good nor beautiful, do not any the more for that reason suppose he must be ugly and bad, she said, but rather something between these two.

And yet, I said, everybody agrees he is a great god.

You mean everybody who doesn't know, or also those who know? she said.

Why, absolutely everybody.

She laughed and said, And how would he be agreed to be a great c   god, Socrates, by those who say he is not even a god at all?

Who are these people, I said.

You're one, she said, and I'm another.

And I said, How can you say that?

Easily, she replied. For tell me: don't you claim that all gods are happy and beautiful? Or would you dare deny that any god is beautiful and happy?

Emphatically not, I said.

But you say that it is those who possess good and beautiful things who are happy?

Of course.

d   Moreover, you have agreed that Eros, by reason of lack of good and beautiful things, desires those very things he lacks.

Yes, I have.

How then would what is without portion of[223] beautiful and good things be a god?

In no way, it seems.

Then you see, she said, that even you do not acknowledge Eros to be a god?

Then what is he? I said. A mortal?

Hardly.

But what, then?

As I said before, she said, intermediate between mortal and immortal.

223. ἄμοιρος, an unusual word used by Agathon at 197d; cf. 181.

Eros as Daimon (202d–203a)

What is he, Diotima?

A great divinity, Socrates; for in fact, the whole realm of divinities is intermediate between god and mortal.

e   Having what power? I said.

Interpreting and conveying things from men to gods and things from gods to men, prayers and sacrifices from the one, commands and requitals in exchange for sacrifices from the other, since, being in between both, it fills the region between both so that the All is bound together with itself. Through this realm moves all prophetic art and the art of priests having to do with sacrifices
203a and rituals and spells, and all power of prophecy and enchantment. God does not mingle with man, but all intercourse and conversation of gods with men, waking and sleeping, are through this realm. He who is wise about such things as this is a divine man, but he who is wise about any other arts or crafts is a mere mechanic.[224] These divinities, then, are many and manifold, and one of them is Eros.

The Myth of Poros and Penia (203a–e)

Who is father and mother?[225] I said.

b   It's a rather long story, she replied; nevertheless, I will tell you. When Aphrodite was born, the gods banqueted, both the others and Poros, Resourcefulness, son of Metis, Wisdom. When they dined, Penia, Want, came to beg, as one would expect when there is a feast, and hung about the doors. Well, Poros got drunk on nectar—for there was as yet no wine—and went into the garden of Zeus where, weighed down by drink, he slept. So Penia plotted to have a child by Poros by reason of her own resourcelessness,
c   and lay with him and conceived Eros. This is why Eros has been a follower and servant of Aphrodite, because he was begotten on the day of her birth,[226] and at the same time it is why he is by nature a lover of beauty, since Aphrodite is beautiful.

224. Cf. *Republic* VI 495d–e.
225. The question arises from the fact that Eros is a "divinity," and so either a god or a child of gods.
226. Dover, *Symposium,* remarks on this passage: "Hesiod's injunction (*WD* 735 f.) 'do not beget offspring when you have come home from a funeral, but from a festival of the immortals,' shows the existence of a belief in some kind of connection between the character or fortunes of a child and the occasion of his or her conception."

Because then Eros is son of Poros and Penia, this is his fortune: first, he is ever poor, and far from being delicate and beautiful, as most people suppose,[227] he on the contrary is rough and hard

d   and homeless and unshod, ever lying on the ground without bedding, sleeping in doorsteps and beside roads under the open sky. Because he has his mother's nature, he dwells ever with want. But on the other hand, by favor of his father, he ever plots for good and beautiful things, because he is courageous, eager and intense, and clever hunter ever weaving some new device, desiring understanding and capable of it, a lover of wisdom through the whole of life, clever at enchantment, a sorcerer and a sophist.[228] And he

e   is by nature neither mortal nor immortal, but sometimes on the same day he lives and flourishes, whenever he is full of resource, but then he dies and comes back to life again by reason of the nature of his father, though what is provided ever slips away so that Eros is never rich nor at a loss . . .

Eros as Philosopher (203e–204c)

. . . and on the other hand he is between wisdom and ignorance. For things stand thus: no god loves wisdom or desires to become

204a   wise—for he is so; nor, if anyone else is wise, does he love wisdom. On the other hand, neither do the ignorant love wisdom nor desire to become wise; for ignorance is difficult just in this, that though not beautiful and good, nor wise, it yet seems to itself to be sufficient. He who does not think himself in need does not desire what he does not think he lacks.

Then who are these lovers of wisdom, Diotima, I said, if they are neither the wise nor the ignorant?

b   Why, at this point it's clear even to a child, she said, that they are those intermediate between both of these, and that Eros is among them. For wisdom is surely among the most beautiful of things, but Eros is love of the beautiful, so Eros is necessarily a philosopher, a lover of wisdom, and, being a philosopher, intermediate between wisdom and ignorance. His birth is the cause of this too: for he is of a wise and resourceful father, but of an unwise and resourceless mother.

227. And as Agathon did, 195c 7.
228. Diotima is herself said to be "most wise," and her mode or reply compared to "an accomplished sophist" at 208b–c.

This then is the nature of the divinity, my dear Socrates; but
c   there is nothing surprising about what you thought Eros is. You
thought, as I gather from what you say, that Eros is what is loved,
not the loving. That is why, I think, Eros seemed utterly beautiful
to you. In fact, it is what is beloved that is really beautiful and
charming and perfect and deemed blessed; but loving has this
other character, of the sort I described.

Eros as Wish for Happiness (204c–205a)

And I said: Very well then, my dear lady; you speak beautifully.
But if Eros is of this sort, what usefulness does he have for men?
d   That's the next thing I will try to teach you, Socrates, she said.
For since Eros is of this sort and this parentage, he is of beautiful
things, as you say. But suppose someone asked us, Why is Eros of
beautiful things, Socrates and Diotima? I will ask still more clearly:
Why does he who loves, love beautiful things?
And I replied, To possess them for himself.
But the answer still longs for the following kind of question, she
said: What will he have who possesses beautiful things?
I still can't quite readily answer that question, I said.
e   But suppose someone changed "beautiful" to "good," she said,
and then inquired: Come, Socrates, he who loves, loves good
things. Why does he love them?
To possess them for himself.
And what will he have who possesses good things?
This I can answer more easily, I said. He will be happy.
205a   Yes, she said, for the happy are happy by possession of good
things, and there is no need in addition to ask further for what
purpose he who wishes to be happy wishes it. On the contrary, the
answer seems final.
True, I replied.

Diotima's Definition of Eros (205a–206a)

Do you think this wish and this love are common to all men, and
that everyone wishes to possess good things for themselves forever?
Yes, I said: it is common to everyone.
b   Why is it then, Socrates, she said, that we do not say that every-

one loves, if indeed everyone loves the same things, and always, but we rather say that some love and some do not?

I'm also surprised myself, I said.

Don't be, she said. It is because we subtract a certain species of eros and name it Eros, applying the name of the whole, but we use other names for the others.

As what? I said.

As this. You know that making [poiesis] is something manifold; for surely the cause of passing from not being into being for anything whatever is all a making, so that the productions of all the arts are makings, and the practitioners of them are all makers [poietai].

True.

But nevertheless, she said, you know that they are not called makers [poietai] but have other names, while from all making one single part has been subtracted, that concerned with music[229] and meter, and given the name of the whole. For this alone is called poetry [poiesis], and those who have this part of making are called poets [poietai].

True, I said.

So also then for Eros. In general, it is every desire for good things and happiness, "Eros most great, and wily[230] in all"; but those who turn to him in various other ways, either money-making or athletics or philosophy, are neither said to love nor to be lovers, while those who sedulously pursue one single species get the name of the whole, Eros, and are said to love and be lovers.

Very likely true, I said.

Yes, and a certain story is told, she said, that those in love are seeking the other half of themselves. But my account is that love is of neither half nor whole, my friend, unless it happens to be actually good, since people are willing to cut off their own hands and feet if they think these possessions of theirs are bad. For they each refuse, I think, to cleave even to what is their own, unless one calls what is good kindred and his own, and what is bad alien;[231] because there is nothing else that men love than the good. Do you agree?

229. μουσική (scilicet τέχνη) was any art over which the Muses preside, but especially poetry, which was sung. Cf. *Republic* II 376e.

230. δολερός. The adjective is otherwise rare in Plato, but applied at *Hippias Minor* 365c to Odysseus. See above, 203d.

231. Cf. *Lysis* 210b–c, 221d–222e.

206a   I most certainly do, I said.

Then one may state without qualification that men love the good? she said.

Yes, I said.

Really? Is it not to be added, she said, that they also love the good to be their own?

It must.

And not only to be theirs, she said, but also to be theirs forever?

This too is to be added.

In sum, then, she said, Eros is of the good, being his own forever.

Very true, I replied.

The Works of Eros: Begetting in Beauty
(206b–207a)

b   Then given that Eros is ever this, she said, in what way, and in what activity, would eagerness and effort among those pursuing it be called Eros? What does this work happen to be? Can you say?

No, I said. If I could, I would not admire your wisdom so much, Diotima, and keep coming to you to learn these very things.

But I will tell you, she said: this work is begetting[232] in beauty, in respect to both the body and the soul.

What you say needs divination, I said, and I don't understand.

c   Why, I'll put it more clearly, she said. All men are pregnant in respect to both the body and the soul, Socrates, she said, and when they reach a certain age, our nature desires to beget.[233] It cannot beget in ugliness, but only in beauty. The intercourse of man and woman is a begetting. This is a divine thing, and pregnancy and procreation are an immortal element in the mortal living creature.

d   It is impossible for birth to take place in what is discordant. But ugliness is in discord with all that is divine, and beauty concordant. So the Goddess of Beauty is at the birth Moira, Fate, and Eilithyia, She Who Comes in Time of Need. That is why, when what is pregnant draws near to the beautiful, it becomes tender and full of gladness and pours itself forth and begets and procreates; but when it draws near to the ugly, it shrivels in sullen grief and turns away and goes slack and does not beget, but carries with difficulty

232. Or bearing children, τόκος.
233. τίκτειν, the verb of which τόκος is the corresponding noun.

the conception within it. Whence it is that one who is pregnant and already swollen is vehemently excited over the beautiful, be-

e   cause it releases its possessor from great pangs. For Socrates, she said, Eros is not, as you suppose, of the beautiful.

But what, then?

It is of procreation and begetting of children in the beautiful. Very well, I said.

To be sure, she said. But why of procreation? Because procreation is everlasting and immortal as far as is possible for something

207a   mortal. Eros necessarily desires immortality with the good, from what has been agreed,[234] since its object is to possess the good for itself forever. It necessarily follows from this account, then, that Eros is also love of immortality.

Immortality and the Mortal Nature (207a–208b)

All these things she taught me at various times when she discoursed about matters of love. Once she asked, Socrates, what do you think is cause of this love and desire? Or are you not aware how strangely all beasts are disposed, footed and winged, when

b   they desire to reproduce—all sick and erotically disposed, first for intercourse with each other and next for the nurture of the offspring? In their behalf the weakest are ready to do battle with the strongest, to die in their behalf,[235] to be racked with hunger themselves so as to feed them, to do anything else. One might suppose, she said, that men do these things on the basis of reflection; but what is the cause of beasts being erotically disposed this way? Can you tell?

c   And I again used to say I didn't know.

She said, Then do you think you'll ever become skilled in the things of love if you don't understand this?

Why, that's why I keep coming to you, Diotima, as I just now said,[236] knowing I need instruction. Please tell me the cause of this, and other things concerning matters of love.

If then you are persuaded, she said, that love is by nature of what we have often agreed, do not be surprised. For here, in the

d   animal world, by the same account as before, the mortal nature

234. 206a.
235. Compare Phaedrus's speech, 179b.
236. 206b.

seeks so far as it can to exist forever and be immortal. It can do so only in this way, by giving birth, ever leaving behind a different new thing in place of the old, since even in the time in which each single living creature is said to live and to be the same—for example, as a man is said to be the same from youth to old age—though he never has the same things in himself, he nevertheless is called the same, but he is ever becoming new while otherwise perishing, in respect to hair and flesh and bone and blood and the entire body.

e   And not only in respect to the body but also in respect to the soul,[237] its character and habits, opinions, desires, pleasures, pains, fears are each never present in each man as the same, but
208a   some are coming to be, others perishing. Much more extraordinary still, not only are some kinds of knowledge coming to be and others perishing in us, and we are never the same even in respect to the kinds of knowledge, but also each single one among the kinds of knowledge is affected in the same way. For what is called studying exists because knowledge leaves us; forgetting is departure of knowledge, but study, by introducing again a new memory in place of what departs, preserves the knowledge so that it seems to be the same.[238]

       For it is in this way that all that is mortal is preserved: not by
b   being ever completely the same, like the divine, but by leaving behind, as it departs and becomes older, a different new thing of the same sort as it was. By this device, Socrates, she said, what is mortal has a share of immortality both body and everything else; but what is immortal by another device. Do not be surprised, then, if everything by nature values its own offshoot; it is for the sake of immortality that this eagerness and love attend upon all.

Creation in Respect to Body and Soul
(208b–209e)

       When I heard this account I was surprised and said, Why really, my most wise Diotima, are these things actually true?
c   And she replied as the accomplished sophists do, Know it well, Socrates. Since indeed if you will look to the love of honor among

237. Application of the claim to the second case distinguished at 206b.
238. Compare Aristotle's account of perception, memory, and experience at *Metaphysics* I 980a 29ff., *Posterior Analytics* II 99b 35ff.

men, you'd be surprised by the unreasonableness of which I've spoken, unless you keep in mind and reflect on how strangely disposed men are by Eros to make a name and "lay up store of immortal glory for everlasting time"; for this they are ready to run

d every risk, even more than for their children, to spend money, to perform labors of every sort, to die for it. Do you think, she said, that Alcestis would have died for Admetus, or Achilles after Patroclus, or our own Cadmus for his children's kingdoms, if they had not thought the fame of their own virtue, which we now cherish, would be immortal?[239] Far from it, she said; rather, I think, it is for immortal virtue and the sort of fame which brings glory that everyone does everything, and the more insofar as they are better.

e For they love the immortal.

Some men are pregnant in respect to their bodies, she said, and turn more to women and are lovers in that way, providing in all future time, as they suppose, immortality and happiness for themselves through getting children. Others are pregnant in respect to

209a their soul—for there are those, she said, who are still more fertile in their souls than in their bodies with what it pertains to soul to conceive and bear. What then so pertains? Practical wisdom and the rest of virtue—of which, indeed, all the poets are procreators, and as many craftsmen as are said to be inventors. But the greatest and most beautiful kind of practical wisdom by far, she said, is that concerned with the right ordering of cities and households, for which the name is temperance and justice.

On the other hand, whenever one of them is pregnant of soul

b from youth, being divine,[240] and reaches the age when he then desires to bear and beget, he too then, I think, goes about seeking the beautiful in which he might beget; for he will never beget in the ugly. Now, because he is fertile, he welcomes beautiful rather than ugly bodies, and should he meet with a beautiful and noble and naturally gifted soul, he welcomes the conjunction of both even more, and to this person he is straightway resourceful in speaking about virtue, and what sort of thing the good man must be concerned with and his pursuits; and he undertakes to educate him.

239. Diotima here contradicts Phaedrus's speech (179b–180a), arguing that Alcestis and Achilles sacrificed themselves not for love, but for love of honor, in order to be remembered.

240. Reading θεῖος with BTW Oxy. and Bury, against Parmentier's emendation ἤθεος, accepted by Burnet and Dover. The reading is supported by *Meno* 99c–d and anticipated by 206c.6.

c   For I think that in touching the beautiful [person] and holding
familiar intercourse with it [him], he bears and begets what he has
long since conceived, and both present and absent he remembers
and nurtures what has been begotten in common with that
[him],[241] so that people of this sort gain a far greater communion
with each other than that of the sharing of children, and a more
steadfast friendship, because they have held in common children
more beautiful and more immortal. Everyone would prefer for
himself to have had such children as these, rather than the human

d   kind, and they look to Homer and Hesiod and the rest of our good
poets and envy offspring of the sort they left behind, offspring
which, being such themselves, provide immortal fame and remembrance.

But if you wish, she said, look at the sort of children Lycurgus
left behind in Sparta, saviors of Sparta and, one might almost say,
of Greece.[242] Solon also is honored among you because of his begetting of the Laws,[243] and other men in other times and many

e   other places, both in Greece and among the barbarians, who have
displayed many beautiful deeds and begotten every sort of virtue;
for whom, also, many temples and sacred rites have come into
being because of children such as these, but none because of children merely human.

The Ladder of Love (209e–210e)

Into these things of love, Socrates, perhaps even you may be

210a   initiated; but I do not know whether you can be initiated into the
rites of and revelations for the sake of which these actually exist
if one pursues them correctly. Well, I will speak of them and spare
no effort, she said; try to follow if you can.

It is necessary, she said, for him who proceeds rightly to this
thing to begin while still young by going to beautiful bodies; and
first, if his guide[244] guides rightly, to love one single body and beget

241. This sentence is purposefully ambiguous: it refers to the beloved, but also
anticipates what will be said in the Greater Mysteries of Eros about Beauty itself.

242. Diotima speaks as a native of Mantinea, located in the Peloponnesus and
allied with Sparta. Lycurgus, like Solon in Athenas, was supposed to have given laws
to Sparta, and those laws are here regarded as his children.

243. The Laws of Athens were often referred to as the Laws of Solon, though
there had been (sometimes unacknowledged) changes since his time. Plato was a di-
rect and lineal descendant of Solon.

244. Cf. 210c, e, 211c.

there beautiful discourses; next, to recognize that the beauty on
b   any body whatever is akin to that on any other body, and if it is
necessary to pursue the beautiful as it attaches to form, it is quite
unreasonable to believe that the beauty on all bodies is not one
and the same. Realizing this, he is constituted a lover of all beautiful bodies and relaxes this vehemence for one, looking down on
it and believing it of small importance.

After this he must come to believe that beauty in souls is more
to be valued than that in the body, so that even if someone good
c   of soul has but a slight bloom, it suffices for him, and he loves and
cares and begets and seeks those sorts of discourses that will make
the young better, in order that he may be constrained in turn to
contemplate what is beautiful in practices and laws and to see that
it is in itself all akin to itself, in order that he may believe bodily
beauty a small thing.

After practices, he[245] must lead him to the various branches of
knowledge, in order that he may in turn see their beauty too, and,
d   looking now to the beautiful in its multitude, no longer delight
like a slave, a worthless, petty-minded servant, in the beauty of
one single thing, whether beauty of a young child or man or of
one practice; but rather, having been turned toward the multitudinous ocean of the beautiful and contemplating it, he begets
many beautiful and imposing discourses and thoughts in un-
grudging love of wisdom, until, having at this point grown and
waxed strong, he beholds a certain kind of knowledge which is
e   one, and such that it is the following kind of beauty. Try, she said,
to pay me the closest attention possible.

The Ascent to Beauty Itself (210e–212a)

He who has been educated in the things of love up to this point,
beholding beautiful things rightly and in due order, will then, suddenly, in an instant, proceeding at that point to the end of the
things of love, see something marvelous, beautiful in nature: it is
that, Socrates, for the sake of which in fact all his previous labors
existed.

211a   First, it ever is and neither comes to be nor perishes, nor has it
growth nor diminution.

245. That is, the guide mentioned at 210a.

Again, it is not in one respect beautiful but in another ugly, nor beautiful at one time but not at another, nor beautiful relative to this but ugly relative to that, nor beautiful here but ugly there, as being beautiful to some but ugly to others.[246]

Nor on the other hand will it appear beautiful to him as a face does, or hands, or anything else of which body partakes, nor as any discourse or any knowledge does, nor as what is somewhere in something else, as in an animal, or in earth, or in heaven, or in

b anything else; but it exists in itself alone by itself, single in nature forever, while all other things are beautiful by sharing in *that* in such manner that though the rest come to be and perish, *that* comes to be neither in greater degree nor less and is not at all affected.

But when someone, ascending from things here through the right love of boys,[247] begins clearly to see *that*, the Beautiful, he would pretty well touch the end. For this is the right way to pro-

c ceed in matters of love, or to be led by another[248]—beginning from these beautiful things here, to ascend ever upward for the sake of *that*, the Beautiful, as though using the steps of a ladder, from one to two, and from two to all beautiful bodies, and from beautiful bodies to beautiful practices, and from practices to beautiful studies, and from studies one arrives in the end at *that* study which is nothing other than the study of *that*, the Beautiful itself, and one knows in the end, by itself, what it is to be beautiful. It is there, if

d anywhere, dear Socrates, said the Mantinean Stranger, that human life is to be lived: in contemplating the Beautiful itself. If ever you see it, it will not seem to you as gold or raiment or beautiful boys and youths, which now you look upon dumbstruck; you and many another are ready to gaze on those you love and dwell with them forever, if somehow it were possible, not to eat nor drink but only to watch and be with them.[249]

What then do we suppose it would be like, she said, if it were

e possible for someone to see the Beautiful itself, pure, unalloyed, unmixed, not full of human flesh and colors, and the many other kinds of nonsense that attach to mortality, but if he could behold the divine Beauty itself, single in nature? Do you think it a worth-

246. Or "as being thought beautiful by some but ugly by others." ὡς with participle: Smyth, 2086b; cf. 2996.
247. In contradiction to Pausanias's sexualized pederasty.
248. Cf. 210a, c, e.
249. Diotima directly recalls the speech of Aristophanes, 191a, 192b–d.

212a less life, she said, for a man to look *there* and contemplate *that* with
that by which one must contemplate it,[250] and to be with it? Or are
you not convinced, she said, that there alone it will befall him, in
seeing the Beautiful with that by which it is visible, to beget, not
images of virtue, because he does not touch an image, but true
virtue, because he touches the truth? But in begetting true virtue
and nurturing it, it is given to him to become dear to god, and if
any other among men is immortal, he is too.

Socrates' Peroration (212b–c)

b   These then, Phaedrus and you others, are the things Diotima
said, and I am persuaded. Being persuaded, I try also to persuade
others that one would not easily get a better partner for our human nature in acquiring this possession than Eros. Therefore I
say that every man should honor Eros, and I myself honor and
surpassingly devote myself to the things of love and summon others to do so; now and always, I praise the power and courage of
c   Eros so far as I am able. Consider this speech then, Phaedrus, if
you will, an encomium to Eros, or if you prefer, name it what you
please.

After Socrates said this, the rest praised him, but Aristophanes
tried to say something, because Socrates in speaking alluded to his
own speech.[251]

Interlude: The Arrival of Alcibiades (212c–215a)

And suddenly, there was a loud knocking at the courtyard door,
as of revelers, and they heard the voice of a flute-girl.

d   So Agathon said, Boys, won't you see about it? And if it's one
of our friends, invite him in; if not, say that we're not drinking
but about to retire.

A moment later we heard in the courtyard the voice of Alcibiades, very drunk and shouting loudly, asking, Where is Agathon? and saying, Take me to Agathon. So they led him in to us,
the flute-girl supporting him, with certain others of his followers,
e   and he stood in the doorway crowned with a bushy wreath of ivy

250. That is, by mind or intelligence. See *Republic* VI 490a–b, VII 518c, 533c–d.
251. 205e.

and violets[252] and a multitude of fillets[253] on his head, and said,
Greetings, gentlemen. Will you accept a man already quite drunk
as a drinking companion? Or shall we leave after crowning Agathon alone, which is what we came to do? I couldn't come yesterday, he said, but I'm here now, with fillets on, to take a wreath
from my own head and put it on the head of the wisest and most
beautiful man here, if I may so speak of him—will you laugh at
me for being drunk? Even if you do laugh, I still know I speak the
213a   truth. Tell me right now—do I come in on these terms or not?
Will you drink with me or not?

Well, everybody applauded and bid him come in and recline,
and Agathon invited him. And he did come in, led by his retinue,
and because he was untying the fillets to put them on Agathon,
he had them in front of his eyes and didn't see Socrates, but sat
b   down beside Agathon, between him and Socrates, for Socrates
moved over when he saw him. He sat down and embraced Agathon and crowned him.

So Agathon said, Boys, take off Alcibiades' shoes so he can recline as a third here.

By all means, said Alcibiades. But who's our third drinking companion? And at that he turned around, caught sight of Socrates,
jumped up and said, Heracles! What's this! Socrates here! Lying
c   in ambush for me again, suddenly appearing as you usually do
where I least expect you will be. And why do you come now? And
again, why lie here, and not beside Aristophanes or somebody else
who's funny and wishes to be? Instead, you've contrived to lie next
to the most beautiful person in the room.

And Socrates said, See if you can protect me, Agathon; because
my love for this fellow has been no light matter. Ever since I fell
d   in love with him, it's no longer been possible for me even to look
at or talk to a single beautiful person, not even one, or this fellow
here is jealous of me and envious, and does extraordinary things,

252. Ivy was associated with Dionysus, and appropriate to a drunken reveler. Violets were associated with Aphrodite—fittingly enough, as we shall soon see—but also
with Athens itself, "Violet-Crowned." The violets are *Viola hymettia*, the blossoms
bright yellow and white against the dark green of the ivy. At present these violets
bloom in March, and it is customary to identify the month Gamelion, on the twelfth
day of which the Lenaea was celebrated, with January—the nights were long (223c).
But the Athenian solar-lunar year made the dates of months in relation to the year
as variable as Easter now is, and the presence of violets in the crown of Alcibiades
indicates the first stirrings of spring.
253. Headbands or ribbons worn in sign of victory or sacrifice to the god.

upbraiding me and only just restraining himself from laying both hands on me. See to it then that he doesn't also start something now; reconcile us, or if he tries to use force, protect me, because I very much tremble at his madness and his love for having lovers.

Why, it's impossible to reconcile you and me, said Alcibiades. But I'll exact a penalty from you for that another time. Right now,

e   Agathon, he said, give me back some of those fillets, so that I may crown his head too, this wonderful head, and he won't blame me because I crowned you when he is victorious in speech over all mankind, not only the other day as you were, but always, and I still didn't crown him.

And with that he took some of the fillets and crowned Socrates, and lay down.

After he had laid down, he said, Very well then, gentlemen. It seems to me you're sober. We can't have that, so drink up; for that was our agreement. I choose to take charge of the drinking myself until you've drunk enough. If there is a big wine bowl, Agathon, let it be brought. No, that's unnecessary. Boy, he said, observing that it held more than eight cups, Bring that wine cooler here instead.[254]

214a   When it was filled, he drank it down first and then ordered them to pour again for Socrates, and at the same time said, My piece of cleverness won't work for Socrates, gentlemen. He'll drink as much as one bids and never be a bit more drunk for it.

Well, after the boy poured, Socrates drank.

Eryximachus said, What are we doing, Alcibiades? Aren't we

b   going to say something over the cup, or sing something? Do we simply drink up as if we were thirsty?

So Alcibiades said, Hello there, Eryximachus, most excellent son of a most excellent and most temperate father.

Hello to you too, said Eryximachus. But what do we do?

Whatever you say. One must after all obey you: "For a healer is a man worth many others."[255] So command what you wish.

Listen then, said Eryximachus. Before you came, it seemed best that each of us, from left to right, should give the most beautiful

c   speech about Eros he could and offer an encomium. The rest of us have all spoken; but since you haven't and you've finished your drink, you ought to speak too. Once you've done so, you can pre-

---

254. Wine was always drunk mixed with water; the wine was kept in a cooler before being mixed. Alcibiades is calling for approximately two quarts of wine, straight.
255. *Iliad* xi 514.

scribe for Socrates as you wish, and he for the man on his right, and so on for the rest.

Why, Eryximachus, said Alcibiades, that's a beautiful suggestion, but perhaps it isn't fair to compare a drunken man to the speeches of the sober. At the same time, my friend, do you believe

d   anything Socrates just now said? Don't you know it's all just the opposite of what he was saying? Because he's the one who won't keep his two hands off me if I praise anyone in his presence, either a god or a man other than him.

What a thing to say! said Socrates.

By Poseidon, said Alcibiades, don't add another word, because I couldn't praise one other person with you present.

Why, if you wish, do that, said Eryximachus. Praise Socrates.

e   Do you mean it? said Alcibiades. Do you think I should, Eryximachus? Should I punish the man and inflict a penalty on him in front of you?

Whoa! said Socrates. What have you got in mind? To praise me in order to poke fun at me? Is that what you'll do?

I'll tell the truth. Just see if you allow it.

Why certainly I allow the truth, he said, and I insist you tell it.

I can hardly wait to start, said Alcibiades. But you must do this: if I say anything untrue, interrupt me right in the middle, if you wish, and say that I said it falsely; for I won't willingly say anything

215a   false. If, however, in recollecting, I say one thing here and another there, don't be surprised; because it's no easy thing for someone in my condition to enumerate your peculiarities fluently and in good order.

The Speech of Alcibiades (215a–222b)
Praise by Images (215a–216c)

I will undertake to praise Socrates in this way, gentlemen, through images. Perhaps he'll think it's to poke fun at him, but the image will be for the sake of truth, not laughter.

I say that Socrates is exactly like those silenes sitting in the stat-

b   uary shops, the kind the craftsmen manufacture holding flutes or pipes, but when opened in the middle, they prove to hold within them images of gods. And I say on the other hand that he is like the satyr Marsyas.[256]

---

256. Silenus appears in early Attic vase painting as a shaggy bearded man, with

That at least you look like them, Socrates, surely not even you yourself would dispute.[257] But next hear how you're like them in other ways too. You're outrageous.[258] No? Because if you don't agree I'll offer witnesses. But you're not a flutist? Yes, and one far
c   more marvelous than Marsyas. He charmed people by the power of his mouth, using instruments, and those who play his music do so even now; for I claim that what Olympus used to play belonged to Marsyas—Marsyas was his teacher—but whether played by a good flutist or a worthless flute-girl, his music alone causes possession and reveals, because it is divine, those who need the gods and rites of initiation.

You differ from him only in this, that you accomplish the same thing by bare words without instruments. When we hear some
d   other speaker, at any rate, even quite a good orator, speaking other words, it hardly matters to anyone at all; but when someone hears you or someone else repeating your words, then even if the speaker is quite worthless and whether it be man, woman, or child who hears, we are amazed and possessed. At any rate, gentlemen, if I weren't in danger of seeming completely drunk, I'd state to you on oath how I've been affected by his words, how I'm still
e   affected even now. For when I hear him my heart leaps up, much more than those affected by the music of the Corybantes,[259] and tears flow at his words—and I see many another affected the same way too.

I heard Pericles and other good orators and I believe they spoke well, but I was not affected at all like this, nor was my soul disturbed and angered at my being in the position of a slave; but due
216a   to this Marsyas here I've often been put in that position, so that

---

the ears and sometimes the legs and tail of a horse, much given to pursuing nymphs. He knows important secrets, and if he is caught he can sometimes be forced to tell, but he was also associated with drunkenness, bestiality, and the worship of Dionysus.

Satyrs are very like silenes, but usually young rather than old, and they took from Pan the attributes of a goat. By the time they appear in satyr plays, such as Euripides' *Cyclops* and Sophocles' *Ichneutae*, they are clearly human beings, with attributes of horses or, in Sophocles, perhaps of dogs.

Marsyas was a satyr who in his hubris competed in music with Apollo, and was worsted and flayed alive for his presumption.

257. Socrates had a snub nose and protruding eyes. *Theaetetus* 143e.

258. Recalling Agathon's challenge. Agathon had said exactly the same thing (175e) in suggesting that Dionysus would decide between himself and Socrates. See also 213c–d, where Socrates in effect brings this charge against Alcibiades, and 214d, where Alcibiades returns it. But see also 219c.

259. Cf. *Ion* 533e–534a, 536c, *Euthydemus* 277d, *Crito* 54d, *Laws* VII 790d.

it seemed to me it was not worth living to be as I am.[260] And this, Socrates, you will not deny to be true.

And still even now, I am conscious that if I were willing to give ear I could not hold out against him; I would suffer the same things. For he compels me to agree that though I am myself much in need, I neglect myself and attend to the affairs of Athens. So I stop my ears by force as if against the Sirens[261] and run away, in order that I may not grow old sitting here beside him. Before him

b alone among men I suffer what one might not have supposed is in me—shame before anyone. Before him alone I feel ashamed. For I am conscious that I cannot contradict him and say it isn't necessary to do what he bids, but when I leave him, I am worsted by the honors of the multitude. So I desert him and flee, and when I see him I am shamed by my own agreements. I'd often gladly

c see him dead, but I'm well aware that if it happened I'd be much more distressed; so I don't know what to do about this man.

Irony and Seduction (216c–219d)

I and many another have been thus affected by the flutings of this satyr. But hear from me how alike he is in other respects to those to whom I compared him, and how wondrous is his power.

d Be assured that not one of you knows him. But I'll reveal him, since I've begun. You see how erotically disposed Socrates is toward handsome people, and always around them, and smitten; and on the other hand that he is ignorant of everything and knows nothing. As to his appearance—isn't it Silenus-like? Of course it is. His outside covering is like a carved statue of Silenus, but when he is opened, gentlemen and drinking companions, can you guess how he teems with temperance within? Do you know that it doesn't matter to him in the slightest if someone is beautiful, that he despises it to a degree one could scarcely imagine—or if someone is

e wealthy or has any other distinction counted fortunate by the multitude? He thinks all these possessions are worthless and that we are nothing, I assure you, but he is sly and dishonest and spends his whole life playing with people. Yet, I don't know whether any-

260. Cf. 211d.
261. As Odysseus stopped the ears of his crew with wax and had himself lashed to the mast, so that they would not hear the Sirens' song and stay with them (*Odyssey* xii 37–54, 154–200). Alcibiades is an example of Aristotle's ἀκρατής, the incontinent man: he knows what is good, but acts otherwise. For incontinence as to honor, see *Nicomachean Ethics* VII 1147b 29–35.

one else has seen the images within when he is in earnest and opened up, but I saw them once, and I thought they were so divine and golden, so marvelously beautiful, that whatever Socrates might bid must, in short, be done.

217a

Believing he was earnestly pursuing my youthful beauty, I thought it was a stroke of luck and my wonderful good fortune, because by gratifying Socrates I could learn everything he knew; for I was amazingly proud of my vernal bloom. So with this in mind, though previously I wasn't accustomed to be alone with him unattended, I then dismissed my attendant and was with him

b

alone—for I have to tell you the whole truth. Pay attention, Socrates, and if what I say is false, refute me—so we were alone with each other, gentlemen, one on one, and I thought at that point he would converse with me as a lover might converse in private with his beloved, and I rejoiced. But not a bit of it. Instead, he'd converse with me in his usual way, and after spending the day together he'd get up and go away.

c

Next I invited him to exercise with me, and we did; I expected to accomplish something there. Well, he exercised and wrestled with me many times when no one was present. And what must I report? I got no farther.

Since I'd accomplished nothing at all this way, I thought I had to attack the man directly and not give up, since I'd taken the matter in hand; at that point I had to know how things stood. So I invited him to dine, exactly like a lover laying a plan for his beloved. Even in this he didn't yield to me quickly, but in time, he nonetheless obeyed.

d

When he came the first time, he wished to leave after dinner. At that point I was embarrassed and let him go; but I laid plans for him again, and when we had dined I kept on talking far into the night, and when he wished to leave I used the excuse that it was late and made him stay. So he lay down on the couch next to mine, the couch on which he'd dined, and there was no one else sleeping in the room except us.

e

Well, up to this point it would be fit to tell the story to anyone; but from here on you wouldn't hear a word from me if it were not that, first, wine with or without slaves[262] is truthful, as the saying

262. παίδων. The word translated "slaves" is also the word for children, and the underlying proverb probably was "Wine and children are truthful." But slaves, and perhaps others, are present, and asked not to listen (218b). This is dramatic foreshadowing: Plato's audience would have recalled that Alcibiades was to be prosecuted

goes, and next, if it didn't appear wrong in me to continue praising Socrates while concealing his arrogant deed. Then, too, I'm
almost affected like a man who's been bitten by a snake. They say
that anyone who's suffered it is unwilling to tell what it was like
except to those who've been bitten, because they alone will sym-

218a pathize and understand if one was driven to do and say everything
in his pain. Well, I'd been bitten by something more painful, and
in the most painful place one can be bitten—in the heart or soul
or whatever one should name it, struck and bitten by arguments
in philosophy that hold more fiercely than a serpent, when they
take hold of a young and not ill-endowed soul and make him do
and say anything whatever[263]—but again, I see here people like

b Phaedrus and Agathon, Eryximachus and Pausanias and Aristodemus and Aristophanes; and what should be said about Socrates
himself and the rest of you? For you have all shared in philosophical madness and Bacchic frenzy[264]—so listen, all of you; for
you will sympathize with the things then done and now told.

But let the servants, and anyone else profane and vulgar, put
great gates over their ears.

Well, gentlemen, when the lamp was out and the slaves with-

c drew, I thought I shouldn't dissemble but tell him freely what I
thought. And I nudged him and said, Socrates, are you asleep?

Of course not, he said.

Do you know what I think?

What, exactly? he said.

I think that you alone, I said, are worthy to become my lover,
and you appear to shrink from saying it to me. But this is how it
is with me: I believe I'd be very foolish not to gratify you in this,
or if you may need anything else from my estate or my friends.

d For there is nothing more important to me than to become as good
as possible, and I do not think there's anyone who can help me in
this more authoritatively than you. I'd feel much more shame before wise men if I did not gratify such a man than before an ignorant multitude if I did.

during the next year, in 415 B.C., for mocking the Eleusinian Mysteries in the course
of a drunken party, on the evidence of slaves and metics who were present. Thucydides VI 28 1.

263. Here and in what follows there is considerable inconsequentiality—anacol-
outhon—in Alcibiades' speech. He is under considerable emotion, and he is very
drunk. Yet it will be observed that his speech as a whole is beautifully constructed.

264. In the plural, Bacchic orgies. Madness and Bacchic frenzy are, of course,
precisely what, in Socrates' view, philosophy is not.

When he heard this, he said, with the usual sly dishonesty that is typical of him, My dear Alcibiades, you are really not to be taken lightly, if indeed what you say about me happens to be true, and

e there is in me some power through which you might become better; you would then see inconceivable beauty in me, even surpassing your own immense comeliness of form. But if, seeing it, you are trying to strike a bargain with me to exchange beauty for beauty, then you intend to take no slight advantage of me: on the contrary, you are trying to get possession of what is truly beautiful instead of what merely seems so, and really, you intend to trade

219a bronze for gold.[265] But please, dear friend, give it more thought, lest it escape your notice that I am nothing. The sight of the mind begins to see sharply when that of the eyes starts to grow dull; but you're still a long way from that.

I heard this and said, That's how it is with me; I've only said what I think. Since that's so, you yourself must consider whatever you think is best for you and me.

Why, you're right, he replied. We'll in future consider and do

b what appears best to ourselves about these and other things.

In hearing and saying this, I'd loosed my arrows, as it were, and I thought I'd wounded him; I got up without letting him say another word, and I wrapped my own cloak around him—for it was winter—and I lay down on his threadbare coat, and I put my two arms around this genuine divinity, this wonderful man, and lay

c there the whole night through. And again, Socrates, you will not say I speak falsely. But when I did this, he was so contemptuously superior to my youthful bloom that he ridiculed and outrageously insulted it; and in that regard, at least, I thought I was really something, gentlemen and judges—for you are judges of the arrogance of Socrates—for know well, by gods and by goddesses, when I

d arose after having slept with Socrates, it was nothing more than if I'd slept with a father or an elder brother.

Can you imagine my state of mind after that? I considered myself affronted, and yet I admired his nature, his temperance and courage, having met a man of a sort I never thought to meet in respect to wisdom and fortitude. The result was that I could neither get angry and be deprived of his company nor yet find a way

e to win him over. For I well knew he was far more invulnerable to

265. Cf. *Iliad* vi 236, where Glaucus foolishly trades golden armor for bronze.

money than Ajax ever was to iron, and he'd escaped me in the only way I thought he could be caught. So I was at a loss, and I went around enslaved by this man as no one ever was by any other.

Courage and Contemplation (219d–221c)

All this happened to me before, and afterward we served together on the campaign to Potidaea,[266] and we were messmates there. Well, first of all, he not only surpassed me but everyone else in bearing hardship—whenever we got cut off somewhere, as happens on campaign, and had to go without food, the others were nothing in respect to fortitude—but again, in times of good cheer, he alone was able to enjoy them to the full: in particular, though unwilling to drink, he beat everybody else at it when compelled to, and what is most remarkable of all, no man has ever seen Socrates drunk. I think that will be tested right now. Then again, there was his fortitude in winter—the winters there are dreadful. He did other amazing things, but one time there was a truly terrible frost and everybody stayed inside and didn't go out, or if they did they wore an amazing amount of clothes and put on shoes after wrapping their feet in felt and fleeces, but he went around outside among them with the same sort of cloak he was accustomed to wear before, and got around on the ice without shoes more easily than the others did shod. But the soldiers looked askance at him, thinking he despised them.[267]

So much for that. "But here is a task such as that strong man endured and accomplished,"[268] once there on campaign. It's worth hearing. One time at dawn he began to think something over and stood in the same spot considering it, and when he found no solution, he didn't leave but stood there inquiring. It got to be midday, and people became aware of it, wondering at it among themselves, saying Socrates had stood there since dawn thinking about something. Finally some of the Ionians, when evening came, after they'd eaten—it was then summer—carried their bedding out to sleep in the cool air and to watch to see if he'd also stand there all night. He stood until dawn came and the sun rose; then he offered a prayer to the sun, and left.

266. In 432 B.C. Alcibiades would then have been eighteen, Socrates not quite forty.

267. Some of those soldiers doubtless voted at Socrates' trial; the *Symposium,* then, suggests that this was one source of the prejudice against him, one that he himself could scarcely have mentioned.

268. *Odyssey* IV 242 (trans. Richmond Lattimore). Cf. IV 271.

But if you wish, take battles—it is only just to give him this.
Because when the battle occurred after which the generals gave
e   me the award for valor, no other man saved me but him; I was
wounded and he refused to leave, but saved both me and my armor.[269] I told the generals even at the time, Socrates, to give the
award to you, and for this you'll surely neither fault me nor say
I'm not telling the truth. But when the generals wished to give me
the prize for valor out of regard for my rank and station, you yourself were more eager than the generals that I should receive it
instead of you.

Still again, gentlemen, it was worth seeing Socrates when the
221a   army made its disorderly retreat from Delium;[270] I happened to
be mounted, but he was in the heavy infantry. Well, as the men
were scattering, he and Laches together gave ground. I happened
to be nearby, and as soon as I saw them I told them to have courage
and said I wouldn't desert them. But here I could watch Socrates
even better than at Potidaea—for I was myself less afraid because
I was on horseback—and first, I saw how much he surpassed even
b   Laches in self-possession, and then again, to quote that line of
yours, Aristophanes, I thought that he proceeded there just as he
does here too, "head held high, casting his eyes about,"[271] calmly
surveying both friend and foe, making it clear to everyone, and
at quite a distance, that if anybody touched this man he'd defend
himself quite stoutly. That's why he and his comrade got away safe;
they don't usually touch people who defend themselves like that
c   in battle, but pursue those who flee headlong.

The Strangeness of Socrates (221c–222b)

Well, one could praise Socrates for many other remarkable
things; with respect to other activities one might also perhaps say
the same sort of thing about someone else, but unlikeness to any
other man, past or present, is worthy of all wonder. One might
compare the sort of man Achilles was to Brasidas[272] and others,

269. Loss of arms in battle was a disgrace. "With your shield or on it" was no light
saying; you could run faster without it.
270. In 424 B.C.
271. Cf. *Clouds* 362 (not an exact quotation, at least from our present text). Laches
himself, a general, refers to this incident and pays tribute to Socrates' courage at
Delium in the *Laches* 181a–b. Socrates mentions his service at Potidaea, Amphipolis,
and Delium as an indication of his faithfulness to duty imposed by Athens, even to
death. *Apology* 28d–e.
272. A distinguished Spartan general killed at Amphipolis in 422 B.C.

and Pericles, again, to Nestor and Antenor, and there are others
d   one might compare in the same way. But the sort of man this is
and his strangeness, both himself and his words, one couldn't
come close to finding if one looked, neither among people present
nor past, except perhaps if one were to compare him to those I
mention—not any man, but silenes and satyrs, him and his words.

Actually, I left this out at first, that even his arguments are ex-
e   actly like silenes that have been opened. For if one is willing to
listen to Socrates' arguments, they'd appear quite ridiculous at
first; they're wrapped round on the outside with words and
phrases like the hide of an outrageous satyr. He talks about pack-
asses and smiths and cobblers and tanners, and forever appears
to be saying the same things in the same ways, so that an inex-
222a   perienced and unreasonable man might ridicule his arguments.[273]
But if the arguments are opened, and one sees them from the
inside, he will find first that they are the only arguments with any
sense in them, and next, that they contain within themselves utterly divine and multitudinous images of virtue, and that they are
relevant to most or rather to all things worth considering for one
who intends to be noble and good.

This then, gentlemen, is my praise of Socrates. On the other
hand, I've also mixed in the faults I find in him, and told you of
his outrageous insult to me. It isn't just me he's treated this way,
b   however, but also Charmides, son of Glaucon, and Euthydemus,
son of Diocles, and many another as well, whom he seduces as a
lover and ends up himself as beloved instead of lover. I warn you,
Agathon, don't be deceived by him, but learn from our own experiences and watch out, instead of, as the proverb has it, learning
by dumb suffering.[274]

Socrates Replies (222c–223b)

c   After Alcibiades said this, they laughed at his frankness, because he seemed still in love with Socrates. So Socrates said, I think
you're sober, Alcibiades. Otherwise, you'd never try to disguise
your intention so cleverly and conceal why you've said all this, and
put it at the end as if it were merely an afterthought—as though

273. As Callicles does at *Gorgias* 490c–491a; but perhaps there is also a reference
to Aristophanes and the *Clouds*.
274. *Iliad* xvii 32; Hesiod *Works and Days* 218.

d   you hadn't said it all to cause Agathon and me to quarrel, because
you think I should love you and nobody else, and that Agathon
should be loved by you and not one single other person. But you
don't fool me; the point of your satyr play[275]—or rather your Silenus play—is perfectly obvious. My dear Agathon, don't let him
get away with it; don't let anyone cause you and me to quarrel.

e   So Agathon said, Why really, Socrates, maybe you're right. I
offer as proof the fact that he lay down between you and me in
order to keep us apart. Well, he won't get away with a thing; I'll
come lie next to you.

Yes, do, said Socrates. Come lie here below me.[276]

Zeus! said Alcibiades. The things I suffer from this man! He
thinks he has to get the better of me in every way. If nothing else,
my friend, at least let Agathon be set down between us.

Impossible, said Socrates. You praised me, and I have to praise
the person to my right. So if Agathon lies below you, won't he have
to praise me again instead of being praised by me? Let him go,

223a my friend. Don't begrudge the lad my praises, for I very much
want to offer him an encomium.[277]

Yes, Alcibiades! said Agathon. I can't possibly stay here. I'll absolutely have to change places in order to be praised by Socrates.

It's the same old story, said Alcibiades. When Socrates is around,
it's impossible for anyone else to get a share of the beauties. And
now what a convincing argument he's found, and so resourceful,
too, to make this fellow sit next to him!

b   So Agathon got up to sit next to Socrates.

Conclusion (223b–d)

But at this point, suddenly, a mob of revelers came to the doors,
and when they found them open because someone was leaving,
they came straight in to us and lay down. Everything was in an

---

275. Tragic trilogies at the Dionysia closed with a humorous phallic play in which
the chorus dressed as satyrs.

276. The original order of places was Agathon–Socrates (175c–d), and Alcibiades
upon entering seated himself between them (213a–b), so that the order became Agathon–Alcibiades–Socrates. Socrates now invites Agathon to change his position so
that the order becomes Alcibiades–Socrates–Agathon.

277. Alcibiades has suggested the order Alcibiades–Agathon–Socrates. Socrates
objects, pleading the rule of procedure suggested by Eryximachus at 214b–c (cf.
177d).

uproar, there was no longer any order, and everyone was compelled to drink a great deal of wine.

Aristodemus said that Eryximachus and Phaedrus and some
others got up and left, and he fell asleep and slept quite a while,
c   because the nights were long, but he woke up toward daybreak,
at cock-crow, to see some asleep and others gone. Only Agathon
and Aristophanes and Socrates were still awake, drinking from a
large bowl, and passing it from left to right.

Well, Socrates was discussing with them. Aristodemus said he
couldn't remember the other arguments—he wasn't there at the
d   beginning, and he was drowsy—but the main point, he said, was
that Socrates was making them agree that the same man knows
how to compose comedy and tragedy, and he who is a tragic poet
by art is a comic poet too.[278] Compelled to these admissions, and
not quite following, they drowsed, and Aristophanes fell asleep
first, and then, just as it was becoming light, Agathon.

So after putting them to sleep, Socrates got up and left, and
Aristodemus as usual followed him. He went to the Lyceum and
bathed, passed the rest of the day as he would any other, and after
that he went home in the evening and rested.

278. The argument must have been that tragedy and comedy are opposites; the
same art has knowledge of opposites; therefore, anyone who is by art a tragic poet is
a comic poet too. The conclusion superficially contradicts *Ion* 531e–534e; but the *Ion*
denies that the actor, and by implication the poet, has an art.

INDEX

References to author's comments are given according to the pagination of this book. References in italic are to Plato's *Symposium*, and are given by Stephanus pages in the margin of the translation; these pages are subdivided according to the letters *a, b, c, d, e,* answering to divisions in the original folio page.

Virtue (*continued*)
88–89; of Eros, 14, 16, 17, 40, *196b–c*; happiness as consisting in, 65; possession of, and love, 12, *178c–180b*; Protagoras and, 11. *See also* Courage; Justice; Temperance; Wisdom
Vlastos, Gregory, 17n, 99

Wholeness, desire for, 31, 33–35, 77, *192c–e*, *205e*
Wicking, and wisdom, 107, *175d*
Wilamowitz, Ulrich von, 46–47
Wisdom: desire for, and Eros, 53–54; Dionysus as judge of, 6, 20, 44, 108, *175e*, *215b*; happiness and, 55; of Socrates,

106–108; and temperance, *209a*; wicking and, 107, *175d*
Wish: vs. desire, 56–57, 58, 62–65; the Primary Valuable and, 62–65
Women: Plato's views of, 46n; segregation of, 18, 19, *176e*; status of, in Athens, 18–19; subjugation of, and Dionysus, 18n; willingness to die for love, 12, *178b–c*. *See also* Agave; Alcestis; Aspasia; Diotima

Xenophon, *Symposium*, 14

Zeus: father of Aphrodite Pandemus, *180e*; guidance of Eros and, *197b*; human procreation and, 31, 32; nature of ancient men and, *190d–191b*